# TYPES OF AUTHORITY IN FORMATIVE CHRISTIANITY AND JUDAISM

Two well-known scholars, in New Testament and Rabbinic Judaism respectively, ask the question: what does it mean to translate a theory of God's presence in the social order into a concrete doctrine of everyday authority? What sort of politics, what theory of on-going and everyday religious encounter, and what modes of persuasive intellectual exchange embody the conviction that God is present among us and that our community is made holy by obedient response to that Presence? The holy community, the presence of God's representatives on earth, and the compelling power of certain kinds of evidence and arguments – these provide the outlines of an answer to that question. Politics come first. But both communities also looked to the authority of God embodied in persons, validated by miraculous events, or otherwise certified by gifts of the spirit. And, finally, both Christianity and Rabbinic Judaism deemed Christ and the Torah respectively to embody the logos of reason or the rules of right thought. Both maintained that well-expounded, probative evidence and compelling argument formed the best source of authority – compulsion exercised from within, by intellect.

**Bruce Chilton** is Bernard Idding Bell Professor of Religion at Bard College, New York.

**Jacob Neusner** is Distinguished Research Professor of Religious Studies at the University of South Florida and Professor of Religion at Bard College, New York.

# TYPES OF AUTHORITY IN FORMATIVE CHRISTIANITY AND JUDAISM

*Bruce Chilton and
Jacob Neusner*

London and New York

First published 1999
by Routledge
11 New Fetter Lane, London EC4P 4EE

Simultaneously published in the USA and Canada
by Routledge
29 West 35th Street, New York, NY 10001

Typeset in Garamond by Routledge
Printed and bound in Great Britain by
Creative Print and Design (Wales), Ebbw Vale

*British Library Cataloguing in Publication Data*
A catalogue record for this book is available from the British
Library

*Library of Congress Cataloguing in Publication Data*
A catalogue record for this book has been requested

ISBN 0–415–17325–6 (hbk)
ISBN 0–415–17326–4 (pbk)

# CONTENTS

# CONTENTS

# PREFACE

This partnership of an Anglican/Episcopalian priest and a rabbi (bearing no denominational affiliation) aims at making possible a new approach to the analytical study of Orthodox, Catholic Christianity and Rabbinic Judaism in late antiquity, when both took shape as the West would know them. We regard as insufficient the study of formative Christianity out of communication with Rabbinic Judaism, or of formative Judaism out of phase with Christianity. Since both heirs of the same Scripture formed, each for itself, a category-formation in important aspects corresponding to that of the other, neither can be fully understood in its broadest context wholly on its own. So here we continue a project in the systematic comparison and contrast of kindred religions.

We do so by reason of two convictions. First, religions are best studied in a comparative framework, not in isolation from the rest of the world of religious history and culture. Second, religions that are compared and contrasted have to begin with to intersect, and Judaism and Christianity are joined together from their mutual origin in Scripture and never really part company. Hence our work of comparison of history, religion, and theology, in a set of systematic studies. We maintain that since both religious traditions took shape in response to the same Scripture – "the Old Testament" of Christianity, "the written Torah" of Rabbinic Judaism – they not only share a common heritage but also take up a joint set of concerns, dictated by Scriptural imperative to them both equally. Accordingly, studying their formative history ought to require a constant encounter of each with the other in a systematic labor of comparison and contrast. We mean to provide academic, descriptive ways of studying the formation of Christianity in the framework of the formation of Rabbinic Judaism, of gaining perspective on that

Judaism by constant reference to counterpart issues and events in Catholic and Orthodox Christianity of the same time and place.

This is not a work of theological comparison and contrast; we have undertaken that elsewhere. In fact, we are currently engaged in a three-part project in the re-framing of the study of each foundation: two principal religions of the West in relationship to one another. The first, as explained, involves comparative religion, the second, comparative history, and the third, comparative theology.

*Comparative Religion*   In our studies of comparative religion, we have systematically addressed principal issues in the description of the two religious traditions, pointing up likenesses and differences and so gaining perspective upon each tradition. Of those studies, in logical order, the present volume is the fourth, introducing as it does principal documents and doctrines of the one in comparison and contrast with those of the other, as we explain in the Introduction. The four titles are as follows:

*Common Heritage, Diverse Dispositions. Judaic and Christian Classics Doctrinally Compared*, London: Routledge (in preparation)
*Judaism in the New Testament. Practices and Beliefs*, London: Routledge, 1995
*The Intellectual Foundations of Christian and Jewish Discourse: The Philosophy of Religious Argument*, London: Routledge, 1997
*Types of Authority in Formative Christianity and Judaism. Institutional, Charismatic, and Intellectual*, London: Routledge, 1999

We begin with our basic introduction, proceed to read the New Testament in the way in which we should examine the principal writings of any other religion, then take up modes of thought shared in some ways but not in others by the two kindred religions, and finally, address the issue of authority governing the mediation of Scripture and its revelation to each of the competing heirs thereto. Clearly, the present volume is a progressive continuation of the inquiry we began some years ago.

*Comparative History*   In our comparison of the histories of formative Christianity and Rabbinic Judaism in its formative age, we have asked whether the histories follow a common course or show marks of change and interchange. Some have held that the histories run parallel, so that what took place in the history of the one has a counterpart in what happened for the other. But we hold that the two religions traded places, the one ending up its formative history in the situation confronted by its counterpart at the very outset of its formative age. This work is as follows:

*Trading Places: The Intersecting Histories of Christianity and Rabbinic Judaism*, Cleveland: Pilgrim Press, 1996
*Trading Places. A Reader and Sourcebook on the Intersecting Histories of Christianity and Rabbinic Judaism*, Cleveland: Pilgrim Press, 1996

*Comparative Theology* We have, finally, produced four works of description in comparative theology. These works identify categories that are shared by the theologians of the two traditions and show how each takes on its own definition and character in the encounter with Scripture.

*Christianity and Judaism: The Formative Categories*. I. *Revelation: The Torah and the Bible*, Valley Forge: Trinity Press International, 1995
*Christianity and Judaism: The Formative Categories*. II. *The Body of Faith: Israel and the Church*, Valley Forge: Trinity Press International, 1996
*Christianity and Judaism: The Formative Categories*. III. *God in the World*, Harrisburg: Trinity Press International, 1997
*Jewish-Christian Debates. God, Kingdom, Messiah*, Minneapolis: Fortress Press, 1998

In these ways we have undertaken to describe and analyze the formative age of the two religions within a shared frame of reference, a common categorical structure.

So much for the shared work of comparison and contrast for academic purposes. But we also practice Christianity and Judaism, respectively. Not only so, but living in the second generation after the end of the Holocaust, each of us, faithful to his own tradition and its revelation, recognizes the promise of the new day that has been born in the aftermath of the Holocaust. The first generation, shocked by what Germany and its allies did to the Jewish people and cognizant of the enormous contribution of Christian anti-Judaism and anti-Semitism to that work, found Christianity asking itself exceedingly painful questions. These led, in Roman Catholic and Anglican and Protestant Christianity as well as in some

Orthodox Christian circles, to the recognition that Judaism, after nearly 2,000 years, really does constitute a vital and living religion. Judaic response in that day meant to encourage that recognition. From 1945 to 1970 many people traveled long distances toward a new relationship.

But it was left for the second generation to translate the new attitudes and theological convictions into the language of the academy, into the work of learning and a new episteme. The new dialogue – one of academic and intellectual substance – takes place because we live in an age in which Christianity has now radically revised its understanding of "Israel after the flesh" and the eternity of the Torah, and in which Judaism as practiced in the Western democracies has proposed to respond constructively to gestures of respect. Learning is called for; that explains why ours has been not only a labor of history and of the history of religion, comparison and contrast, description and analysis, but also a work of religious dialogue carried on through shared learning. Theology cannot go forward, however, unless religious thinking, not only academic learning, takes account of the new age.

In our shared teaching at Bard College, we have experimented in not only descriptive courses in the comparison of religion but also in theological studies in the framing of a religious language of dialogue. One result is the essays emerging from a Bard College course and conference that took up systematic discussion of the future of Judaic-Christian religious encounter, yielding:

*Forging a Common Future: Catholic, Judaic, and Protestant Relations for a New Millennium*, Cleveland: Pilgrim Press, 1997

This same long-term work motivates the multi-volume project, with Bruce Chilton as editor in chief, Jacob Neusner as chairman of the editorial board, and Craig Evans as managing editor, entitled *The Synoptic Gospels in Rabbinic Context,* in which a sizable team of scholars reopens questions of the exegesis of the Gospels in light of Rabbinic literature. This project will begin to be published shortly by E.J. Brill, Leiden, in separate volumes.

On the Judaeo-Christian dialogue, in addition, Jacob Neusner has followed a logical course of work of his own. Looking backward at the intellectual legacy of Judaeo-Christian dialogue and finding it wanting, he began with two works of criticism of the dialogue before our day:

*Jews and Christians: The Myth of a Common Tradition*, New York and
    London: Trinity Press International and SCM Press, 1990
*Telling Tales: Making Sense of Christian and Judaic Nonsense. The
    Urgency and Basis for Judaeo-Christian Dialogue*, Louisville:
    Westminster-John Knox Press, 1993

Concluding – as had others before – that the way to enter into
substantive religious interchange required a new form, he then
proceeded to a constructive theological dialogue in the form of
story-telling. This took place through the encounter of the Bible
and the Torah, first, in an imaginary dialogue with Jesus as
portrayed in the Gospel of Matthew, and with Paul writing on who
and what is Israel in Romans. A further exercise required joint
study of Scripture with a great contemporary Roman Catholic
theologian. These titles are as follows:

*A Rabbi Talks with Jesus. An Intermillennial, Interfaith Exchange*, New
    York: Doubleday, 1993 (also in German, Swedish, Italian,
    Polish, and Portuguese)
*Children of the Flesh, Children of the Promise. An Argument with Paul
    about Judaism as an Ethnic Religion*, Cleveland: Pilgrim Press,
    1995
*Common Ground. A Priest and a Rabbi Read the Scriptures Together*,
    Cleveland: Pilgrim Press, 1996 (second edition, revised, of *The
    Bible and Us. A Priest and a Rabbi Read the Scriptures Together*,
    with Andrew M. Greeley, New York: Warner Books, 1990)
    (also in Portuguese)

In these various projects, both authors have undertaken what they
believe to be that labor of conciliation and reconciliation, through
both historical and theological learning, that the hour both makes
possible and also requires.

Bruce Chilton's comparative work began within his study of
Jesus and Christian origins. In previous works, he has shown –
against current fashion in North America – that Jesus cannot be
assessed except within his Judaic milieu. His preaching of the
kingdom of God took up the actual vocabulary of the Aramaic
translation of the book of Isaiah (the Targum) which was current in
an oral form within the synagogues of his time (Chilton, *God in
Strength. Jesus' Announcement of the Kingdom*, Studien zum Neuen
Testament und seiner Umwelt 1, Freistadt: Plöchl, 1979; reprinted
in "The Biblical Seminar", Sheffield: JSOT, 1987). In much of

Jesus' characteristic teaching, the phrasing of that Aramaic Targum shines through the Greek text of the Gospels as we can read it today (Chilton, *A Galilean Rabbi and His Bible. Jesus' Use of the Interpreted Scripture of His Time*, Wilmington: Glazier, 1984; also published with the subtitle, *Jesus' Own Interpretation of Isaiah*, London: SPCK, 1984). The influence of Galilean Judaism is not only evident in Jesus' words, but in his deeds: by occupying the Temple in order to insist upon his own view of purity, Jesus courted his own execution (Chilton, *The Temple of Jesus. His Sacrificial Program Within a Cultural History of Sacrifice*, University Park: The Pennsylvania State University Press, 1992). Indeed, his entire preaching of the kingdom is to be seen in the context of a quest for the purity God demands as eschatological king, a quest which finds a complete language of expression in the book of Psalms (Chilton, *Pure Kingdom. Jesus' Vision of God*, Studying the Historical Jesus 1, Grand Rapids and London: Eerdmans and SPCK, 1996).

One of the great fears which come into play in the historical study of Jesus is religious and theological: if we locate him in Judaism, does that involve giving up a Christian spirituality? Chilton understands that fear, but in his experience the result of critical work is just the opposite. Jesus' Judaism involved an emphatic discipline of spirituality. In *Jesus' Prayer and Jesus' Eucharist. His Personal Practice of Spirituality* (Valley Forge: Trinity Press International, 1997), Chilton has shown how Jesus' Aramaic model of prayer and his development of fellowship in meals[1] provided definite examples, commended for emulation and further development among those who follow him. Spirituality is not just an intellectual exercise, it is a communal and practical matter. That is one of the principal results of appreciating Jesus within a Judaic context.

Chilton's most recent book along that line of inquiry is *Jesus' Baptism and Jesus' Healing. His Personal Practice of Spirituality* 2 (Harrisburg: Trinity Press International, 1998). Because Judaism was concerned with humanity as pure before God, prepared in a state to be compatible with divine holiness, Jesus could not and did not ignore the issue of purity. *Jesus' Prayer and Jesus' Eucharist* has already shown that in regard to fellowship in meals. *Jesus' Baptism and Jesus' Healing* deals with the practice of immersion (baptism), one of the more characteristic elements of Judaism in the time of Jesus. What has become increasingly plain is that historical and exegetical work can only proceed when attention is also afforded to the religious dimensions of the meanings which the texts generate, and to the committed, theological practices and beliefs which were involved.

Obviously, this work together is made possible because we share a happy academic home at Bard College, where undergraduates in our joint courses have allowed us to try out our ideas, both educational and scholarly, and to clarify our thought. The undergraduates also participate in the scholarly conferences we organize to explore ideas and advance learning. We are proud of our students. To the President of Bard College, Leon Botstein, we offer our thanks for making this work possible.

In addition, Jacob Neusner enjoys an appointment as Distinguished Research Professor of Religious Studies at the University of South Florida and the very ample research opportunities that that vast, highly professional university affords. He expresses gratitude for the many acts of support and generosity accorded by his university. Both Bard College and the Church of St John the Evangelist have afforded Bruce Chilton just the academic support he has found indispensable to his work, and of late the Pew Charitable Trusts have provided him with a fellowship under the Evangelical Scholars Program which has been of enormous value and a great encouragement.

Finally, we have found at Routledge a constant source of wisdom and support in our editor, Richard Stoneman, to whom, and to whose highly professional staff, we say "thank you".

Bruce Chilton
Bard College and the Church of St John the Evangelist
Jacob Neusner
University of South Florida and Bard College

# INTRODUCTION

For Judaism, Moses, and, for Christianity, Jesus, uniquely embodied authority, and their teachings conveyed God's will. The Torah revealed by God to Moses at Sinai set forth that will; Jesus Christ, God Incarnate, embodied and taught it. So the community of sages and their disciples asked all Israel to accept God's will and thus form that sacred society that God designed Israel to be. And the bishops and priests, holy men, theologians, and councils of Christianity spoke, too, in God's name to the Church, God's people. In maintaining such conceptions, both Rabbinic Judaism and Orthodox, Catholic Christianity aspired to establish the Israel which Scripture had portrayed, a holy community governed by God, be it through the prophet-king, Moses, or through kings designated and recognized by God, or through the establishment of Temple priests in God's service.

The actuality of a voluntary community scarcely able to administer more than its own trivial affairs made slight impact upon how the sages of Judaism and the theologians of Christianity imagined matters to be. Both undertook to frame in concrete and immediate terms the theory of the holy community, embodying God's will, that possessed the authority to define its own character and, within the framework of God's will, to shape its own destiny. So God in the Torah or God in Christ embodied the authority that defined the holy Israel of Rabbinic Judaism and the Body of Christ of Christianity, respectively. And that is why the issue of authority contains within itself the dynamics, the inner workings of the imaginative life of Christianity and Rabbinic Judaism. The way people thought about authority conveys the practical theology that shaped the everyday life of the community: imitate God as God is made manifest in the Torah and sanctified in Israel, imitate Christ as God is made manifest on the cross and made real in the life of the Church.

1

That is where matters become complicated, for these claims regarding the nature of God's dominion in the here-and-now, self-evidently true to the faithful, ought to complete any treatment of authority in formative Christianity and Rabbinic Judaism. But what does it mean to translate a theory of God's presence in the social order into a concrete doctrine of everyday authority? What sort of politics, what theory of ongoing and everyday religious encounter, and what modes of persuasive intellectual exchange embody the conviction that God is present among us and that our community is made holy by obedient response to that Presence? These are the questions that define the present exercise in exposition, comparison and contrast.

The accounts of the Judaic and Christian theories of the politics of the holy community, the presence of God's representatives on earth, and the compelling power of certain kinds of evidence and arguments – these provide the outlines of an answer to that question. Politics come first, because neither Rabbinic Judaism nor Christianity constituted wholly voluntary communities, lacking legitimate means of coercion. Both could impose the will of the community upon individuals at least to some degree, and neither found itself unable to effect its public policy. The sages of the Torah served as officials of the Jewish administrations recognized by both the Roman and Iranian empires. For the centuries before Christianity became licit, and subsequently gained status as the dominant religion of the Roman empire, Church order was enforced through institutional media. But both communities, living at the outer edge of everyday encounter with the living Presence of God, also looked to the authority of God embodied in persons, validated by miraculous events, or otherwise certified by gifts of the spirit. And, finally, both Christianity and Rabbinic Judaism deemed Christ and the Torah to embody the logos of reason or the rules of right thought respectively. That is why both, in theory and in the writings that conveyed theory, responded to sound argument and weighty criticism in the formation of opinion, attitude, and action. Both took for granted that the faith operated in a world of reason, and both maintained that well-expounded, probative evidence and compelling argument formed the best source of authority – compulsion exercised from within, by intellect.

We deal therefore with the practical side of theology, the impact of faith upon the social order. The issue of this study, a work of exposition and of comparison and contrast, accordingly emerges at the meeting point of revelation and reason, power politics and persuasion, charisma and routine. That issue is simply phrased: what are the bases in the institutional, spiritual and intellectual theory of formative Christianity and Rabbinic Judaism to compel someone to do or refrain from doing a given action? We propose to describe the more important conceptions that the principal documents set forth, leaving for later inquiry a concrete account of how things actually took shape. To answer that question of the theory of authority for the formative age of the West – the first six centuries of the Common Era that mark late antiquity in Christianity and Judaism – we identify the three indicated types of authority.

Because the two religious worlds taking shape appealed to the same holy Scripture, what we learn is how diverse heirs disposed of a common heritage, the potentialities of a single set of writings to generate conflicting results. But if each community defined matters in its own way, both adopted a single category-formation, asking the same questions but producing different answers. Accordingly we describe, for purposes of comparison and contrast, the contents of those shared categories of authority as set forth by the two religious constructions that rested on the common revealed Scripture of ancient Israel, Orthodox, Catholic Christianity and Rabbinic Judaism. In this way we understand the points on which Rabbinic Judaism and Christianity concurred, and where they differed.

Like ancient Israelite prophecy, formative Christianity and Rabbinic Judaism laid heavy emphasis upon matters of attitude, intentionality, and will. Ultimately, they held, it is not coercive action but correct attitude that leads to right action on the part of the individual and to correct public policy for the community. The Judaic sages taught that the commandments were given only to purify the heart of Man, and they maintained that what God really wants of Man is the heart. Paul's profound meditations on the uncertain heart – "the good that I would, that I do not" – correspond to Jeremiah's reflections on the devices of the heart as well. So considerations of force, such as politics introduce into public affairs, conceptions of divine intervention into the world of nature, such as charismatic personalities invoke, and conventions of coercive argument leading to conformity by reason of persuasion, such as are defined by authority worked through intellect – these come together in a single large category: attitude. That is hardly surprising, since neither Rabbinic Judaism through its formative age nor Christianity until the fourth century could invoke much power beyond admonition, argument, and intangible appeal to the will of Heaven. So "authority" takes on its own dimensions when we address weak and marginal groups, better able to give orders than to enforce them.

That makes all the more poignant the adoption, by both groups, of the same political metaphor of divine power, "the kingdom of Heaven" for Rabbinic Judaism, "the kingdom of God," for Christianity, which identified Jesus Christ as, among other things, King of the Jews. Both Christian faithful and Judaic sages accepted the dominion of Heaven – the rule of God – as authoritative. To imitate Christ, for the Christian, or to imitate God, for the Judaist (the Jew who practiced Judaism, to distinguish from the Jew by reason of ethnic origin), would explain why the community of the faithful formed the kind of community that it did or engaged in the acts of commission or omission that it did. Both found it expedient – and right – to turn necessity into a virtue by urging the believers to conform out of free will, voluntarily to make God's will their own. Obey the law of the Torah or accept the authority of Christ, not by reason of coerced obedience, the result of political power, charismatic force, or coercive argument, but by reason of one's own conviction, character, and conscience – another kind of authority altogether, an internal kind. So the sages of Judaism recommend in so many words:

> Antigonos of Sokho received [the Torah] from Simeon the Righteous. He would say, (1) "Do not be like servants who serve the master on condition of receiving a reward, (2) "but [be] like servants who serve the master not on condition of receiving a reward. (3) "And let the fear of Heaven be upon you."
>
> (Tractate Abot 1:3)

> [Rabban Gamaliel, son of R. Judah the Patriarch,] would say, "Make his wishes into your own wishes, so that he will make your wishes into his wishes. Put aside your wishes on account of his wishes, so that he will put aside the wishes of other people in favor of your wishes."
>
> (Tractate Abot 2:4)

> R. Yohanan Hassandelar says, "Any gathering which is for the sake of Heaven is going to endure. And any which is not for the sake of Heaven is not going to endure."
>
> (Tractate Abot 4:11)

These and counterpart sayings in Christian classics leave no doubt of the ideal state of affairs: people will do the right thing for the right motive and will not have to be coerced.

Jesus' advice puts the matter simply, and is resonant with the teaching of the sages:

> But who among you, having a servant who plows or shepherds will say to him when he comes in from the field, Right away, enter and enjoy a repast? But will he not say, Prepare what I shall dine on and serve me girded until I have eaten and drunk, and after this you yourself shall eat and drink? Is there credit to a servant because he has done what is commanded? So you also, when you have done all that is commanded of you, say, We are useless servants, we have done what we were obliged to do.
>
> (Luke 17:7–10)

Near the same time that the Gospel according to Luke was composed (that is, around 90 CE) a letter composed in the name of Peter would spell out the socio-economic medium of the imitation of Christ:

> Domestics, be submitted in all fear to masters, not only to the good and kind, but also to the unscrupulous. For this is credit, if on account of God's conscience one bears griefs, suffering unjustly. For what sort of fame is it if you endure beating, having sinned? But if you do good and endure suffering, this is credit before God. For to this you were called, because Christ also suffered for you, leaving you a model, so that you might follow in his footsteps.
>
> (1 Peter 2:18–21)

By the end of the period that concerns us, there would be practically no situation of social life – from domestics to the Imperial court – which had not been baptized by Christianity with the understanding that it was possible to serve God in a Christ-like manner within that station.

Sages urged the faithful to imitate God out of love and fear of God, not out of personal inclination or volition.

> "You shall be holy to me, for I the Lord am holy" (Lev. 19:2):

"Just as I am holy, so you be holy.

"Just as I am separate, so you be separate."

"...and have separated you from the peoples, that you should be mine":

"If you are separated from the nations, lo, you are for my Name, and if not, lo, you belong to Nebuchadnezzar, king of Babylonia, and his associates."

R. Eleazar b. Azariah says, "How do we know that someone should not say, 'I do not want to wear mixed fibers, I don't want to eat pork, I don't want to have incestuous sexual relations.'

"Rather: 'I do want [to wear mixed fibers, I do want to eat pork, I do want to have incestuous sexual relations.] But what can I do? For my father in heaven has made a decree for me!'

"So Scripture says, 'and have separated you from the peoples, that you should be mine.'

So one will turn out to keep far from transgression and accept upon himself the rule of Heaven."

(Sifra CCVII:II)

But appealing to the mythic life made possible by Scripture and theology opens questions of a this-worldly character, for God's rule worked its way from Heaven to earth through diverse paths. This sense of the mystery of how God's loving rule was to be worked out was an explicit feature of the consciousness of early Christianity:

Look what wonderful love the Father has given us, that we should be called God's children: and we are. For this reason the world does not know us, because it did not know him. Beloved, now we are God's children, and it has not yet appeared what we shall be. But when it does appear, we shall be like him, because he shall see him just as he is. And everyone who has this hope sanctifies himself upon him, just as that one is holy.

(1 John 3:1–3)

This is the same epistle, produced within the circle of John near the turn of the first and second centuries, which came to the deceptively simple formulation that "God is love" (1 John 4:8):

> Beloved, let us love one another, because love is from God, and everyone who loves has been fathered by God and knows God. One who does not love does not know God, because God is love.
>
> (1 John 4:7–8)

Christianity and Rabbinic Judaism understood that tangible media claimed to mediate God's authority and exercise power in God's name. There were, to be sure, powerful sources of resistance to these media, because God's rule was far from fully revealed, but the fact of the partial manifestation of his sovereignty was the only victory that mattered.

In practical terms we spell out how these media of authority took shape in three distinct ways. First in our presentation come political institutions – ongoing modes of political organization that claimed the right legitimately to commit acts of violence (physical, emotional, social) to enforce the rules. These, as we said, we present not in their multifaceted concrete reality but only in unitary theory: how the sages of Judaism and the apostolic leaders of Christianity defined matters. Then we take note of charismatic personalities that exercised enormous influence through example. Here Rabbinic Judaism and Christianity part company, because the former took the view that prophecy ceased with Malachi and the other latter-day prophets, while Christianity began with the advent of the greatest personality of all: God Incarnate, authorizing a new age of prophecy. But in practice both Rabbinic Judaism and Christianity recognized supernatural events and personalities in the here and now of ordinary life – and appealed to them to impose the authority of the Torah or of the Church upon the community of the faithful. Finally we turn to the inner life of intellect and examine modes of argument and reasoning that compelled intellectual concurrence. Consequently, in our picture of both heirs of ancient Israel, God ruled, in a concrete way, through political structures, personalities, and persuasion of a certain order. People then would submit, imitate, or accept the view and will of the other – all in God's name.

We provide a simple account of how Judaism and Christianity mediated God's authority to the holy community constituted by the respective faiths. The three parts of the book proceed logically, following the order of our analysis.

In Part 1, we take up the character of institutional authority as theoretically portrayed. Neither Rabbinic Judaism nor Catholic,

Orthodox Christianity found in Israelite Scripture the models that would dictate the shape of its politics. Both adopted the premises of Scripture – God rules the community through chosen instruments of His will – but worked them out in quite different ways.

Part 2 examines the working of charismatic authority: divine intervention, the holy man or saint, the Holy Spirit, prophecy. Here we address the continuity with Scripture, which portrayed in an elaborate way the authority of God's representatives in the here and now, the prophets and wonder-workers who could accomplish miracles to validate their instructions. Scripture spoke of direct divine revelations to men and women. How did Rabbinic Judaism and Christianity take over that account and carry forward its conviction concerning the immediacy of God's presence through prophecy and other charismatic media?

Part 3 moves onward to the realm of intellect. Just as Scripture presented a God who reasons and argues – the case of Abraham and God dealing with the fate of Sodom suffices to make the point – so both Christian and Judaic theologians and sages appealed to reason. Arguments from nature, from history, from Scripture, and from reason bore the burden of proving the case for the faith, thereby persuading the faithful to accept the authority of God's rule as mediated by the Torah and Christ, respectively.

# Part 1

# INSTITUTIONAL
# AUTHORITY

# 1

# RECOVERING EDEN: THE THEORETICAL POLITICS OF RABBINIC JUDAISM

If for Christianity Christ represented the Last Adam, restoring humanity to Eden, for Rabbinic Judaism, Israel the holy people stood for the counterpart of Adam, the Land of Israel for Eden, the expulsion by the Babylonians in 586 BCE and by the Romans in 70 CE for Adam's fall from grace. Then the challenge of politics was to restore Israel to grace and hence to the Land, thus bringing Adam back to Eden once more. Through its political theory, exposed in the Mishnah, *c.* 200 CE, Rabbinic Judaism made the statement that Israel had lost its land by reason of sin but could regain it by means of atonement and reconciliation, so restoring Adam to the place that the Creator had prepared for him and her. That is why the initial document of Rabbinic Judaism set forth a theoretical politics that focused upon the sin of rebellion and reconciliation through humble atonement. What the Mishnah presents is not merely a mythic and theological picture but also a political structure, and authority mediated through that political structure would shape the public life of this Israel into Eden. To make that statement politics provided an ideal medium, since the issues of politics – the forma-tion of institutions to define and preserve the social order – encompassed the inherited model of the ideal state, Israel under God's rule en route to and arrived in the Land, under Moses and Joshua, respectively. When people would speak of "a state of (being) Israel," therefore, they would also address "a state of (constituting) the State of Israel," the Judaic State, such as the Torah recorded for the age of Moses.

The politics of Judaism began in the imagination of a generation of intellectuals who, in the aftermath of the Jerusalem government's and Temple's destruction (70 CE) and the military defeat Jews suffered three generations later (132–5), had witnessed the end of

11

the political system and structure that the Jews had known for the preceding millennium. Initially set forth in the Mishnah, a second-century philosophical treatise in the form of a law-code, the political theory of Judaism laid out political institutions and described how they should work. In that way these intellectuals, who enjoyed no documented access to power of any kind and who certainly seem to have been unable to coerce many people to do very much, sorted out issues of power. They took account, in mind at least, of the issues of legitimate coercion within Israel, the holy people, which they considered more than a voluntary association, more than a community formed around a cult.[1]

The task undertaken by the political myth of Rabbinic Judaism is not only to make power specific and particular to cases. It is especially a labor of differentiation of power, indicating what agency or person has the power to precipitate the working of politics as legitimate violence at all. When, therefore, we understand the differentiating force of myth that imparts to politics its activity and dynamism, we shall grasp what everywhere animates the structures of the politics and propels the system. In the case of the politics of Rabbinic Judaism, we shall work our way downward, into the depths of the system, toward a myth of taxonomy of power. Appealing to a myth of taxonomy, the system accomplishes its tasks by explaining why this, not that, by telling as its foundation story a myth of classification for the application of legitimate violence. The myth appeals in the end to the critical bases for the taxonomy, among institutions, of a generalized power to coerce. Let me make these somewhat abstract remarks more concrete.

Specifically, we analyze the mythic foundations of sanctions. And when we move from sanctions to the myth expressed and implicit in the application and legitimation of those sanctions, we see a complex but cogent politics sustained by a simple myth. This somewhat protracted survey of sanctions and their implications had best commence with a clear statement of what we shall now uncover.

The encompassing framework of rules, institutions and sanctions is explained and validated by appeal to the myth of God's shared rule. That dominion, exercised by God and his surrogates on earth, is focused partly in the royal palace, partly in the Temple, and partly in the court. For us, the issue here is the differentiation of power, which is to say, which part falls where and why. Helpfully, the political myth of Rabbinic Judaism explains who exercises legitimate violence and under what conditions, and furthermore specifies the source for differentiation. The myth consequently serves a particular purpose – which is to answer that particular question. Indeed, the Judaic political myth comes to expression in its details of differentiation, which permit us to identify, and of course to answer, the generative question of politics.

How then are we to identify, on the basis of what the Mishnah does tell us, the generative myths to which the system is supposed to appeal? A myth explains the exercise of legitimate power. Now, we know, power comes to brutal expression when the state kills or maims someone or deprives a person of property through the imposition of legal sanctions for crime or sin.[2] But the Mishnah presents rules and does not contain myths, so where shall we begin? In the absence of a myth of power, we begin with cases of the exercise of power itself. We shall work our way back from the facts of power to the intimations, within the record of legitimately violent sanctions, of the intellectual and even mythic sources of legitimation for the exercise and use of that legitimate violence. For it is at the point of imposing sanctions, of killing, injuring, denying property, excluding from society, that power operates in its naked form. Then how these legitimate exercises of violence are validated will set before us such concrete evidence of the myth. And, so far as there is such evidence, that will identify the political myth of Rabbinic Judaism.

Analyzing myth by explaining sanctions draws our attention to the modes of legitimate violence that the system identifies. There we find four types of sanctions, each deriving from a distinct institution of political power, each bearing its own mythic explanation. The first comprises what God and the Heavenly court can do to people. The second comprises what the earthly court can do to people. That type of sanction embodies the legitimate application of the worldly and physical kinds of violence of which political theory ordinarily speaks. The third comprises what the cult can do to the people. The cult through its requirements can deprive people of their property as legitimately as can a court. The fourth comprises conformity with consensus – self-imposed sanctions. Here the issue is, whose consensus, and defined by whom? Across these four types of sanction, four types of coercion are in play. They depend on violence of various kinds – psychological and social as much as physical. Clearly, then, the sanctions that are exercised by other than judicial–political agencies prove violent and legitimately coercive, even though the violence and coercion are not the same as those carried out by courts.

13

On this basis we can differentiate among types of sanctions – and hence trace evidences of how the differentiation is explained. Since our data focus upon who does what to whom, the myth of politics must explain why various types of sanctions are put into effect by diverse political agencies or institutions. As we shall see, the exercise of power, invariably and undifferentiatedly in the name and by the authority of God in Heaven to be sure, is kept distinct. And the distinctions in this case signal important differences which require explanation. Concrete application of legitimate violence by, first, Heaven covers different matters from parts of the political and social world governed by the policy and coercion of, second, the this-worldly political classes. And both sorts of violence have to be kept distinct from the sanction effected by, third, the community through the weight of attitude and public opinion. Here again we find a distinct set of penalties applied to a particular range of actions. When we have seen the several separate kinds of sanction and where they apply, we shall have a full account of the workings of politics as the application of power, and from that concrete picture we may, I think, identify the range of power and the mythic framework that has to have accommodated and legitimated diverse kinds of power.

Our task therefore is to figure out on the basis of sanctions' distinct realms – Heaven, earth, and the mediating range of the Temple and sacrifice – which party imposes sanctions for (in modern parlance) what crimes or sins. Where Heaven intervenes, do other authorities participate, and if so, what tells me which party takes charge and imposes its sanction? Is the system differentiated so that where earth is in charge, there is no pretense of appeal to Heaven? Or do we find cooperation in coextensive jurisdiction, such that one party penalizes an act under one circumstance, the other the same act under a different circumstance? A survey of the sanctions enables us to differentiate the components of the power-structure before us. So we wonder whether each of these three estates that enjoy power and inflict sanctions of one kind or another – Heaven, earth, Temple in-between – governs its own affairs, without the intervention of the others, or whether, working together, each takes charge in collaboration with the other, so that power is parceled out and institutions simultaneously differentiate themselves from one another and also intersect. The survey of sanctions will allow us to answer these questions and so identify the myth of politics and the exercise of power that Rabbinic Judaism promulgated through the Mishnah.

What has been said about the relationship of the Mishnah to Scripture – the system makes its own choices within the available revelation – imposes the first task. We must address this obvious question: can we not simply open the Hebrew Scriptures and choose, therein, the operative political myth? No, we cannot. Why? First, the system-builders choose what they find useful and ignore what they do not. Second, Scripture presents for a political myth pretty much everything and its opposite; it allows for government by the prophet (Moses), the king (David), the priest (Ezra). So if we are to appeal to Scripture in our search for myth, we can do so only by showing that, in the very context of the concrete exercise of power, the framers of the Mishnah turn to Scripture. They then will tell us where to look and why. In fact, our authorship does represent the entire system as the realization of God's dominion over Israel. And this representation is specific and detailed. It thus justifies an inquiry, once we have identified the questions the myth must answer, into how, in Scripture, we find responses to just those questions.

Simply knowing that everything is in accord with the Torah and that God wants Israel to keep the laws of the Torah – the point at which the Introduction has left us – does not reveal the systemically active component of the political myth. On the one hand, the propositions are too general; on the other hand, they do not address the critical question. The sequence of self-evident premises that runs (1) God revealed the Torah, (2) the political institutions and rules carry out the Torah, and therefore (3) people should conform, hardly sustains a concrete theory of just where and how God's authority serves the systemic construction at hand. The appeal to Scripture, therefore, reveals no incisive information about the Mishnah's validating myth.

This conclusion is reinforced by the references we find here and there to "the kingdom of Heaven"[3] that appeal to God's rule in an everyday framework. These form a mere allegation that, in general, what the political authorities tell people to do is what God wants them to do illuminates not at all. For example, at M. Ber. 2:5, the following statement is attributed to Gamaliel, "I cannot heed you to suspend from myself the kingdom of Heaven even for one hour." Now as a matter of fact that is not a political context – there is no threat of legitimate violence, for instance – for the saying has to do with reciting the prayer, the *shema*: "Hear O Israel, the Lord is our God, the one God." No political conclusions are drawn from that allegation. Quite to the contrary, Gamaliel, head of the collegium of sages, is not thereby represented as relinquishing power to Heaven, only as expressing his obedience to divine rule even when he does not have to. Indeed, "the kingdom of Heaven" does not form a political category, even though, as we shall see, in the politics of Rabbinic Judaism, all power flows from God's will and law, expressed in the Torah. In this Rabbinic Judaism the manipulation and application of power, allowing the impositions of drastic sanctions in support of the law for instance, invariably flow through institutions, on earth and in Heaven, of a quite concrete and material character. "The kingdom of Heaven" may be within, but violate the law deliberately and wantonly and God will kill you sooner than you should otherwise have had to die. And, as a matter of fact, the Mishnah's framers rarely appeal in the context of politics and the legitimate exercise of violence to "the kingdom of Heaven," which, in this setting, does not form a political institution at all.

Indeed, while the Pentateuch presupposes a political Israel, we can hardly construct from the Pentateuchal writings the particular politics, including the mythic component thereof, that operates in the Mishnah's (or any other) Judaism. First of all, the Pentateuch does not prepare us to make sense of the institutions that the politics of Rabbinic Judaism for its part designs – government by king and high priest, rather than, as in the Pentateuch, prophet. Second, and concomitantly, the Pentateuchal myth that legitimates coercion – rule by God's prophet, governance through explicitly revealed laws that God has dictated – plays no active and systemic role whatsoever in the formulation and presentation of the Mishnah's politics of Judaism. Rather, of the types of political authority contained within the scriptural repertoire, the Mishnah's philosophers reject prophetic and charismatic authority and deem critical authority to be exercised by the sage's disciple who has been carefully nurtured in rules, not in gifts of the spirit. The authority of sages in the politics of Rabbinic Judaism does not derive from charisma, (revelation by God to the sage who makes a ruling in a given case, or even from general access to God for the sage). The myth we shall presently explore in no way falls into the classification of a charismatic myth of politics.

Is God's direct intervention (e.g., as portrayed in Scripture) represented as a preferred or even available sanction? Yes and no, but mostly no.[4] For in our system what is important is that the myth of God's intervention on an *ad hoc* and episodic basis in the life of the community hardly serves to explain obedience to the law in the here and now. What sort of evidence would indicate that God intervenes in such wise as to explain the obedience to the law on an everyday basis? Invoking God's immediate presence, a word said, a miracle performed, would suffice. But in the entirety of the more than five hundred chapters of the Mishnah, no one ever prays to have God supply a decision in a particular case. More to the point, no judge appeals to God to put to death a convicted felon. If the judge wants the felon killed, he kills him. When God intervenes, it is on the jurisdiction assigned to God, not the court. And then the penalty is a different one from execution.

It follows that an undifferentiated myth explaining the working of undifferentiated power by appeal to God's will, while relevant, is not exact and does not explain this system in its rich detail. How the available mythic materials explain the principles of differentiation now requires attention. The explanation must be both general and specific. That is to say, while the court orders and carries out the execution, the politics works in such a way that all three political institutions, God, the court and the Temple, the three agencies with the power to bestow or take away life and property and to inflict physical pain and suffering, work together in a single continuum and in important ways cooperate to deal with the same crimes or sins. The data to which we now turn will tell us who does what to whom and why, and, in the reason why, we shall uncover the political myth we seek.

Predictably, when we work our way through sanctions to recover the mythic premises thereof, we begin with God's place in the institutionalization and execution of legitimate violence. Of course, the repertoire of sanctions does encompass God's direct intervention, but that is hardly a preferred alternative or a common one. Still, God does commonly intervene when oaths are violated, for oaths are held to involve the person who invokes God's name and God. Further, whereas when faced with an insufficiency of valid evidence under strict rules of testimony, the earthly court cannot penalize serious crime, the Heavenly court can and does impose a penalty. Clearly, then, God serves to justify the politics and account for its origin. Although God is never asked to join in making specific decisions and effecting policy in the everyday politics of the state, deliberate violation of certain rules provokes God's or the Heavenly court's direct intervention. Thus obedience to the law clearly represents submission to God in Heaven. Moreover, forms of Heavenly coercion such as we shall presently survey suggest a complex mythic situation, with more subtle nuance than the claim that, overall, God rules, would indicate. A politics of rules and regulations cannot admit God's *ad hoc* participation, and this system did not do so. God joined in the system in a regular and routine way, and the rules took for granted God's part in the politics of Rabbinic Judaism.

Precisely how does the intervention of God into the system come to concrete expression? By appeal to the rules handed down at Sinai as an ultimate reference in legal questions, for instance. This is the case in the story about R. Simeon of Mispah, who sowed his field with two types of wheat. Simeon's problem is that he may have violated the law against sowing mixed seeds in a single patch. When the matter came before Rabban Gamaliel, the passage states:

[C] They went up to the Chamber of Hewn Stone and asked [about the law regarding sowing two types of wheat in one field].

[D] Said Nahum the Scribe, "I have received [the following ruling] from R. Miasha, who received it from his father, *who received {it} from the pairs, who received {it} from the prophets, {who received} the law {given} to Moses on Sinai,* regarding one who sows his field with two types of wheat...'

(M. Peah. 2:6) (my emphases)

Here, the law's legitimacy clearly depends on its descent by tradition from Sinai. But that general principle of descent from Sinai was invoked only rarely. Indeed, R. Simeon's case undermines the Mishnah's relation to God's intervention. R. Simeon's problem is minor. Nothing important requires so drastic a claim to be made explicit. That is to say, it is a mere commonplace that the system appeals to Sinai.

But though revelation in the here and now takes place in Rabbinic Judaism, this is not a politics of revelation, for a politics of revelation consistently and immediately appeals to the myth that God works in the here and now, all the time, in concrete cases. That appeal is not common in the Mishnah's statement of its system and, consequently, that appeal to the myth of revelation does not bear important political tasks and is not implicit here. Indeed I do not think it was present at all, except where Scripture made it so (for example, with the ordeal inflicted on the wife accused of adultery). Why the persistent interest in legitimation other than through the revelation of the Torah for the immediate case? The answer to that question draws upon the traits of philosophers, who are interested in the prevailing rule governing all cases and the explanation for the exceptions, rather than upon those of historian-prophets, who are engaged by the exceptional case which is then represented as paradigmatic. Our philosophers appeal to a myth to explain what is routine and orderly, and what they wish to explain is what is ordinary and everyday: institutions and rules, not cases and *ad hoc* decisions yielding no rule at all.

The traits of the politics of Rabbinic Judaism then emerge in the silences as much as in the acts of speech, in the characteristics of the myth as much as in its contents. The politics of Rabbinic Judaism appeals not to a charismatic but to a routine myth, in which is explained the orderly life of institutions and an administration, and by which are validated the rules and the workings of a political structure and system. True, all of them are deemed to have been founded on revelation. But what kind of revelation? The answer derives from the fact that none of the political institutions appeal in the here and now to God's irregular ("miraculous") intervention. Treatment of the rebellious elder and the false prophet as we shall see tells us quite the opposite. The political institutions not only did not invoke miraculous intervention to account for the imposition of sanctions, they would not and did not tolerate the claim that such could take place.

It is the regularity and order of God's participation in the politics that the character of the myth of the politics of Rabbinic Judaism maintains we have to understand and account for. Mere allegations in general that the law originates with God's revelation to Moses at Sinai do not serve to identify that middle-range myth that accounts for the structure and the system. If God is not sitting at the shoulder of the judge and telling the judge what to do (as the writers of Exodus 21ff. seem to suppose), then what legitimacy attaches to the judge's decision to give Mr Smith's field over, or back, to Mr Jones? And why (within the imaginary state at hand) should people support, sustain, and submit to authority? Sages' abstract language contains no answers to these questions. And yet the sages' system presupposes routine and everyday obedience to power, not merely the utilization of legitimate violence to secure conformity. That is partly because the systemic statement to begin with tells very few stories. Matters that the Pentateuchal writers expressed through narrating a very specific story about how God said thus and so to Moses in this particular case, rewarding the ones who obeyed and punishing those who did not, come to expression in the Mishnah in language of an allusive and philosophical, generalizing character.

Here, too, we discern the character of the myth even before we determine its contents. While we scarcely expect that this sort of writing is apt to spell out a myth, even though a myth infuses the system, we certainly can identify the components of the philosophical and theological explanation of the state that have taken mythic form. Even here, to be sure, the evidence proves sparse. First, of course, in the mythic structure comes God, who commands and creates, laying out what humanity is to do, exercising the power to form the social world in which humanity is to obey. God then takes care of God's particular concerns, and these focus upon deliberate violation of God's wishes. If a sin or crime is inadvertent, the penalties are of one order, if deliberate, of a different order. The most serious infraction of the law of the Torah is identified not by what is done but by the attitude of the sinner or criminal.[5] If one has deliberately violated God's rule, then God intervenes. If the violation is inadvertent, then the Temple imposes the sanction. And the difference is considerable. In the former case, God through the Heavenly court ends the felon's or sinner's life. Then a person who defies the laws – as these concern one's sexual conduct, attitude toward God, relationships within the family – will be penalized either (if necessary) by God or (if possible) by the earthly court. This means that the earthly court exercises God's power, and the myth of the system as a whole, so far as the earthly court forms the principal institutional form of the system, emerges not merely in a generality but in all its specificity. These particular judges, here and now, stand for God and exercise the power of God. In the latter case, the Temple takes over jurisdiction; a particular offering is called for, as the book of Leviticus specifies. But there is no need for God or the earthly court in God's name to take a position.

Now come the data of real power, the sanctions. We may divide sanctions just as the authorship of the Mishnah did, by simply reviewing the range of penalties for law-infraction as they occur. These penalties, as we mentioned above, fall into four classifications: what Heaven does, what political institutions do, what religious institutions do, and what is left to the coercion of public opinion, that is, consensus, with special attention to the definition of that "public" that has effective opinion to begin with. The final realm of power, conferring or withholding approval, proves constricted and, in this context, not very consequential.

Let us begin with the familiar, with sanctions exercised by the earthly court as they are fully described in Mishnah-tractates Sanhedrin and Makkot. We will review at length the imposition of sanctions as it is represented by the earthly court, the Temple, the

Heavenly court, the sages. This review allows us to identify the actors in the system of politics – those with power to impose sanctions, and the sanctions they can inflict. Only from this perspective will the initial statement of Rabbinic Judaism, in its own odd idiom, be able to make its points in the way its authorship has chosen. When we take up the myth to which that statement implicitly appeals, we shall have a clear notion of the character of the evidence, in rich detail, on which our judgment of the mythic substrate of the system has been composed.

The most impressive mode of legitimate violence is killing; it certainly focuses our attention. The earthly court may justly kill a sinner or felon. This death-dealing priority accorded to the earthly court derives from the character of the power entrusted to that court. The earthly court enjoys full power to dispose of the property and life of all subject to its authority – in the context imagined by Rabbinic Judaism, of all residing in territory that comes under the state's control. Imposing the death penalty is described in the following way:

### Mishnah-tractate Sanhedrin 7:1–3

{A}     Four modes of execution were given over to the court [in order of severity]:

{B}     (1) stoning, (2) burning, (3) decapitation, and (4) strangulation.

{C}     R. Simeon says, "(2) Burning, (1) stoning, (4) strangulation, and (3) decapitation."

(M. San. 7:1)

The passage leaves no doubt that the court could put people to death. Only the severity of suffering imposed by each mode of execution is in question. Thus, Simeon's hierarchy of punishments [C] differs from that of [B] in the degradation and suffering inflicted on the felon, not in the end result. The passage details four modes of execution, that is, four forms of legitimate violence. In the account, the following is of special interest. I have emphasized the key-words.

{A}     The religious requirement of decapitation [is carried out as follows]:

{B}     They would cut off his head with a sword,

{C}     just as the government does.

21

{D}     *R. Judah says, "This is disgusting.*

{E}     "But they put the head on a block and chop it off with an ax."

{F}     *They said to him, "There is no form of death more disgusting than this one."*

{G}     The religious requirement of strangulation [is carried out as follows:]

{H}     They would bury him in manure up to his armpits, and put a towel of hard material inside one of soft material, and wrap it around his neck.

{I}     This [witness] pulls it to him from one side, and that witness pulls it to him at the other side, until he perishes.

(M. San. 7:3)

In among all the practical detail, Judah's intervention stands out. It leaves no doubt that carrying out the law ("way of life") realizes a particular world view. Specifically, his language implies that the felon remains a human being, in God's image. Clearly, then, at stake in the theoretical discussions at hand is how to execute someone in a manner appropriate to his or her standing after the likeness of God. This problem obviously presupposes that in imposing the penalty in the first place and in carrying it out, the court acts wholly in conformity with God's will. This being the case, a political myth of a dominion belonging to God and carrying out God's plan and program certainly stands behind the materials at hand.

But that observation still leaves us struggling with a mere commonplace. On the strength of our knowledge that God stands behind the politics and that the consideration that human beings are in God's image and after God's likeness applies even in inflicting the death penalty, we still cannot identify the diverse media by which power is carried out. More to the point, we can hardly distinguish one medium of power from another, which we must do if we are to gain access to the myth that sustains what we shall soon see is the fully differentiated political structure before us. We do well at this turning point to remember the theoretical basis for this entire inquiry: a politics is a theory of the ongoing exercise of the power of coercion, including legitimate violence. Sanctions form the naked exercise of raw power – and hence will require the protection and disguise of a heavy cloak of myth.

How to proceed? By close attention to the facts of power and by sorting out the implications of those facts. A protracted journey through details of the law of sanctions leads us to classify the sanctions and the sins or crimes to which they apply. What precisely do I think requires classification? Our project is to see who does what to whom and, on the basis of the consequent perception, to propose an explanation for that composition. For from these sanctions of state, that is, the legitimate exercise of coercion, including violence, we may work our way back to the reasons adduced for the legitimacy of the exercise of coercion, which is to say, the political myth. The reason is that such a classification will permit us to see how in detail the foci of power are supposed to intersect or to relate: autonomous powers, connected and related ones, or utterly continuous ones, joining Heaven to earth, for instance, in the person of this institutional representative or that one. What we shall see is a system that treats Heaven, earth, and the mediating institution, the Temple, as interrelated, thus, connected, but that insists, in vast detail, upon the distinct responsibilities and jurisdiction accorded to each. Once we have perceived that fundamental fact, we may compose for ourselves the myth, or, at least the point and propositions of the myth, that accounted for the political structures of Rabbinic Judaism and persuaded people to obey or conform even when there was no immediate threat of penalty.

A survey of (1) types of sanctions, (2) the classifications of crimes or sins to which they apply, and (3) who imposes them, now yields these results. First come extirpation (death before one's allotted time) and the death-penalty:

|  | HEAVEN | EARTH |
| --- | --- | --- |
| *Sanction*: | *Extirpation (for deliberate actions)* | *Death-penalty* |
| For these crimes or sins: |  |  |
| sexual crimes: | incest, violating sex taboos (bestiality, homosexuality) | in improper relationships, incest |
| religious crimes against God: | blasphemy, idolatry, magic, sorcery, profaning the Sabbath | blasphemy, idolatry, magic, sorcery, profaning the Sabbath |
| religious sins against family: |  | cursing parents |
| social crimes: |  | murder, communal apostasy, kidnapping |

social sins:

religious sins, deliberately committed against God:

public defiance of the court, false prophecy

unclean person who ate a Holy Thing, uncleanness in sanctuary, violating food taboos, making offering outside of Temple, violating taboos of holy seasons, replicating Temple incense or oil outside

| | EARTH | TEMPLE | COMMUNITY |
|---|---|---|---|
| *Sanction*: | *flogging or exile* | *obligatory offering and/or flogging for inadvertent action* | *shunning or approbation* |
| For these crimes or sins: | manslaughter, incest, violation of menstrual taboo, marriage in violation of caste rules, violating food taboos, removing dam with offspring, violating negative commandments | uncleanness, eating Temple food in violation of the law, replicating Temple oil or incense outside, violating Temple food taboos, violating taboos of holy days (Passover, atonement) uncleanness (Zab, mesora etc.), Nazirite, sex with bondwoman, unclean Nazirite, false oath of testimony, false oath of deposit | repay moral obligation (debt cancelled by sabbatical year), stubbornly rejecting majority view, opposing majority will, opposing the patriarch, obedience to majority or patriarch |

The operative distinction between inflicting a flogging and requiring a sacrifice (Temple sanctions against person or property), and the sanction of extirpation (Heavenly death-penalty), is made explicit as follows: "For those [transgressions] are people liable, for deliberately doing them, to the punishment of extirpation, and for accidentally doing them, to the bringing of a sin-offering, and for not being certain of whether or not one has done them, to a suspensive guilt-offering." (That distinction is suspended in a few instances, as indicated at M. Ker. 2:1–2.)

This summary yields a simple and clear fact, and on the basis of that simple fact we may now reconstruct the entire political myth on which the politics of Rabbinic Judaism rested. Let me emphasize: some of the same crimes or sins for which the Heavenly court imposes the penalty of extirpation are those that, under appropriate circumstances (for instance, sufficient evidence admissible in court) the earthly court imposes the death-penalty. That is, the Heavenly court and the earthly court impose precisely the same sanctions for the same crimes or sins. The earthly court therefore forms down here the exact replica and counterpart, within a single system of power, of the Heavenly court up there. This no longer looms as an empty generalization; it is a concrete and systemically active and indicative detail, and the system speaks through its details.

But this is not the entire story. There is a second fact, equally indicative for our recovery of the substrate of myth. We note that there are crimes for which the earthly court imposes penalties, but for which the Heavenly court does not, as well as vice versa. The earthly and Heavenly courts share jurisdiction over sexual crimes and over what I classify as serious religious crimes against God. The Heavenly court penalizes with its form of the death-penalty religious sins against God, in which instances a person deliberately violates the taboos of sanctification.

That fact calls our attention to a third partner in the distribution and application of power, the Temple with its system of sanctions that cover precisely the same acts subject to the jurisdiction of the Heavenly and earthly courts. The counterpart on earth is now not the earthly court but the Temple. This is the institution that, in theory, automatically receives the appropriate offering from the person who inadvertently violates these same taboos of sanctification. But this is an odd choice for the Mishnah, since there is now no Temple on earth. The juxtaposition appears then to involve courts and Temple, and the upshot is that both are equally matters of theory. In the theory at hand, then, the earthly court, for its part, penalizes social crimes against the community that the Heavenly court, on the one side, and the Temple rites, on the other, do not take into account at all. These are murder, apostasy, kidnapping, public defiance of the court, and false prophecy. The earthly court further imposes sanctions on matters of particular concern to the Heavenly court, with special reference to taboos of sanctification (for example, negative commandments). These three institutions, therefore, exercise concrete and material power, utilizing legitimate violence to kill someone, exacting penalties against property, and inflicting pain. The sages' modes of power, by contrast, stand quite apart, apply mainly to their own circle, and work through the intangible though no less effective means of inflicting shame or paying honor.

The facts we have in hand draw us back to the analysis of our differentiation of applied and practical power. In the nature of the facts before us, that differentiation tells us precisely for what the systemic myth will have to give its account. Power flows through three distinct but intersecting dominions, each with its own concern, all having some interests in common. The Heavenly court attends to deliberate defiance of Heaven, the Temple to inadvertent defiance of Heaven. The earthly court attends to matters subject to its jurisdiction by reason of sufficient evidence, proper witnesses, and the like, and these same matters will come under Heavenly jurisdiction when the earthly court finds itself unable to act. Accordingly, we have a tripartite system of sanctions – Heaven cooperating with the Temple in some matters, with the court in others, and, as noted, each bearing its own distinct media of enforcing the law as well. What then can we say concerning the systemic myth of politics? The forms of power and the modes of mediating legitimate violence draw our attention to a single political myth, one that we first confronted, if merely as a generality and commonplace to be sure, at the very outset. The unity of that myth is underlined by the simple fact that the earthly court enters into the process right alongside the Heavenly court and the Temple; as to blasphemy, idolatry, and magic, its jurisdiction prevails. So a single myth must serve all three correlated institutions.

It is the myth of God's authority infusing the institutions of Heaven and earth alike, an authority diffused among three principle foci or circles of power, Heaven's court, the earthly court, and the Temple in between. Each focus of power has its own jurisdiction and responsibility, Heaven above, earth beneath, the Temple in the position of mediation – transmitting as it does from earth to

Heaven the penalties handed over as required. And all media of power in the matter of sanctions intersect at some points as well: a tripartite politics, a single myth drawing each component into relationship with a single source and origin of power, God's law set forth in the Torah. But the myth has not performed its task until it answers not only the question of why, but also the question of how. Specifically, the details of myth must address questions of the details of power. Who then tells whom to do what? And how are the relationships of dominion and dominance to compliance and obedience made permanent through myth?

We did not require this sustained survey to ascertain that God through the Torah has set forth laws and concerns. That generality now may be made quite specific, for it is where power is differentiated and parceled out that we see the workings of the political myth. So we ask, how do we know who tells whom to do, or suffer, what sanction or penalty? It is the power of myth to differentiate that defines the generative question. The key lies in the criterion by which each mode of power, earthly, mediating, and Heavenly, identifies the cases over which it exercises jurisdiction. The criterion lies in the attitude of the human being who has done what he or she should not: did he act deliberately or unintentionally?

I state the upshot with heavy emphasis: the point of differentiation within the political structures, supernatural and natural alike, lies in the attitude and intention of a human being. We differentiate among the application of power by reference to the attitude of the person who comes into relationship with that power. A person who comes into conflict with the system, rejecting the authority claimed by the powers that be, does so either deliberately or inadvertently. The myth accounts in the end for the following hierarchization of action and penalty, infraction and sanction: (1) if the deed is deliberate, then one set of institutions exercises jurisdiction and utilizes supernatural power; (2) if the deed is inadvertent, another institution exercises jurisdiction and utilizes the power made available by that same supernatural being.

A sinner or criminal who has deliberately violated the law has by his or her action challenged the politics of Rabbinic Judaism. Consequently, God or God's surrogate imposes sanctions – extirpation (by the court on high), or death or other appropriate penalty (by the court on earth). A sinner or criminal who has inadvertently violated the law is penalized by the imposition of Temple sanctions, losing valued goods. People obey because God wants them to and has told them what to do, and when they do not obey, a differentiated political structure appeals to that single hierarchizing myth. The components of the myth are two: first, God's will, expressed in the law of the Torah; second, the human being's will, carried out in obedience to the law of the Torah or in defiance of that law.

Have we come so far and not yet told the story that the myth contains? I have now to explain and spell out the story that conveys the myth of politics in Rabbinic Judaism. It is not in the Mishnah at all. Do I find the mythic foundation in Scripture, which accounts for the uses and differentiation of power that the Mishnah's system portrays? Indeed I do, for, as we realize, the political myth of Rabbinic Judaism has to explain the differentiation of sins or crimes, with their associated penalties or punishments, and so sanctions of power. And in Scripture there is a very precise answer to the question of how to differentiate among sins or crimes and why to do so. Given the position of the system of the Mishnah, the point of differentiation must rest with one's attitude or intentionality. And, indeed, I do have two stories of how the power of God conflicts with the power of humanity in such a way as to invoke the penalties and sanctions in precisely the differentiated modes we have before us. Where do I find such stories of the conflict of wills, God's and humanity's?

The first such story of power differentiated by the will of the human being in communion or conflict with the word of the commanding God comes to us from the Garden of Eden. We cannot too often re-read the following astonishing words:

> The Lord God took the man and placed him in the garden of Eden...and the Lord God commanded the man, saying, "Of every tree of the garden you are free to eat; but as for the tree of knowledge of good and bad, you must not eat of it; for as soon as you eat of it, you shall die."
>
> ...When the woman saw that the tree was good for eating and a delight to the eyes, and that the tree was desirable as a source of wisdom, she took of its fruit and ate; she also gave some to her husband, and he ate...
>
> The Lord God called out to the man and said to him, "Where are you?"
>
> He replied, "I heard the sound of You in the garden, and I was afraid, because I was naked, so I hid."
>
> Then He asked, "Who told you that you were naked? Did you eat of the tree from which I had forbidden you to eat?"

...And the Lord God said to the woman, "What is this you have done!"

So the Lord God banished him from the garden of Eden...

(Genesis 2:15 – 3:23)

Now a reprise of the exchange between God, Adam, and Eve, tells us that at stake was responsibility: who has violated the law, but who bears responsibility for deliberately violating the law:

"The woman You put at my side – she gave me of the tree, and I ate."

"The serpent duped me, and I ate."

Then the Lord God said to the serpent, "because you did this..."

(Genesis 3:12–14)

The ultimate responsibility lies with the one who acted deliberately, not under constraint or on account of deception or misinformation, as did Adam and Eve. Then the sanction applies most severely to the one who by intention and an act of will has violated God's intention and will.

The political myth of Rabbinic Judaism now emerges in the Mishnah in all of its tedious detail as a reprise – in now-consequential and necessary, stunning detail – of the story of God's commandment, humanity's disobedience, God's sanction for the sin or crime, and humanity's atonement and reconciliation. The Mishnah omits all explicit reference to myths that explain power and sanctions, but invokes in its rich corpus of details the absolute given of the story of the distinction between what is deliberate and what is mitigated by an attitude that is not culpable, a distinction set forth in the tragedy of Adam and Eve, in the failure of Moses and Aaron, and in countless other passages in the Pentateuch, Prophetic Books, and Writings. Then the Mishnah's is a politics of life after Eden and outside of Eden. The upshot of the matter is that the political myth of Rabbinic Judaism sets forth the constraints of freedom, the human will brought to full and unfettered expression, imposed by the constraints of revelation, God's will made known.

Since it is the freedom of humanity to make decisions and frame intentions that forms the point of differentiation among the political media of power, we are required, in my view, to return to the paradigmatic exercise of that same freedom, that is, to Eden, to the moment when Adam and Eve exercise their own will and defy God. Since the operative criterion in the differentiation of sanction – that is, the exercise of legitimate violence by Heaven or earth or the Temple – is the human attitude and intention in carrying out a culpable action, we must recognize that the politics before us rehearses the myth of Adam and Eve in Eden – it finds its dynamic in the correspondence between God's will and humanity's freedom to act however it chooses, thus freely incurring the risk of penalty or sanction for the wrong exercise of freedom.

At stake is what Adam and Eve, Moses and Aaron, and numerous others intend, propose, plan, for that is the point at which the politics intervenes, making its points of differentiation between and among its sanctions and the authorities that impose those penalties. For that power to explain difference, which is to say, the capacity to represent and account for hierarchy, we are required, in my opinion, to turn to the story of the fall of Adam and Eve from Eden and to counterpart stories. The reason is that the political myth derives from that same myth of origins its points of differentiation and explains by reference to the principal components of that myth – God's and humanity's will and power – the dynamics of the political system at hand. God commands, but humanity does what it then chooses, and in the interplay of those two protean forces, each power in its own right, the sanctions and penalties of the system apply.

Power comes from two conflicting forces, the commanding will of God and the free will of the human being. Power expressed in immediate sanctions is also mediated through these same forces, Heaven above, human beings below, with the Temple mediating between the two. Power works its way in the interplay between what God has set forth in the law of the Torah and what human beings do, whether intentionally, whether inadvertently, whether obediently, whether defiantly. That is why the politics of Rabbinic Judaism is a politics of Eden. True, as we shall now see, we listen in vain in the creation myth of Genesis for echoes resounding in the shape of the institutions such as those the politics of Rabbinic Judaism actually invents. But the points of differentiation of one political institution from another will serve constantly to remind us of what, in the end, serves to distinguish this from that, to set forth not a generalized claim that God rules through whoever is around with a sword (or the right, that is, Roman sponsorship).

The careful descriptions of, and distinctions among, institutions, through a vastly and richly nuanced account of concrete and enduring institutions, will once more emphasize the main point. It is how people know that power lies here, not there, is exercised by this bureau, not that, that we find our way back to the myth of differentiation and hierarchization. In what is to follow, we shall see how effectively the politics of Judaism distinguishes one institution from another, just as, in our survey of sanctions, we recognize the points of intersection and of separation. At every point we shall therefore be reminded of the most formidable source of power, short of God, in all. That always is the will of the human being. And he and she are never mentioned as paramount actors, even though, in this politics, humanity is what is at issue. For in the end, as we shall now see, politics makes a statement of theological anthropology: just exactly what do we conceive Man to be?

To what end? The politics of this Judaism finds its teleology in eternity; its account of the theory of power over the nation, Israel, appeals in the end to the conception of an entire nation outliving the grave. This is stated very simply in the opening lines of the protracted account of who gets, and who does not get, a share in the world to come. The importance of the passage requires us to consider it in full detail. It is the single most important political statement in the Mishnah. It is also quintessentially a political statement about the state of the people, Israel, and about the state that they create, complete with the program of sanctions, spelled out in Mishnah-tractate Sanhedrin, of which the following comes as the climactic formulation:

### Mishnah-tractate Sanhedrin 10:1–3

[A]  All Israelites have a share in the world to come,

[B]  as it is said, *Your people also shall be all righteous, they shall inherit the land forever; the branch of my planting, the work of my hands, that I may be glorified* (Is. 60:21).

The proof-text at [B] bears a definition of the world to come, with its reference to (1) the land, to (2) permanent possession of the land, to (3) Israel's possession of the land as God's doing. Here then is the world to come: locativity attained at the end, the fulfillment of a utopian politics in some one place. But that one place is not of this world at all. It finds its boundaries not in space but in time and space joined in union with God. It constitutes life eternal in the land of Israel under God's protection. And this offers a vision of eternity that is, as a matter of fact, deeply political in its essence. For the system's teleology speaks of a political entity, this people forming a nation,

31

that is, "Israel," with its system of penalties and sanctions – its politics – located in a particular place, the "land," and a permanent possession of enduring life in that community, that "people" that is "your people" and "righteous." But, we note, the principle is static, not dynamic. No matter what happens now or in the short term, and without regard to who does or does not do what is expected, all Israel has a share in that coming world. Clearly, we have here a politics of eternity, not a politics of time at all.

So here is the systemic teleology and source of passion, in politics in particular, fully exposed in a simple assertion that everybody will get that "world to come" that is none other than the "Israel" of the here and now. They will never die and (by way of definition) they will always possess the sanctified territory in which God does God's planting. No wonder that death at the hands of the earthly court or extirpation by the Heavenly court prove ephemeral; everybody, that is, every Israelite, will live forever pretty much in the place and in the manner of the present, except that all will be righteous, none will die, and God will secure the society and state of that unending present coming in the indeterminate future.

Then, if that is the systemic teleology, is there any political penalty at all? Of course there is, and it is specifically defined for kings and for ordinary folk alike (but never for identified priests – the Mishnah refers only to a wicked high priest – or for sages, identified or otherwise). First, some actions permanently exclude a person from ongoing existence, from life beyond the grave:

[C] And these are the ones who have no portion in the world to come:

[D] (1) He who says the resurrection of the dead is a teaching which does not derive from the Torah, (2) and the Torah does not come from Heaven; and (3) an Epicurean.

[E] R. Aqiba says, "Also: he who reads in heretical books,

[F] "and he who whispers over a wound and says, *I will put none of the diseases upon you which I have put on the Egyptians, for I am the Lord who heals you* (Ex. 15:26)."

[G] Abba Saul says, "Also: he who pronounces the divine Name as it is spelled out."

(M. 10:1)

Clearly, the true mortal sins comprise doctrinal violations directed against God. These include, for example, denying the resurrection of the dead as a teaching of the Torah. Such a denial effectively denies the world to come – and what one denies one cannot have. As for denying that the Torah comes from God, practicing the sin of Epicureanism, reading heretical books, using God's name in healing, or expressing God's ineffable name, these form mere concretizations of the same species of sin. Unlike sins or crimes committed against other human beings – or even against the law of the Torah and the social order – these sins or crimes directly and immediately engage God. They misuse God's name, deny God's Torah, and above all and first of all, reject the view that God has provided life as the permanent condition of creation. Why should my utterances in these matters make so profound a difference, over-riding all other crimes or sins? Because in misusing God's name and in denying the Torah, the Israelite places his or her will over the will of God in an explicit and articulated way.

So the systemic passion expresses a theological anthropology. Indeed, the various forms of blasphemy that provoke political penal-ties (whether from Heaven or on earth) deny that the human being is like God – if the Torah does not teach that the human being gets "the world to come," which is to say, lives beyond the grave, then the Torah does not represent the human being as like God, who lives forever. These two notions unite into a single sanc-tion: denying eternal life for the human being means rejecting the image of God as it defines human beings, and, species of the same genus of crime and sin, misusing the name or the image of God provokes the same odious penalty. So the teleological reading of the sanctions at hand allows us clear entry into the passionate concern of the politics as a structure and system. What motivates the politics is the issue of death or life.

No wonder, then, that those who have no access to "the world to come," in this context, in light of the definitive proof-text, to eternal life beyond the grave, require specification. Kings and commoners, prophets and ordinary people, all are listed, with their crimes or sins alongside. The kings are those who caused Israel to sin. Then come entire political entities, complete communities, "the generation of the flood," "the generation of Babel," "the men of Sodom." These are gentiles, but not individuals. They are political entities, and what these have in common is that as entire communi-ties, they form counterparts to Israel as a whole nation.[6] They rebelled against God, so they lost eternal life. Then come individual Israelites too.

Which Israelites lose the world to come? The counterpart to rejecting God is rejecting the Land. In light of the definitive proof-text with which we began, that hardly presents a surprise. The spies who rejected the land have lost their portion in the world to come. So too have the generation of the wilderness, which did not believe and trust. Clearly, then, the counterpart to the kings who made Israel sin and the gentiles who warred against God, are the Israelites who rejected the Land, on the one side, or who rejected God, on the other.

[A] Three kings and four ordinary folk have no portion in the world to come.

[B] Three kings: Jeroboam, Ahab, and Manasseh.

[C] R. Judah says, "Manasseh has a portion in the world to come,

[D] "since it is said, *And he prayed to him and he was entreated of him and heard his supplication and brought him again to Jerusalem into his kingdom* (2 Chron. 33:13)."

[E] They said to him, "To his kingdom he brought him back, but to the life of the world to come he did not bring him back."

[F] Four ordinary folk: Balaam, Doeg, Ahitophel, and Gahazi.

(M. 10:2)

[I A] The generation of the flood has no share in the world to come,

[B] and they shall not stand in the judgment,

[C] since it is written, *My spirit shall not judge with man forever* (Gen. 6:3) –

[D] neither judgment not spirit.

[II E] The generation of the dispersion has no share in the world to come,

[F] since it is said, *So the Lord scattered them abroad from up there upon the face of the whole earth* (Gen. 11:8).

[G] *So the Lord scattered them abroad* – in this world.

[H] *and the Lord scattered them from there* – in the world to come.

[III I] The men of Sodom have no portion in the world to come,

[J] since it is said, *Now the men of Sodom were wicked and sinners against the Lord exceedingly* (Gen. 13:13) –

[K] *Wicked* – in this world,

[L] *And sinners* – in the world to come.

[M] But they will stand in judgment.

[N] R. Nehemiah says, "Both these and those will not stand in judgment,

[O] "for it is said, *Therefore the wicked shall not stand in judgment, nor sinners in the congregation of the righteous* (Ps. 1:5) –

[P] *"Therefore the wicked shall not stand in judgment* – this refers to the generation of the flood.

[Q] *"Nor sinners in the congregation of the righteous* – this refers to the men of Sodom."

[R] They said to him, "They will not stand in the congregation of the righteous, but they will stand in the congregation of the sinners."

[IV S] The spies have no portion in the world to come,

[T] as it is said, *Even those men who brought up an evil report of the land died by the plague before the Lord* (Num. 14:37) –

[U] *Died* – in this world.

[V] *By the plague* – in the world to come.

[V W] (1) "The generation of the wilderness has no portion in the world to come and will not stand in judgment,

[X] "for it is written, *In this wilderness they shall be consumed and there they shall die* (Num. 14:25)," the words of R. Aqiba.

[Y] R. Eliezer says, "Concerning them it says, *Gather my saints together to me, those that have made a covenant with me by sacrifice* (Ps. 50:5)."

[Z] (2) "The party of Korah is not destined to rise up,

[AA] "for it is written, *And the earth closed upon them* – in this world.

[BB] *"And they perished from among the assembly* – in the world to come," the words of R. Aqiba.

[CC] And R. Eliezer says, "Concerning them it says, *The Lord kills and resurrects, brings down to Sheol and beings up again* (1 Sam. 2:6)."

[DD] (3) "The ten tribes are not destined to return,

[EE] "since it is said, *And he cast them into another land, as on this day* (Deut. 29:28). Just as the day passes and does not return, so they have gone their way and will not return," the words of R. Aqiba.

[FF] R. Eliezer says, "Just as this day is dark and then grows light, so the ten tribes for whom it now is dark – thus in the future it is destined to grow light for them."

(M. 10:3)

As we review the catalog of those who have lost life beyond the grave, we notice a curious disjuncture between the initial catalog and the illustrative materials. Our account of who has no share in the world to come begins with those who commit crimes or sins against God. Such crimes or sins are individual, since they concern matters of conviction, on the one side, and misappropriation of divine power by the individual, on the other. But the account goes on to deal with kings and ordinary folk, as public figures. Its kings are those who made Israel sin; its ordinary folk are false prophets, again, persons who have access to legitimate power and who have misused it. And then, as if to underline the utterly public and shared political sanction at hand, the catalog provides a series of gentile, then Israelite political entities that are denied eternal life. This means that a share in the world to come is something one gains, or loses, as part of an entire community, and that the condition of the public interest dictates the fate of the private person. Entire generations of gentiles, groups and an entire generation of Israelites form such entities.

So the passion and motivation point to the proposition that the political entity, Israel, will endure forever. That political entity, Israel, moreover is made up of persons who will never really die, in that, in the world to come, they will live forever. And my characterization of matters is right at the surface, even though, admittedly, evidences of passion and encompassing concern prove difficult to locate in a document so laconic as the Mishnah and in a system so centered upon stability and order as the initial politics of Rabbinic Judaism. Wanting to find out what people so cared about as to identify with the purpose of shared society and collective action yields only one ineluctable result. People individually did not want to die, and collectively wanted to stay right where they were and do pretty much what they then were doing. So, as we saw in those simple, but definitive words, "life in the world to come" means life in the Land, secured by God, living and not dying.

Now one may ask what such a teleology has to do with the politics of the here and now. In light of the account of sanctions now reviewed, the question bears its own self-evidently valid answer. The system as a whole is meant to secure that here-and-now of life in the Land, the life of the people sustained by the Land, the life beyond death for individuals and for nation alike. And that teleological and eschatological vision forms not only the goal of politics but also the explanation and justification for the most violent media available to the political entity, which is denial of life. None then can miss the appropriate quality of the passion and its complement, the pathos, of the politics of this Judaism: to live forever, to lose life forever. That is to say, to live forever, like God, or to lose life forever, unlike God. Faced with such a choice, who could remain indifferent?

To conclude: a tripartite plan, in which Heaven, earth, and mediating Temple collaborate to realize a complete political structure and system bespeaks a single passion. Constant caring about what people do, passionate concern to correct and sustain right thought and right action, flow from the paramount appeal to the systemic theory of God in relationship to the Israelite individual and also to the entire holy society, Israel. The task of the social order, and thus of its politics, requires people working together in a holy community to aim at the sanctification of the here and now. In line with the sanctification of creation on the eve of the seventh day, when all things were in place and subject to their correct name, sanctification is understood as the stable and proper ordering of all things in the plan and program of Heaven. But the here and the now form the vestibule, prologue to the eternal life of Israel, political entity and social fact, through all time.

From their intellects, the Mishnah's system-builders of Rabbinic Judaism have composed a world at rest, perfect and complete, made holy because it is complete and perfect. In mythic terms, the Mishnah confronts the fall from Eden with Eden, with the world on the eve of the Sabbath of Creation:

> Thus the heavens and the earth were finished and all the host of them. And on the seventh day God finished his work which he had done, and he rested on the seventh day from all his work which he had done. So God blessed the seventh day and hallowed it, because on it God rested from all his work which he had done in creation.
>
> (Genesis 2:1–3)

The Mishnah's framers have posited an economy embedded in a social system awaiting the seventh day, and that day's divine act of sanctification which, as at the creation of the world, would set the seal of holy rest upon an again complete creation. There is no place for action and actors when what is besought is no action whatsoever, but only unchanging perfection. There is room only for a description of how things are, for the present tense, for a sequence of completed statements and static problems. All the action lies within, in how these statements are made. Once they stand fully expressed, when nothing remains to be said, nothing remains to be done.

# 2

# APOSTLES AND BISHOPS: A POLARITY OF POWER IN EARLIEST CHRISTIANITY

Institutional authority appears in no uncertain terms during the emergence of Christianity in its Classical and Orthodox form. Indeed, the certain and even absolute terms of reference which are claimed only emphasize an equally remarkable feature of Christian institutions of political authority: *different* institutions, sometimes concurrently, claim comprehensive authority over the Church. For that reason, our task in this chapter is to understand the grounds and the forms which institutional authority took in the Church at its earliest stages. Only by grasping that diversity will this complex phenomenon be understood. Two forms of authority will concern us here: the authority of apostles, and the authority of bishops. Each form takes Jesus as its ground of authority, but in a distinctive sense; each understands that its horizon of power is bounded only by heaven. There are, to be sure, other forms of institutional authority within early Christianity, some reflected within the New Testament itself. They could be equally trenchant in their claims (as we will see in some of the examples taken up in Chapter 4), or susceptible of incorporation within an apostolic or episcopal paradigm (as we will also see in Chapter 4), but the tension between apostolic authority and episcopal authority marks the principal polarity of tension within the institutional understanding of the Church in its classic form. The concern of the present chapter is simply to understand those two poles, how they came to be and how they functioned. How they related to one another and other forms of authority in the Church is the concern of Chapter 4. We also leave aside, until Chapter 6, a discussion of the authority of the Emperor, on the understanding that it was a late development which reflects more the environment within which episcopal authority was exercised than a genuine competitor in the day-to-day discipline of the Church.

## Jesus, the kingdom, and his apostles

Jesus' teaching focused plainly and without apology on the kingdom of God. That is both the incentive and the challenge to an understanding of authority, since the kingdom must be seen, whatever else it is, as political. At no point within the authentic sayings of Jesus is there a prosaic description of the kingdom, the moment or the method of its coming. It is out there in the future, but near, within us and outside us. Jesus himself cast out demons in its name and thereby provided a root of christology, but in his sayings leaven is the kingdom's image as much as he himself is; it is implausible to claim that the underlying meaning of the kingdom was Jesus' exalted status. Rather, God's own activity is the center and focus of the kingdom. We are to be ready for what we cannot see, and pure by standards Jesus refuses to set. The radiance of the kingdom is to shelter us, even as we risk all to storm in. Deliberate paradox is obviously part and parcel of Jesus' message.

The place of paradox in Jesus' teaching has been investigated keenly in recent years.[1] Paradox, of course, can be used as an occasion to see things in a new way, to break through habits of thought which are not appropriate to the apprehension of a new reality. But the breakthrough which animated Jesus was not simply cognitive. He understood the kingdom of which he spoke to be final, all-pervading, perfect, holy, and radiant. It was to consume all that is, even as it opened itself to all.

Yet he spoke, not in exclusively visionary terms, but of the promise of the kingdom in the midst of the ordinary. Although final, the kingdom is also near. A host of small disclosures intimate what is to be immanent, even as finite acts of love herald the perfect justice which is to be. The ordinary purity of Israel at table is as much a seal of the kingdom's sanctity as a mustard seed is proof of its eventual consummation.

Precisely because Jesus emphasized the ordinary as the medium of the divine, his teaching of the kingdom seems strangely indeterminate. He neither embraces nor (at first) challenges the Temple as the center of God's sanctity; he neither accepts nor rejects the Roman Imperium as the legitimate instrument of political power. He will not be pinned down in regard to when the kingdom will be, where it is or will be, what acts precisely will insure entry, how purity consistent with the kingdom is to be maintained, or who finally will be able to nest in its shelter. Almost any other Judaic theology of the kingdom will answer those questions more clearly than Jesus does. Only he will turn to the pragmatics of daily living, and insist that the kingdom is to be found there, on its way to culmination.

In Jesus' teaching, the kingdom is presented as the ways in which God is active with his people. Because God as kingdom is active, response to him is active, not merely cognitive. The kingdom of God is a matter of performing the hopeful dynamics of God's revelation to his people. For that reason, Jesus' teaching was not only a matter of making statements, however carefully crafted and remembered. He also engaged in characteristic activities, a conscious performance of the kingdom, which invited Israel to enter into the reality which he also portrayed in words.

Because his distinctive theology was that God was revealing himself definitively in the leaven, in the graspings of a child, in his own exorcisms, in the mustard seed, and in the way we might pray for the kingdom and consequently see it, any limitation on the understanding of how the kingdom might potentially be revealed was inappropriate. Jesus was not explicitly a universalist; had he been, the controversies concerning circumcision and rules of purity within the Church could not have occurred.[2] But Jesus thought so consistently within the terms of reference of what could be seen, heard, or otherwise experienced, that the significance of social boundaries in the world outside – Jew and non-Jew, Roman and subject, priest and peasant – receded into the background.

Writing during the third century, Origen, the theologian who resided first in Alexandria, then in Caesarea, denied that God could be described as bodily, although he is the source of all nature and mind, because he is spirit (*On First Principles* 1.2.8.).[3] Mystical theology since Origen has described God as a sphere whose center is nowhere and whose circumference is everywhere.[4] The focus on the nature of God's revelation caused Origen to deny locality and limit in speaking of God. Jesus engaged in a similar distortion of conventional geometry, the usual language of the kingdom, in his insistence on consuming the formulation of boundaries within the details of experience.

Once experience and activity are taken to be the terms of reference of the kingdom, what one actually does is also an instrument of its revelation, an aspect of its radiance. Jesus' awareness of that caused him to act as programmatically as he spoke, to make of his total activity a parable of the kingdom. That, too, was appreciated by Origen, who referred to Jesus as *autobasileia*, the kingdom itself.[5] Jesus, in speaking of his exorcisms, approached that statement himself (Matthew 12:28; Luke 11:20), although in his own conception, that made him no better than mustard seed or leaven.

Still, on any reckoning (including his own), Jesus was the principal agent of the kingdom of God. Personal, continuous contact with him was therefore not only a matter of discipleship, that following of Jesus which could enable one to enter into the kingdom oneself: it was also a matter of apostleship, that being commissioned by Jesus which brought his own activity by means of his delegates to places where he himself was not present. As a rabbi of his period, Jesus quite naturally had his disciples, his *talmidim*. In that regard, his activity might be regarded as typically Judaic. But in the institution of the apostle or delegate, the *shaliah*, Jesus broke new ground.[6] What had been a matter of occasional representation by a delegate (for purposes of business and personal matters, as well as in religious contexts) becomes in the practice of Jesus a programmatic method of extending what he says and does in regard to the kingdom to a new constituency beyond the range of his personal contact. One of the earliest sources within the Gospels is the best guide to this development.

Recent discussion of the source known as "Q" has brought about a remarkable consensus that at least some of the sayings within it were circulated a few years after the crucifixion, around the year 35 CE. It was at base a collection of sayings (today represented by some two hundred verses in the Gospels according to Matthew and Luke, but absent – apart from possible echoes – from the Gospel according to Mark), much in the manner of a mishnah which a rabbi might have his disciples learn. Indeed, it is plausible that the organization of what we call "Q" (after the German term *Quelle*, meaning "source") was initiated by Jesus himself, to instruct the disciples he sent out on his behalf as delegates. A recent study includes in the earliest version of Q a charge to Jesus' disciples (Luke 10:3–6, 9–11, 16), a strategy to cope with resistance to their message (Luke 6:27–35), examples of how to speak of the kingdom (Luke 6:20b-21, 11:2–4, 14–20, 13:18–21), curses to lay on those who reject people sent in the name of the kingdom (Luke 11:39–48, 52), and a section relating John the Baptist and Jesus as principal emissaries of the kingdom (Luke 7:24b-26, 28a, 33–4).[7]

The reconstruction proposed by Leif Vaage follows in the wake of the recent fashion of proposing multiple versions of Q prior to the composition of Matthew and Luke. He cites John Kloppenborg's hypothesis of three redactions of Q prior to the Gospels, but in Vaage's own analysis his concern is to distinguish the formative stage from the redaction more generally. In that approach, Vaage's work is comparable to the more conservative contribution of David Catchpole, which appeared in the previous year.[8]

Catchpole isolates the formative material of the charge to Jesus' disciples much as Vaage does (Luke 10:3, 4, 5–7, 9, 10a, 11a, 12). He sees that as "an integrated whole stemming from Jesus himself," which has been layered over with additional material (Luke 10:2, 13–15, 16). The additional material represents the especial concerns of Q: christology, eschatology, and the final mission to Israel on Jesus' behalf.[9]

The agreement between Vaage and Catchpole in regard to the formative stage of Q makes their profound disagreement in regard to the cultural milieu of Q all the more striking. Two statements, placed side by side, will illustrate their dissonance:

> Like the Cynics, the "Galilean upstarts" whom Q's formative stratum represents conducted in word and deed a form of "popular" resistance to the official truths and virtues of their day.
>
> (Vaage, p. 106)

> ...there is a preoccupation with a mission to Israel, which needs to be expanded by means of yet more charismatically endowed missionaries sent out by a settled but charismatic community with the authority of God himself.
>
> (Catchpole, p. 188)

The nearly polar opposition seen here is even greater than may appear at first reading, for while Vaage is characterizing the formative stage of Q, Catchpole is speaking of the redactional product. Vaage's Jesus, and therefore his Q, never had anything to say to or about Israel; Catchpole's Jesus, Catchpole's Q, never had anything but Israel in mind.

Both these perspectives are too rigid, and distort a critical reading of Q. Vaage relies extensively and unreflectively on recent work in North America which has arbitrarily ignored the Judaic milieu of Jesus' activity. Catchpole, on the other hand, understands the "confrontational sense" of such statements as John the Baptist's claim that God could raise up children for Abraham from stones in order to replace those of Israel who refused to repent (Luke 3:8), but he does not adequately allow for the distance from Israel in the final orientation of Q that such a threat implies.

Q is better seen as evolving in two distinct stages. In the first, Jesus' teaching was arranged in the form of a mishnah by his disciples. They took up a ministry in Jesus' name which was addressed to Israel at large after the resurrection. The mishnaic form of Q was preserved orally in Aramaic, and explained how the twelve were to discharge their mission. It included just the materials which have already been detailed – instructions to Jesus' disciples, a strategy of love to overcome resistance, paradigms to illustrate the kingdom, threats directed towards enemies, and a reference to John the Baptist which would serve as a transition to baptism in the name of Jesus. As specified, that is probably the original, mishnaic order of Q. It is the order that accords with Q's purpose within the mission to Israel.

At the final stage, Q's order was changed to become quasi-biographical, in accordance with the order of the Petrine teaching which provided the sequencing of material which the Synoptic Gospels generally follow. At that stage of Q, for example, material concerning John the Baptist was moved to the beginning, and the story of Jesus' temptations (Luke 4:1–13) was added, in order to make the transition to an unequivocal focus upon Jesus rather than John. The final redaction of Q probably took place a decade after the mishnaic stage of Q was composed, probably in Syria, an environment in which both Aramaic and Greek were spoken.

Catchpole and Vaage are both competent guides in the attempt to understand Luke 10:1–12, that is, the commission of the seventy or seventy-two disciples (the number varying with the manuscripts which are followed). Whether one accepts the reading seventy or seventy-two, of course, what is startling is that the number is not twelve, the initial number of the apostles whom Jesus sent out, corresponding to the twelve tribes of Israel (see Matthew 10:1–15; Mark 6:7–13; Luke 9:1–6). Although Luke 10:1–12 is rightly taken by Catchpole, Vaage and others to represent the text of Q more accurately than Matthew does, the number seventy or seventy-two has a later, symbolic significance – representing the non-Jews incorporated within the Church by baptism – which we will address below.

Catchpole adduces much Rabbinic material to elucidate the text, while Vaage cites a range of Cynic sources. Both sorts of analogy are

43

helpful in understanding the literary shape of the commission, but the focus here is different. Our purpose is to understand the commission of the disciples in terms of the kingdom (the foundational category of authority in Jesus' teaching), and the kingdom in terms of the commission. If, as seems to be the case, Q in its mishnaic phase represents Jesus' charge to his disciples as he sent them out to be his representatives, it should reflect his own programmatic activity more lucidly than any inference which we might draw regarding his intentions. Jesus' commission is the closest thing there is to his own commentary on his actions and the actions of his apostles.

What the disciples are told to do seems strange, unless the image of the harvest at the beginning of the charge (Luke 10:2) is taken seriously. Because they are going out as to rich fields, they do not require what would normally be required on a journey: purse, bag, and sandals are dispensed with (Luke 10:4). Their charge is to treat Israel as a field in which one works, not as an itinerary of travel; greeting people along the way (which would only lead to diversions from the task) is even proscribed in Luke 10:4.

In addition, staffs are also prohibited, although they were normally used on journeys for support and protection. That is a detail which we actually know from Luke 9:3, the commission of the twelve (rather than the seventy). Luke 9:3 also prohibits carrying a bag, a provision of bread, money, or a change of clothing. Matthew 10:9–10 agrees in regard to money, a bag, clothing, sandals, and staff, but nothing prohibits bread. Mark 6:8–9 prohibits bread, bag and money, but both a staff and sandals are positively prescribed!

All the additional privations comport with the command to go without sandals, and were a part of the original charge. Each Gospel then softens the stringent requirements somewhat. Matthew omits the prohibition of bread; Luke divides the prohibitions between the twelve (9:1–6) and the seventy (10:1–12). In a more radical way, Mark 6:9 turns the prohibition of sandals into a command to wear them. By the same transformation, Mark 6:8 specifies that a staff "alone" should be carried, so that the imagery of discipleship shifts, from treating all Israel as one's household, to passing through territory which might prove hostile. Such variations reflect differences in primitive Christian practice and in conceptions of discipleship. Similarly, the number of disciples in Luke 10:1, seventy or seventy-two, accommodates to the traditional number of the nations of the world,[10] while the earlier figure of 12 in Matthew 10:5 and Mark

6:7 (and, for that matter, Luke 9:1) represents both the intention of Jesus to address all Israel and the mishnaic stage of Q. The image of Israel as a field ripe for harvest dominates the details of the charge to the disciples in the earliest form of the commission, Jesus' mishnah (cf. the use of the image as applied by Rabbi Tarfon in Avoth 2:15).

Another, powerful analogy is at work within the commission. The Mishnah reflects the common practice in Jerusalem of prohibiting pilgrims to enter the Temple with the bags and staffs and purses with which they had traveled (Berakhoth 9:5).[11] All such items were to be deposited prior to worship, so that one was present simply as a representative of Israel. Part of worship was that one was to appear in one's simple purity. The issue of purity also features prominently in the charge to the disciples (although it is overlooked far too often).

The very next injunction (Luke 10:5–8) instructs the disciples to go into any house of a village they enter, and to offer their peace. They are to accept hospitality in that house, eating what is set before them. The emphasis upon eating what is provided is repeated (Luke 10:7, 8), so that it does not appear to be a later, marginal elaboration. Within Pharisaic constructions of purity, such as are reflected in the Mishnah, the foods one ate and the hospitality one offered and accepted were carefully regulated. In the tractate Demai (2:2), which concerns tithing, one who undertakes to be faithful must tithe what he eats, what he sells, and what he buys, and not accept hospitality from a "person of the land." ("Person of the land", 'am ha-aretz, is a phrase which had been used since the time of Zechariah 7:5 to refer to people whose practices could not be trusted.) Demai (2:3) further specifies that a faithful person must not sell a person of the land wet or dry produce, and must not buy wet produce from him. (Wet produce was held to be susceptible to uncleanness.) The passage goes on to make the rule against hospitality more reciprocal, insofar as he cannot have a person of land as a guest when that person is wearing his own (probably impure) garments: he must first change his clothing. These strictures clearly reflect a construction of purity among the "faithful" (haverim) which sets them apart from other Jews by impinging upon the foods one might eat and trade, and the commerce and fellowship one might enjoy.

Jesus' insistence that his disciples accept hospitality in whatever house would accept them is fully consonant with his reputation as a "glutton and a drunkard" (see Matthew 11:19 and Luke 7:34). There is a deliberate carelessness involved, in the precise sense that the disciples are not to have a care in regard to the practices of purity of those who offer hospitality to them. They are true Israelites. When they join in the meals of the kingdom which Jesus' disciples have arrived to celebrate, when they accept and grant forgiveness to one another in the manner of the Lord's Prayer, what they set upon the table of fellowship from their own effort is by definition pure, and should be gratefully consumed. The twelve disciples define and create the true Israel to which they are sent, and they tread that territory as on holy ground, shoeless, without staff or purse.

The activities of the disciples in the fellowship of Israel are essentially to be the activities of Jesus. As Luke presents Q, they are to heal the sick and preach that the kingdom has drawn near (Luke 10:9); as Matthew presents Q, they are to preach that the kingdom has drawn near and heal, raise the dead, cleanse lepers, cast out demons, all the while taking and giving freely (Matthew 10:7–8). As Catchpole observes, the wording of Matthew correlates the disciples' activities with Jesus' activities, and he thinks the correlation was introduced when the Gospel was composed. But the correlation involved is with material in Q: Jesus' statement of what John the Baptist should be told he is doing (Matthew 11:5 and Luke 7:22). For that reason, Matthew at this point may be held to represent the more primitive wording. In any case, the coordination of the disciples' activity with Jesus' is manifestly an organic aspect of the charge in Q.

The extent of the identity between what Jesus does and what the disciples do is clearly represented at the close of the charge, when the disciples are instructed to shake the dust off their feet from any place that does not receive them (Luke 10:11). That gesture is, of course, vivid on any reading. But on the understanding of the charge which we have developed here on the basis of purity, the symbolism is particularly acute. Towns which do not receive the disciples have cut themselves off from the kingdom of God, and can expect worse than what is in store for Sodom (Luke 10:11–12). Taken as a whole, Jesus' charge of the disciples at the mishnaic stage of Q is an enacted parable of the kingdom of God.

The fact that the kingdom has drawn near is the foundation of everything that is commanded, and the disciples are to address the people they gather in towns and villages in order to announce that dawning reality. Their preaching in itself is a witness to the nature of Jesus' eschatology. Likewise, their engagement in a ministry of healing attests to the immanence of the kingdom. The strong man of ailment is bound in order that the stronger man of the kingdom might prevail (see Matthew 12:28–9; Mark 3:27; Luke 11:20–2). That triumphant immanence of the kingdom, whether marked by healing or the wider range of victories indicated in Matthew 10:8 (compare Luke 10:9), appears in the context of purity. The purity of the kingdom is such as to accept that each forgiven and forgiving Israelite is clean in himself and clean in what he produces. Much of the charge to the disciples is arranged to emphasize the under-standing of purity which enables the triumphant immanence of the kingdom. To reject that kingdom, in the shape of its emissaries, alone can render the very dust of the town unclean. Accepting or rejecting the kingdom is the sole ground on which judgment ulti-mately is conducted.

The resurrection of Jesus involved among the apostles in Jerusalem a conviction that they were personally and communally empowered by the spirit of God. As a consequence of the activity of Peter, that spirit was understood to be available to Christians gener-ally in baptism. In his resumé of the usual presentation of Christian baptism in the New Testament, G.B. Caird observes the close connection between immersion and the gift of the spirit of God:

> The case of Cornelius, in which the Spirit came first and baptism followed (Acts 10:47f.), was an exception to the normal pattern (Acts 2:38) that the Spirit followed baptism.[12]

Those two cases, in Cornelius' house and in Jerusalem at Pentecost, do in fact embrace the overall model of baptism as presented within the book of Acts, the principal source for the practice within the earliest Church. The first instance Caird mentions, the baptisms authorized by Peter in the house of the Roman officer Cornelius (Acts 10) represents the principle of the Petrine extension of activity far outside Jerusalem.[13] The other reference is the famous scene of the mass baptisms (of some three thousand people, according to Acts 2:41) following the events at Pentecost.

But before the contrast between those two scenes can be assessed, the underlying unity of their account of what baptism into Jesus' name involves needs to be appreciated. In each case, the principal agent of baptism, and the person who provides the theology to account for the practice and the attendant experience, is Peter. And the theological account he provides is quite coherent as one moves in order from Acts 2 to Acts 10.

At Pentecost, the spirit is portrayed as descending on the twelve apostles (including the newly chosen Matthias), and they speak God's praises in the various languages of those assembled from the four points of the compass for that summer feast of harvest, both Jews and proselytes (Acts 2:1–12). The mention of proselytes (2:11) and the stress that those gathered came from "every nation under heaven" (2:5) clearly point ahead to the inclusion of non-Jews by means of baptism within Acts.[14] But even Peter's explanation of the descent of the spirit does that (Acts 2:14 ff.). He quotes from the prophet Joel (3:1–5 in the Septuagint), "And it will be in the last days, says God, that I will pour out from my spirit upon all flesh."[15] "All flesh," not only historic Israel, is to receive of God's spirit.

Pentecost is the most notable feast (in calendrical terms) of Peter and his circle. Seven weeks after the close of the entire festival of Passover and Unleavened Bread came the feast called Weeks or Pentecost (in Greek, referring to the period of fifty days that was involved; see Leviticus 23:15–22; Deuteronomy 16:9–12). The waving of the sheaf before the Lord at the close of Passover anticipated the greater harvest (especially of wheat; see Exodus 34:22) which was to follow in the summer, and that is just what Weeks celebrates (so Leviticus 23:10–15). The timing of the coming of the Holy Spirit in the recollection of Peter's circle is unequivocal (Acts 2:1–4), and the theme of Moses dispensing of the spirit on his elders is reflected (see Numbers 11:11–29). The association of Weeks with the covenant with Noah (see *Jubilees* 6:1, 10–11, 17–19) may help to explain why the coming of the spirit then was to extend to humanity at large (see Acts 2:5–11). First fruits were celebrated at Weeks (see Numbers 28:26) and they are used to express the gift of spirit and resurrection in Paul's theology (Romans 8:23, 11:16; 1 Corinthians 15:20, 23). We should expect such connections with the Pentecostal theology of Peter in one of Peter's students (see Galatians 1:18), as we should expect him to be especially concerned to keep the feast of Pentecost (see 1 Corinthians 16:8; Acts 20:16) despite what he said about calendrical observations in Galatians (see Galatians 4:9–10; cf. 2:14).

Now we are in a position to see why it was natural within the Petrine circle to use the cultic language of Pentecost. Those who entered into a fresh relationship to God by means of the Holy Spirit were themselves a kind of "first fruits," finding their identity in relation to Christ or spirit as "first fruit" (so Romans 8:23, 11:16, 16:5; 1 Corinthians 15:20, 23, 16:15; James 1:18; Revelation 14:4). The wide range of that usage, which attests the influence of the

Petrine theology, reflects the deeply Pentecostal character of primitive Christianity in its apostolic form. Access to the covenant by means of the spirit meant that believers entered sacrificially "into the name" (*eis to onoma*) of Jesus in baptism. Also within the Petrine circle, eucharist was celebrated in covenantal terms, when one broke bread and shared the cup "into the remembrance of" (*eis ten anamnesin*) of Jesus, a phrase associated with covenantal sacrifice.[16] Both baptism and eucharist are sacrificial in the Petrine understanding, and both intimately involve the spirit of God.

Hartman makes a similar point in regard to the continuing presence of spirit in his discussion of a famous passage from Paul:

> For just as the body is one and has many members, but all the members of the body, being many, are one body, so is Christ. Because by one spirit we were all immersed into one body, whether Jews or Greeks, whether slaves or free, and we were all made to drink one spirit.
>
> (1 Corinthians 12:12–13)

As Lars Hartman observes:

> The last clause of the verse, "We were all made to drink of one Spirit", could as well be translated "We all had the one Spirit poured over us". The Spirit not only brought the baptised persons into the body of Christ, but also remains with them as a divine active presence.[17]

Spirit is understood to be the continuing medium of faithful existence in Christ, and for that reason it is as natural to associate it with eucharist as with baptism. After all, Paul could also say that believers, like the Israelites, drank the same spiritual drink, which came from Christ (1 Corinthians 10:4),[18] and that the Israelites went through their own immersion (1 Corinthians 10:2).

When Peter is speaking in the house of Cornelius in Acts 10, the spirit falls upon those who are listening, and those there with Peter who were circumcised were astounded "that the gift of the Holy Spirit has been poured even upon the nations" (10:44–5). The choice of the verb "to pour" is no coincidence: it is resonant with the quotation of Joel in Acts 2:17. Indeed, those in Cornelius' house praise God "in tongues" (10:46)[19] in a manner reminiscent of the apostles' prophecy at Pentecost, and Peter directs that they be baptized "in the name of Christ Jesus" (10:47–8). That is just the direction Peter gave earlier to his sympathetic hearers at Pentecost (2:37–8). Probably in the case of his speech at Pentecost, and more definitely in the case of his speech in the house of Cornelius, Peter's directions were in Greek, and we should understand that immersion is not in any general sense and that "Jesus" (*Iesous*) has entered the Greek language as a name for Yeshua. Christian baptism, immersion into the name of Jesus with reception of the Holy Spirit, was developed within the practice of the circle of Peter.

In aggregate, the two passages do not suggest any real dispute as to whether the gift of the spirit followed or preceded baptism into Jesus' name. The point is rather that belief in and baptism into him is connected directly with the outpouring of God's spirit. The apparent disruption of the usual model in Acts 10 is intended to call attention to the artificiality (from the point of view of the emergent Petrine theology) of attempting to withhold baptism from those who believe (as Peter actually says in 10:47).[20] Two questions immediately arise at this point. First, why would it have been so natural for Peter to have extended baptism to non-Jews on the basis of the outpouring of spirit, when he was still sensitive to the scruples of Judaism? (And that sensitivity is recorded by Paul, a contemporary witness – see Galatians 2:11–14.[21]) Second, where did Peter understand the new infusion of spirit to have derived from?

As it happens, those two questions have a single answer. The source of the spirit is Jesus as raised from the dead. In Peter's speech at Pentecost, Jesus, having been exalted to the right hand of God, receives the promise of the holy spirit from the Father and pours it out on his followers (2:33). The spirit which is poured out, then, comes directly from the majesty of God, from his rule over creation as a whole. This is the spirit as it hovered over the waters at the beginning of creation (Genesis 1:2), and not as limited to Israel. Because the spirit is of God, who creates people in the divine image, its presence marks God's own activity, in which all those who follow Jesus are to be included. Jesus' own program had involved proclaiming God's kingdom on the authority of his possession of God's spirit.[22] Now, as a consequence of the resurrection, Jesus had poured out that same spirit upon those who would follow him. Baptism in the spirit (see Acts 1:4–5) and baptism into the name of Jesus were one and the same thing for that reason. That was why, as Hartman suggests, believing that Jesus was God's son and calling upon his name were the occasions on which the spirit was to be received.[23] In the new environment of God's spirit which the resurrection signaled, baptism was indeed, as Matthew 28:19 indicates, an activity and an experience which involved the Father (the source of one's identity), the Son (the agent of one's identity), and the Holy Spirit (the medium of one's identity).

The intimate connection between endowment with the spirit of God and the resurrection of Jesus enables us to understand why the actual constituency of the apostles did not have to be strictly limited to those who had been selected by Jesus as such. In Acts 1:21–6, Matthias is chosen with Joseph Barsabbas, as among those who had been associated with the movement from the time of John's baptism. Both are fit to be witnesses of the resurrection, and the casting of lots results in the choice of Matthias, so that the number twelve is made up. Clearly, the apostolic group in Jerusalem maintained the principle of personal familiarity with Jesus prior to the resurrection and with the movement initiated by John, as well as the significance of the number twelve, even as the persons numbered among the twelve changed. That enables us to understand why there should be variations recorded in the names of those chosen by Jesus (see Matthew 10:2–4; Mark 3:16–19; Luke 6:14–16). These lists represent an amalgam of historical memory and the constituency of the twelve as known to the local authorities in Rome around 70 CE (so Mark) or in Damascus around 80 CE (so Matthew) or in Antioch around 90 CE (so Luke).

But not even these variations convey the explosive potential of the conviction that the spirit of God and the resurrection of Jesus, rather than limitation to the number of the tribes of Israel, together function to designate apostles. Paul came to be known as "the Apostle" with the Christian tradition, and yet he was not personally known to Jesus prior to the resurrection. Indeed, Paul himself recognizes that he is "the least of the apostles," and he goes so far as to say that he is not "worthy to be called an apostle" (1 Corinthians 15:9). That confession of unworthiness is mostly grounded in his admission that he had "persecuted the church of God" (see Galatians 1:23 as well as 1 Corinthians 15:9). Still, he puts himself at the end of the list of those to whom the risen Jesus had appeared, and describes himself in vivid terms, writing around 56 CE:

> Because I delivered to you, among the first, what I myself received, that Messiah died for our sins according to the Scriptures, and that he was buried and that he was raised on the third day according to the Scriptures, and that he appeared to Kepha [Peter], then to the twelve, and then he

appeared to more than five hundred brethren at once, among whom most remain until now, and some have slept. And then he appeared to Yakov [James], then to all the apostles. And last of all, as to a fetus, he appeared to me, too.

(1 Corinthians 15:3–8)

The term here rendered "fetus" (*ektroma*) can also refer to a miscarriage: the point is that Paul was simply not developed at the time Jesus appeared to him. He was a persecutor, not a disciple, and yet God called him to preach his Son among non-Jews (so Galatians 1:16).

Paul's vices do not seem to have included false modesty:[24] his self-deprecation here is strategic. The Corinthian correspondence makes it clear that Paul had to frame his own authority against the claims of others who were accepted as apostles. Indeed, at one point he sounds almost plaintive:

Am I not free? Am I not an apostle? Did I not see the Lord Jesus? Are you not my work in the Lord? Even if I am not an apostle to others, yet I am to you, for you are the seal of my apostleship in the Lord.

(1 Corinthians 9:1–2)

Paul goes on to name his opposition: "the rest of the apostles, and the brothers of the Lord and Kepha [Peter]" (1 Corinthians 9:5). Evidently, from their point of view (or from a perspective representing their point of view), Paul was not an apostle. Paul's response is that the appearance of the risen Lord to him with an apostolic commission made him an apostle.

In his assertion of his apostolic rights (including the right not to work, to be sustained, and to have a wife, see 1 Corinthians 9:3–7), Paul includes himself in the same category as Barnabas (9:6): "Or am I alone with Barnabas in not having authority not to work?" By implication, then, Barnabas is an apostle in the same sense Paul is. Barnabas was an important figure within the church in Jerusalem, but he was a Levite from Cyprus, and certainly did not meet the qualifications of a Matthias.[25] Moreover, Paul does not list Barnabas as among those to whom the risen Jesus appeared. Still, Paul does refer to Jesus' appearance to "all the apostles," and Barnabas might be understood among their number. In any case, we do need to rely on Paul's implication to see Barnabas as an apostle: he is actually named as such, with Paul (and before Paul!) in Acts 14:14.

The total list of those to whom the risen Jesus appeared gives us some idea of the extent to which apostolic identity might be claimed far beyond the circle of the twelve, and Paul and Acts confirm that impression. In 2 Corinthians, Paul makes a particular point of the problems caused by those he calls "super-apostles" (*apostoloi huperlian* – 2 Corinthians 11:5; 12:11). It is theoretically possible that Paul has in mind the same apostolic group (including Peter and Barnabas) he compared himself with in 1 Corinthians 9, but his language is different – and at one point theologically violent – when he speaks of the "super-apostles", and it is much more likely he is thinking of yet another apostolic group.

Paul rages against the "super-apostles" because they are promulgating a different Jesus, a different spirit, a different gospel, from what Paul himself brought (2 Corinthians 11:4). The content of their message and work is not specified, but Paul does refer to their being "Hebrews" (that is, Jews whose native language was Aramaic or Hebrew), "Israelites," and "Abraham's seed" (2 Corinthians 11:22). He has no answer to those claims, except to say that he can claim the same attributes. But he also asserts that, if the super-apostles can claim to be "servants" (*diakonoi*) of Christ, he is more so, and he proceeds to relate his own sufferings on account of his faith (2 Corinthians 11:23–33). In addition, Paul relates a vision and revelation in which he was initiated into the third heaven and heard "unutterable sayings, which it is not appropriate for man to speak" (2 Corinthians 12:1–4). Finally, Paul reminds those who received the letter that, when he was with them, "the signs of the apostle were accomplished among you: signs and wonders and powers" (2 Corinthians 12:12). In that respect, as well, Paul claims not to be lacking in comparison to the "super-apostles" (2 Corinthians 12:11).

So four categories of apostolic attribute underlie the dispute between Paul and the "super-apostles," at least in Paul's mind: rootedness in Israel, suffering for Christ as his servant, vision, and the performance of signs. As compared to the qualifications to be enrolled among the twelve, these categories seem broader, and yet they bear a resemblance to the Petrine emphasis on familiarity with the movement from the time of John the Baptist, attestation of the resurrection in an environment of persecution, and the empowering conveyance of the Holy Spirit. Then, too, the continuity with Jesus' charge to the apostles is palpable: the fundamental issue is the manifestation of his own activity in word and deed. The charge was not reduced, it was rather intensified, as a result of the resurrection: now it was the risen Lord who sent apostles with the power of God's own spirit.

That intensity was largely responsible for the extraordinary efforts – including journeys with all their dangers in the ancient world, the endurance of persecution, ostracism, physical punishment, homelessness, and basic want – which characterized the work of many apostles. Paul's outburst in 2 Corinthians 11:23–33 provides us with a glimpse of the terrible dedication which turned Christianity from a local movement within Judaism into a global religion by the end of the century.[26] That was the common achievement of the apostles more than of any other single group, but Paul permits us to appreciate the dreadful competition among them which that could involve:

> For such are false apostles, deceitful workers, transforming themselves into Christ's apostles. And no wonder: for even Satan transforms himself into an angel of light. It is not a big thing if his servants also transform themselves as servants of righteousness, of whom the end will be according to their works.
>
> (2 Corinthians 11:13–15)

The violence of Paul's language, the emphasis upon the "works" of his opponents, as well as their self-recommendation on the grounds of their Judaic pedigree, all suggest that the "super-apostles" were a group of what Paul calls "Judaizers" in his letter to the Galatians.[27] And in 2 Corinthians, as in Galatians, Paul is angry with the recipients of the letter because they are willing to entertain these preachers, who claim a supernatural warrant (see both Galatians 1:6–9 and 2 Corinthians 11:3–5). In Galatians he wishes they would castrate themselves (Galatians 5:12); in 2 Corinthians they are declared messengers of the devil (as we have seen). Whether in the rhetoric of physical or of theological violence, Paul is claiming the absolute nature of apostolic authority.

Reference to Satan is for Paul no merely decorative image. "Satan" is the agent to whom one hands over a member of the community who has been expelled for final punishment. In 1 Corinthians, Paul provides us with a model of how he sees apostolic authority working out, in this case to deal with a person who has had sexual relations with his step-mother:

I personally – while absent in body, but present in spirit –
have already judged – as being present – the person who
has accomplished this thing in this way: in the name of the
Lord Jesus, when you are gathered together, and my spirit
with the power of the Lord, to deliver such a one to Satan
for destruction of the flesh, so that the spirit might be
saved in the day of the Lord. Your boast is not good. Don't
you know that a little yeast leavens the whole dough?
Cleanse out old yeast, so that you might be new dough,
just as you are: unleavened. For Christ our Passover is sacrificed for us. Therefore let us keep the feast, not with old
yeast, neither with a yeast of depravity or wickedness, but
with the unleavened bread of sincerity and truth.

(1 Corinthians 5:3–8)

Paul has the reputation of globally rejecting regulations of purity,
and he does both set aside the usual practices of restriction on
fellowship at meals,[28] and provide the guidance of intellectual
reflection for the evolution of such policy.[29] But here he insists that
the book of Leviticus is correct: intercourse with one's step-mother
is punishable by being cut off from the people (Leviticus 18:8, 29)
which is to say by death (Leviticus 20:11). In Paul's perspective,
exclusion involves exposure to the eschatological travail which is to
come, and there remains an element of hope (at least for the spirit),
but the ferocity of his explicit commitment to purity in the Church
is quite remarkable. In this, he joins the mainstream of Hellenistic
Christianity, which did not discount the importance of purity, but
conceived of the purity required by God as worked out in the
medium of moral intention.[30]

That commitment is worked out on the basis of Paul's full
deployment of his apostolic authority. He goes on in the passage to
insist that the community of Christians at Corinth should refuse to
eat with those who are guilty of the kind of wickedness he has just
dealt with (1 Corinthians 5:9–13). In other words, Paul invokes
exactly the kind of strictures against sexual immorality which he
insists are contrary to the gospel when they are deployed in respect
of fellowship at meals in his dispute with the "Judaizers"!

Paul makes it plain why the triumph of apostolic Christianity
brought with it the crisis of its own authority. The grounding force
of apostolic activity was understood to be the spirit of God, which
apostles conveyed in baptism,[31] teaching, and discipline, but which
could only be received on the basis of the agreement of the

congregations concerned. For that reason, Paul – and any other apostle – had to be concerned with the continuing fidelity to the gospel as he understood it of any congregation he founded. Attempts to limit the understanding of who might claim to be an apostle are therefore quite understandable. Although Paul does not subscribe to the theory of the twelve, he does hold that seeing the risen Lord is a limiting qualification (1 Corinthians 9:1) – but given that he thinks that opens up the field to over five hundred people (1 Corinthians 15:6), it is not surprising that he got involved in controversy with others who could be described as "super-apostles."

Furthermore, once the definition of apostleship is widened to include a Barnabas for example, as Acts does, it raises the question of whether even Paul's looser statement of criteria was universally accepted. If Barnabas was considered an apostle, did anyone hold Priscilla and Aquila in that regard? After all, they are Jews of the Diaspora, associated with Paul in Corinth for a time (Acts 18:1–3); they travel with him and remain in Ephesus, where they correct the teaching of Apollos, described as a Jew from Alexandria, in regard to the reception of the Holy Spirit in baptism (Acts 18:18–19, 24–8). Paul refers to the same Apollos in 1 Corinthians (1:12, 3:4, 5, 6, 22, 4:6), at one point as a "servant" of Christ comparable to Paul (3:5), and once in the same breath with himself and Peter (3:22). Relations with Apollos were obviously difficult for Paul,[32] but he conveys greetings to the Corinthians from Priscilla and Aquila and the congregation of their house (1 Corinthians 16:19), and refers to them in a similar context as his "fellow workers" in Romans (16:3). Paul does not refer to any of these three as apostles, nor does Acts, but their actions show that the spheres of apostolic authority were not easily circumscribed, and that conflict had to be addressed as an inevitable consequence of the success of apostolic Christianity.

## James, the brother of Jesus, and episcopal authority

### *The episcopal office*

The surprising emergence of the apostolate as a consequence of Jesus' ministry is joined by another surprise at the close of the period of the New Testament. Authority comes increasingly to be vested in the hands of people called bishops (*episkopoi*). The term in classical Greek and in Koine had referred to the function of an overseer. That functional designation brought with it an applicability to a patron's oversight, a philosopher's or even a god's, but the term could also refer to high or low levels of management within a given community.[33] The shift from apostolic to episcopal leadership within the Church was dramatic and rather sudden. The roots of the change are obscure. For reasons that will emerge below, the revolutionary move from apostles to bishops is commonly attributed to Paul, but that is an implausible claim. Paul was simply in no position to influence the order of the Church at large.[34]

Clearest access to our second surprise, the emergence of the episcopate, is afforded by 1 Timothy, a letter composed in Paul's name to the follower called Timothy, whom (according to Acts 16:1–3) Paul associated with his work, having circumcised him first because he was the son of a Jewish mother and a Greek father. The letter is widely and rightly regarded as pseudonymous, along with the other Pastoral Epistles (2 Timothy and Titus). In content, style, and thought, they address the situation of the Church around the year 100 CE.[35] Acts itself, of course, was written only some ten years earlier, so what Acts and the Pastorals say in aggregate about Paul and Timothy – a half century earlier – in their relationships, intents and personal backgrounds, must be approached with great caution if one is seeking historical anecdotes. But history in that sense is not our concern here. 1 Timothy, whatever it may say accurately or inaccurately from the point of view of a critical understanding of Paul and Timothy, is a source of the first importance in coming to understand the emergence of episcopal authority.

By the time of this letter, a sense of the institution of being a bishop had become explicit: "The word is reliable, If anyone aspires to the episcopate (*episkope*), he desires a good work" (1 Timothy 3:1). What follows is not an enumeration of duties, however, but a set of qualifications. A bishop is to be of good repute, and that means that corrupt behavior disqualifies one from the office. Addressing the issue of qualification more positively, 1 Timothy insists a bishop should be monogamous, in control of his own house (including his children), and mature (1 Timothy 3:2–7). The emphasis upon control of one's household is helpful in inferring the episcopal functions which are in mind.

The importance of the house (*oikos*) in defining the church, the local congregation, has been increasingly recognized in recent research.[36] Whether we think of Cornelius in Acts 10 or of Aquila and Priscilla in 1 Corinthians 16:19, the identity of a household with Christ, the baptism of entire families and their retainers, must have constituted the most significant advance for the movement centered on the risen Jesus within any city or town we might imagine. The emergence of the episcopate within any such locality corresponds to the need to integrate one household church with another. Who better to do that than someone visibly in charge of his own house? As 1 Timothy itself puts the principle, "But if someone does not know how to conduct his own house, how will he care for the church of God?" (1 Timothy 3:5).

Because a household definition of the church is operative, a bishop must be hospitable, more literally: "a lover of strangers" (*philoxenon*, 1 Timothy 3:2). Hospitality is a virtue especially stressed within the New Testament as the household definition of the church emerges as paradigmatic. The utility of the household was its solidarity and its focus; what needed to be resisted was its tendency to exclude others. What applied to any given household applied doubly to the attempt to coordinate and integrate one congregation with another within a given city or locale. As we have seen above, and have detailed in regard to the conception of Israel within the church in *Judaism in the New Testament*,[37] apostolic Christianity after Paul had to confront the crisis of its own success. The emergence of the Synoptic Gospels, catechetical instruments for the preparation of people for baptism, marked a concerted attempt (probably initiated by the circle of Barnabas in Antioch) to provide for the ecumenical practice of differing kinds of apostolic Christianity with different standards of purity.

As we concluded in *Judaism in the New Testament*:

> By means of their example, the Synoptic Gospels establish a thoroughly christological technique in the interpretation of Scripture as fulfilled. Christ, the guarantor of the kingdom, is the standard by which Scripture is experienced, corrected, and understood to have been fulfilled.
>
> (*Judaism in the New Testament*, p. 116)

That technique did not legislate how one household church or another, or how an association of such congregations, was finally to adjudicate matters of purity and ethics. But it did provide a criterion for such adjudication, and – equally important – it allowed for variation from one community to another in the application of that criterion. The Synoptic Gospels were not only instruments of catechesis, they were also instruments of the first ecumenical effort within the Church (and perhaps the only real example of success in that effort). Two vital and related aspects of life within churches were addressed by the Synoptics in aggregate: how the Scriptures are to be read through the lens of Christ, and how that reading is to provide guidance for the ordering of the community.

What the Synoptic Gospels do not provide, and could not have provided, is an identification of who should be directing that process within the Church. The disciples and apostles who are clearly identified as guardians of the teaching of Jesus, and who provide insight into its understanding (see Matthew 13:10–17; Mark 4:10–12; Luke 8:9–10),[38] are nonetheless not similarly designated to interpret Scripture. That is entirely natural. Jesus' teaching was more experiential than exegetical; his reliance on a fractured and provisional form of Targumic tradition raises the probability that he was personally illiterate. But with the promulgation of the Synoptic catechesis, and the Synoptic Gospels' crafting of a standard of the christological interpretation of Scripture, a new standard of authority came into being within the Church.

That authority was to be articulated by means of an agent unspecified in the Synoptic Gospels, but clearly named in 1 Timothy. In addition to being hospitable, the bishop according to 1 Timothy is also to be "skilled in teaching" (*didaktikon*, 1 Timothy 3:2). The context of the episcopate within what are perceived to be the threats which are most dangerous to the faith makes it apparent that the teaching function is the most crucial concern. Moreover, the substance of teaching is unmistakably identified as interpretative, magisterial instruction on the basis of the Scriptures of Israel.

Teaching is specified in the opening of 1 Timothy as the paramount concern:

> Just as I summoned you to remain in Ephesus, when I was going to Macedonia, so that you would command some not to promulgate heretical teaching, nor to attend to mythologies or endless genealogies, which furnish controversies rather than God's household management in faith. But the end of the commandment is love from a pure heart and a good conscience and unaffected faith, from which some have deviated to pursue empty discussion – wishing to be teachers of the law, understanding neither what they say nor concerning what they insist. And we know that the law is good, if anyone use it lawfully.
>
> (1 Timothy 1:3–8)

Both the intellectual situation of the letter, and the remedy proposed to address that situation, are clearly intimated here. The threat of those who promulgate heretical teaching (*heterodidaskalein*) on the basis of the Torah is to be met by a teacher who knows the end of the commandment which the Torah teaches. The contrast with Paul's own attitude concerning the purely provisional place of the law is striking (cf. Galatians),[39] but that is of lesser categorical importance than the fundamental hermeneutic to which 1 Timothy commits itself at the outset: the Torah continues to be valid by means of, and is only to be interpreted through, faith in Jesus Christ, a faith which shows itself in love and a good conscience (in addition to 1 Timothy 1:5 see 1:19; the central focus on faith within the letter is quite plain).

The adversaries whose threat is to be met in 1 Timothy are apparently Gnostics of some sort.[40] They favor complicated cosmogonies (1 Timothy 1:4) in order not to attribute creation to the Father, the true God, and they urge abstention from marriage and from certain foods (1 Timothy 4:3). Indeed, it is in opposition to their teaching that 1 Timothy extrapolates Paul's teaching about food, and articulates a formal refusal of the consideration of the purity of foods (1 Timothy 4:4–5): "Because every creature of God is good, and nothing is rejected which is taken with thanksgiving (*eukharistia*), for it is sanctified through God's word and prayer." Gone are the Pauline qualifications that it can be wise to abstain from certain foods if their consumption would lead to a misunderstanding (1 Corinthians 8:7–13; Romans 14:15–23).[41] What is now of paramount importance is to insist upon the basic goodness and acceptability of creation, against those who have – in a Gnostic manner – used a reading of the Torah to evolve a distance between God and creation.

That insistence is the very occasion for the charge to "Timothy" (1 Timothy 4:6): "Laying these things down for the brothers, you will be a good servant of Jesus Christ, reared in the words of faith and of good instruction which you have diligently followed." Faith and instruction are "Timothy's" purpose, and the means to attain the purpose are also set out clearly:

> Until I come, attend to reading, to exhortation, to instruction. Do not neglect the gift which is in you, which was given you through prophecy with laying on of hands by the eldership. Take care of these things, be with them, so that your advance might be manifest to all. Take heed to your-

self and the instruction, for doing this you will save both
yourself and those hearing you.

(1 Timothy 4:13–16)

An entire hierarchy is implied here, with Timothy himself designated as the recipient of a spiritual gift – *kharisma*, charismatic
authority. But that line of inquiry, which will include an investigation of how an entire range of institutional functions was articulated
as a matter of *kharisma*, can only occupy our attention in chapter 4.
At the moment our concern is to emphasize that the ministry
Timothy is authorized to conduct and to continue, by laying hands
on others (1 Timothy 5:22), is actually accomplished by means of
study of the Scriptures and teaching on that basis.

Bishops, then, in the succession of Timothy, are to take up their
management of churches (which includes issues of the distribution
of wealth, see 1 Timothy 6:9–10, 17–19) on the basis of their
authoritative reading and instruction. The willingness to take on
this charge is even compared to the courage of Christ himself:

Fight the good fight of faith; lay hold of eternal life, to
which you were called, and you confessed the good confession before many witnesses. I charge you before the God
who made all things alive and before Jesus Christ, who
witnessed the good confession to Pontius Pilate: keep this
commandment without blemish and without reproach
until the appearing of our Lord Christ Jesus.

(1 Timothy 6:12–16)

"The good confession" here is the integrity of the Christian message
(its *homologia*), which is to be attested before friend and enemy alike
in the manner of Christ, and until his coming. The reading and
instructing bishop, mastering the Scriptures – and that means, in
this period, the Scriptures of Israel – within the light of Christ,
actively takes the place of Christ within the community, until he
comes to judge all. The Pastoral Epistles endow the Synoptic
Gospels with the authoritative agency of episcopal teaching, just
what they required to put their interpretation of Scripture into
effect.

## The emergence of the office

In two obvious respects, the episcopate differs from the apostolate, and those two differences are related to one another. First, the bishop by identity stays put: the managerial responsibility, the care for relations and sound instruction within a local community, root him in a particular congregation or set of congregations. Where the apostle is sent, the bishop is called. Second, the source of the bishop's learning is the Scripture in the light of Christ, rather than a commission which comes directly from Christ (whether before or after the resurrection). Evidently, there is an emerging tradition of instruction concerning Jesus which is contemporaneous with the rise of the episcopate; "Timothy" can be charged to keep the example of Jesus before Pilate in mind (1 Timothy 6:13, cited above), and that presupposes that a general program of catechesis such as the Synoptic Gospels represent was common to Christianity at the time the Pastoral Epistles were composed. But the dynamic which Timothy is to put into action – as in the Synoptic Gospels themselves – involves the interplay between Christ and the Scriptures of Israel.

The two distinctive characteristics of the episcopate, the local focus and the interpretative authority, provide a clear profile of how the institution is to function. But nothing 1 Timothy tells us permits us to explain why an institution so distinct from the apostolate emerged as rapidly and generally as it did. To be sure, there was need for such an office to counterbalance the centrifugal forces of faction within the earliest Church (as has been seen in the previous section). But the need alone does not explain the rapid generation of a solution: as will be seen in Chapter 4, there were a host of other offices (such as prophet and elder and deacon and widow and benefactor) which might have served equally well. Some of them could claim greater antiquity – and certainly better biblical warrant – than the office of *episkopos*. Why should such a Hellenistic institution have prospered, and with little to challenge it during the period of the New Testament?

A single figure within the New Testament allows us to answer that question, and to identify the Judaic roots of the episcopate. That figure is James, the brother of Jesus, whom we have already met in *Judaism in the New Testament*.[42] James' status as Jesus' brother and therefore as head of the Christian congregation in Jerusalem, his dedication to worship in the Temple in Jerusalem, and his exercise of authority on the basis of a precise citation of the Scriptures of

Israel are there introduced and explained. To that we now have to add: Eusebius on several occasions refers to James as having been the first bishop of Jerusalem, and once cites a source of the second century to do so.[43] James died in the year 62 CE, so that his example had been there to influence the emerging model of hierarchy within the Church for three decades before the Pastoral Epistles were written. James was clearly a local leader, who made decisions on the basis of Scripture, and the exercise of his authority – owing to his familial relationship – brought with it a personal link to Jesus himself on the basis of his own "good confession" (as the language of 1 Timothy would have us put it) before both friendly and hostile witnesses. The personal model of James as bishop was evidently sufficient to elevate that office above other possible contenders for what was to be the predominant authority within the Church by the end of the first century.

There is, no doubt, a degree of anachronism in Eusebius' portrait of James' episcopal authority. He conceived of it as being a "throne,"[44] in the manner of the image of dominant power which only the fourth century saw fully achieved, and he imagines a formal election as being involved. In fact, if one sees the episcopate as an entirely Hellenistic invention within the life of the Church, it is easy enough to dismiss the entire reference to James as bishop. But that would be a hasty judgment. Eusebius' reference is persistent, and grounded in an identification of James' office from the second century. Moreover, if Eusebius helps us correctly to identify that office (for all his own anachronism), then we can explain the key shift in the hierarchy of the Church during the first century, from apostolate to episcopate.

Still, the objection remains that *episkopos* is an odd title for James – or for any Aramaic-speaker – to bear. In just this regard, a suggestion made many years ago by Joachim Jeremias turns out to be crucially important. Jeremias fastened his attention on the office of the *mebaqqer* at Qumran.[45] That term in fact means "overseer," just as *episkopos* does, and the *mebaqqer* was charged to do many of the same things that an *episkopos* was do to: he was to teach the Torah (even to priests) as well as the particular traditions of the Essenes, administer discipline, and see to the distribution of wealth (see *Damascus Document* 13:7f., 14:8f., 13f.). As Jeremias points out, comparisons are made between the *mebaqqer* and a father and a shepherd (*Damascus Document* 13:9); he does not mention, but the point is worth making, that Christ himself is said to be an *episkopos*, to care as a shepherd does in bringing us to God (1 Peter 2:25 – a letter, shortly before the Pastorals, written around 90 CE). Divine care and the institution of the overseer appear to have been linked in both Essene theology and primitive Christianity.

The connection as Jeremias attempted to make it was vitiated by his surmise that the community at Qumran somehow represented the Pharisaic ethos.[46] In fact, the Essenes pursued their own system of purity, ethics, and initiation, followed their own calendar, and withdrew into their own communities, either within cities or in isolated sites such as Qumran. There they awaited an apocalyptic war when they, as "the sons of light," would triumph over "the sons of darkness": not only the gentiles, but anyone not of their vision (see the *War Scroll* and the *Community Rule*). The culmination of those efforts was to be complete control of Jerusalem and the Temple, where worship would be offered according to their revelation, the correct understanding of the law of Moses (cf. *Damascus Document* 5:17–6:11).

Now James is quite unlike the Essenes in his acceptance of uncircumcised followers of his brother, as well as in his fellowship in Jerusalem with a group centered on the Temple, unassociated with Qumran. But his devotion to the Temple involved tension with the administration there (tension severe enough ultimately to bring about his death), and he appears to have recourse to an interpretation of Scripture which may be compared to that of the Essenes. To see this, we must revisit the book of Acts,[47] which clearly reflects his perspective in regard to both circumcision and the issue of purity (Acts 15), the two principal matters of concern in Galatians 2. The account in Acts 15 is romanticized; one sees much less of the tension and controversy which Paul attests. But once allowance has been made for the tendency in Acts to portray the ancient Church as a body in harmonious unity, the nature and force of James' position become clear.

The two issues in dispute, circumcision and purity, are dealt with in Acts 15 as if they were the agenda of a single meeting of leaders in Jerusalem. (Paul in Galatians 2 more accurately describes the meeting he had with the leaders as distinct from a later decision to return to the question of purity.) The first item on the agenda is settled by having Peter declare that, since God gave his Holy Spirit to gentiles who believed, no attempt should be made to add requirements such as circumcision (Acts 15:6–11). Paul could scarcely have said it better himself, and it is consistent with the version of Paulinism represented in Acts.

The second item on the agenda is settled on James' authority, not

Peter's, and the outcome is not in line with Paul's thought. James first confirms the position of Peter, but he states the position in a very different way: "Symeon has related how God first visited the gentiles, to take a people in his name" (Acts 15:14). James' perspective here is not that all who believe are Israel (the Pauline definition), but that in addition to Israel God has established a people in his name. How the new people are to be regarded in relation to Israel is a question which is implicit in the statement, and James goes on to answer it. The relationship between those taken from the gentiles and Israel is developed in two ways by James. The first method is the use of Scripture, while the second is a requirement of purity. The logic of them both inevitably involves a rejection of Paul's position (along the lines laid out in Galatians 2).

The use of Scripture, like the argument itself, is quite unlike Paul's. James claims that "with this [that is, his statement of Peter's position] the words of the prophets agree, just as it is written" (Acts 15:15), and he goes on to cite from the book of Amos. The passage cited will concern us in a moment; the form of James' interpretation is an immediate indication of a substantial difference from Paul. As James has it, there is actual agreement between Symeon and the words of the prophets, as two people might agree: the use of the verb *sumphoneo* is nowhere else in the New Testament used in respect of Scripture. The continuity of Christian experience with Scripture is marked as a greater concern than within Paul's interpretation, and James expects that continuity to be verbal, a matter of agreement with the prophets' words, not merely with possible ways of looking at what they mean.

The citation from Amos (9:11–12, from the version of the Septuagint, which was the Bible of Luke–Acts) comports well with James' concern that the position of the Church should agree with the principal vocabulary of the prophets:

> After this I will come back and restore the tent of David which has fallen, and rebuild its ruins and set it up anew, that the rest of men may seek the Lord, and all the gentiles upon whom my name is called.
>
> (Acts 15:16–17)

In the argument of James as represented here, what the belief of gentiles achieves is, not the redefinition of Israel (as in Paul's thought), but the restoration of the house of David. The argument is possible because a Davidic genealogy of Jesus – and, therefore, of his brother James – is assumed.

The account given by Hegesippus of James' preaching in the Temple represents Jesus as the Son of Man who is to come from heaven to judge the world. Those who agree cry out, "Hosanna to the Son of David!" Hegesippus shows that James' view of his brother came to be that he was related to David (as was the family generally) and was also a heavenly figure who was coming to judge the world. When Acts and Hegesippus are taken together, they indicate that James contended Jesus was restoring the house of David because he was the agent of final judgment, and was being accepted as such by gentiles with his Davidic pedigree.

But on James' view, gentiles remain gentiles; they are not to be identified with Israel. His position was not anti-Pauline, or at least not at first. His focus was on Jesus' role as the ultimate arbiter within the Davidic line, and there was never any question in his mind but that the Temple was the natural place to worship God and acknowledge Jesus. Embracing the Temple as central meant for James, as it meant for everyone associated with worship there, maintaining the purity which it was understood that God required in his house. Purity involved excluding gentiles from the interior courts of the Temple, where Israel was involved in sacrifice. The line of demarcation between Israel and non-Israel was no invention within the circle of James, but a natural result of seeing Jesus as the triumphant branch of the house of David.

Gentile belief in Jesus was therefore in James' understanding a vindication of his Davidic triumph, but it did not involve a fundamental change in the status of gentiles *vis-à-vis* Israel. That characterization of the gentiles, developed by means of the reference to Amos, enables James to proceed to his requirement of their recognition of purity. He first states that "I determine not to trouble those of the gentiles who turn to God" (15:19) as if he were simply repeating the policy of Peter in regard to circumcision. (The implicit authority of that "I" – we might say, an episcopal "I" – contrasts sharply with the usual portrayal in Acts of apostolic decision as communal.) But he then continues that his determination is also "to write to them to abstain from the pollutions of the idols, and from fornication, and from what is strangled, and from blood" (15:20).

The rules set out by James tend naturally to separate believing gentiles from their ambient environment. They are to refrain from feasts in honor of the gods and from foods sacrificed to idols in the course of being butchered and sold. (The notional devotion of animals in the market to one god or another was a common practice in the Hellenistic world.[48]) They are to observe stricter limits than usual on the type of sexual activity they might engage with, and with whom. (Gross promiscuity need not be at issue here; marriage with cousins is also included within the likely area of concern. That was fashionable in the Hellenistic world, and proscribed in the book of Leviticus – chapter 18 and 20:17–21). They are to avoid the flesh of animals which had been strangled instead of bled, and they are not to consume blood itself. The proscription of blood, of course, was basic within Judaism, and strangling an animal (as distinct from cutting its throat) increased the availability of blood in the meat. Such strictures are consistent with James' initial observation, that God had taken a people from the gentiles (15:14); they were to be similar to Israel and supportive of Israel in their distinction from the Hellenistic world at large.

The motive behind the rules is not separation in itself, however. James links them to the fact that the Mosaic legislation regarding purity is well and widely known (15:21): "For Moses from early generations has had those preaching him city by city, being read in the synagogues every Sabbath." Because the law is well known, James insists that believers, even gentile believers, are not to live in flagrant violation of what Moses enjoined. In the words of Amos, they are to behave as "all the gentiles upon whom my name is called." As a result of James' insistence, the meeting in Jerusalem decides to send envoys and a letter to Antioch, in order to require gentiles to honor the prohibitions set out by James (Acts 15:22–35).

The same chapter of Leviticus which commands, "Love your neighbor as yourself" (19:18) also forbids blood to be eaten (19:26) and fornication (19:29, see also 18:6–30). The canonical (but second-hand) letter of James calls the commandment of love "the royal law" (James 2:8), acknowledging that Jesus had accorded it privilege by citing it alongside the commandment to love God as the two greatest commandments (Mark 12:28–31). In Acts James himself, while accepting that gentiles cannot be required to keep the whole law, insists that they should acknowledge it, by observing basic requirements concerning fornication and blood and idolatry.

It is of interest that Leviticus forbids the eating of blood by sojourners as well as Israelites, and associates that prohibition with how animals are to be killed for the purpose of eating (17:10–16). Moreover, a principle of exclusivity in sacrifice is trenchantly maintained: anyone, whether of Israel or a sojourner dwelling among them, who offers a sacrifice which is not brought to the Lord's honor in the Temple is to be cut off from the people (17:8–9). In other words, the prohibitions of James, involving sacrifice, fornication, strangled meat produce, and blood, all derive easily from the very context in Leviticus from which the commandment to love is derived. They are elementary, and involve interest in what gentiles as well as Israelites do. The position of James as reflected in Acts upholds the integrity of Scripture in the discipline of the Church in a way which recalls both the *mebaqqer* from Qumran and the *episkopos* from the Pastoral Epistles.

James' prohibitions as presented in Acts are designed to show that believing gentiles honor the law which is commonly read, without in any way changing their status as gentiles. Thereby the tent of David is erected again, in the midst of gentiles who show their awareness of the restoration by means of their respect for the Torah. The interpretation attributed to James involves an application of Davidic vocabulary to Jesus, as is consistent with the claim of Jesus' family to Davidic ancestry. The realization of Davidic promises in Jesus is accomplished within an acceptance of the terms of reference of the Scripture generally: to embrace David is to embrace Moses. There is no trace in James' interpretation of the Pauline gambit, setting one biblical principle (justification in the manner of Abraham) against another (obedience in the manner of Moses). Where Paul divided the Scripture against itself in order to maintain the integrity of a single fellowship of Jews and gentiles, James insisted upon the integrity of Scripture, even at the cost of separating Christians from one another. In both cases, the interpretation of Scripture was also – at the same moment as the sacred text was apprehended – a matter of social policy.

In a recent conference at Trinity Western University, John J. Collins referred to the two citations of Amos 9:11 which are attested at Qumran.[49] He relied on his findings in an earlier work that the two exegeses are quite different from one another, and from James' exegesis.[50] For reasons which will emerge shortly, we would be inclined to describe the relationship among the interpretations as complementary. The more recently identified usage (in 4Q174 3:10–13, a florilegium) is the more straightforward, in that the image of the restoration of the hut of David is associated with the promise to David in 2 Samuel 7:13–16 and with the Davidic "branch" (cf. Isaiah 11:1–10), all taken in a messianic sense.[51] Given the expectation of a son of David as messianic king (see

*Psalms of Solomon* 17:21–43), such an application of the passage in Amos, whether at Qumran or by James, is hardly strange. On the other hand, it is striking at first sight that the passage in Amos – particularly, "the fallen hut of David" – is applied in the *Damascus Document* (CD 7:15–17) not to a messianic figure, but to the law which is restored. Now the book of Amos itself makes Judah's contempt for the Torah a pivotal issue (Amos 2:4), and calls for a program of seeking the Lord and his ways (Amos 5:6–15), so it is perhaps not surprising that "the seeker of the law" is predicted to restore it in the *Damascus Document*. Still, CD 7:15–20 directly refers to the "books of the Torah" as "the huts of the king," interpreted by means of the "fallen hut of David." Evidently, there is a precise correspondence between the strength of the messiah and the establishment of the Torah, as is further suggested by the association with the seeker of the law not only here, in the *Damascus Document*, but also in the Florilegium. A contextual reading of the two passages demonstrates a dual focus, on messiah and Torah in each case, such that they stand in a complementary relationship. The possibility of influence on James' interpretation of Amos as presented in Acts 15 may not be discounted.

The conditions of the church in Jerusalem, the most stressful in the Church as a whole prior to the great revolt which culminated in the destruction of the Temple, occasioned the appearance of a new institution. James, the brother of Jesus, whose devotion to the Temple brought him both respect and antagonism in Jerusalem, became the *mebaqqer* of a group whose teaching in regard to the Torah, whose practice of purity, and whose dedication to the sacrificial worship of Israel made for uniqueness. Transferred to a Hellenistic and Christian environment, the Jacobean institution became the episcopate, and saw Christianity through its formative period and beyond.

# Part 2

# CHARISMATIC AUTHORITY

# 3

# WHAT ENDED WITH PROPHECY, AND WHAT HAPPENED THEN IN RABBINIC JUDAISM

Charismatic authority – authority by reason of the gifts of the spirit – takes many forms. But for any Judaism, charisma attests to one basis for demanding conformity: God's will expressed in the word of a holy person, and holiness would be validated by supernatural attestation. Hence, for a Judaism, the model of charismatic authority coincided with the model of political authority, namely, the person of Moses, ruler and prophet at once. And what made Moses charismatic was his supernatural gifts, on the one side, and the repeated allegation that the laws that he set forth in the Torah were dictated to him at Mount Sinai by God: "The Lord spoke to Moses saying, speak to the children of Israel and say to them..." forming the definitive statement of matters. Not only so, but a long line of prophets from Moses forward likewise spoke in God's name and on that basis demanded that people obey their instructions.

Rabbinic Judaism, however, explicitly rejected charismatic authority in the prophetic mode, and some have therefore supposed that Rabbinic Judaism also denied the possibility of an authority based not upon politics, such as we noted in Chapter 1, or upon persuasion and the coercion of strong argument, such as we shall consider in Chapter 5. Charisma, it has been held, disrupts what is routine and orderly, and a religion based on norms of behavior as much as of belief, such as Rabbinic Judaism, cannot find a place for something so irregular as the workings of the spirit, or, in concrete terms, charismatic authority. But rather than surmise, we do better to examine the facts of the matter: exactly how does Rabbinic Judaism define the place for spiritual, as distinct from institutional or intellectual, authority?

For Rabbinic Judaism – the Judaic system portrayed for us in the

Mishnah, Talmuds, and Midrash-compilations of the first six centuries CE – media for direct communication with Heaven did not include prophecy. That point is made in so many words on the Babylonian Talmud's commentary at Mishnah-tractate Sotah 9:12A–D, which follows:

{A}     When the former prophets died out, the Urim and Tummim were cancelled.

{B}     When the sanctuary was destroyed, the Shamir worm ceased and [so did] the honey of supim.

{C}     And faithful men came to an end,

{D}     since it is written, "Help, O Lord, for the godly man ceases" (Ps. 12:2).

In that context, as we shall see in a moment, the Talmud cites a Tannaite formulation that alleges that with the end of the latter prophets, Haggai, Zechariah, and Malachi, the Holy Spirit came to an end in Israel. That statement has ordinarily been understood to mean that prophecy came to an end, which the context surely sustains. The passage has been taken to mean that for all Judaisms prophecy ceased with Haggai and his colleagues. But certainly not all Judaisms concurred, and, among them, Christianity most certainly did not.

So, as to the facts of the matter – did people in general believe in the possibilities of receiving God's word through the media of human statements, "Thus says the Lord," in so many words? – we have to find that allegation surprising. Other Judaic systems, besides that represented by the Mishnah and the Talmud, certainly took it for granted that prophets did continue to grace Israel, and the Gospels attest that this conception was common in the first century, scarcely a hundred years prior to the formation of the Mishnah. What precisely is alleged in this statement must therefore be determined from the standpoint of the system that preserved it and found it factual and authoritative, as, assuredly, from the perspective of other Judaic systems, it was not.

When the final prophets are listed, that constitutes a judgment on the canon of revealed Scripture,[1] excluding from prophecy all candidates for inclusion in the canonical record besides the named figures. That is the force of the systemic statement at hand: no valid prophecy continued. And that judgment forms part of a larger systemic viewpoint. There were no further holy writings, beyond those of the Hebrew Scriptural canon (as then understood). The system could find ample space for teachings of the Torah not in writing, that is, documents alleged to originate in the oral tradition that formed part of the revelation of Sinai – but no more initially written ones. That is the foundation for the insistence that the Mishnah, a free-standing document rarely sustained by citation of proof-texts of Scripture, enjoyed standing as part of the Torah, but the oral part – that is, the part that came down not by direct intervention of God through prophecy but rather by origination at Sinai, along with Scripture. It was handed on through transmission orally, in memory, as tradition, so it is stated in so many words at M. Abot 1:1A–C:

{A}    Moses received Torah at Sinai and handed it on to Joshua, Joshua to elders, and elders to prophets.

{B}    And prophets handed it on to the men of the great assembly.

{C}    They said three things: (1)"Be prudent in judgment." (2)"Raise up many disciples." (3)"Make a fence for the Torah."

The passage contains two points of interest: first, the chain of tradition, encompassing prophecy, and, second, the content of the tradition, which is three sayings not found in Scripture but assigned the standing of Torah nonetheless. So implicitly, this theory of the foundations of the Torah's components that derive from some source other than Scripture set forth by Rabbinic Judaism reaffirms that the Torah continues but prophecy does not.

The allegation that prophecy or the Holy Spirit had ceased to serve, and the conviction that, from the final prophets onward, no further prophetic books were to be recognized, formed two ways of saying one thing. From the Mishnah, *c.* 200 CE, Rabbinic Judaism took the position that from the end of the Scripture's canonical writings up to the Mishnah, no Israelite composition demanded consideration as a valid communication from Heaven. Only tradition from Sinai, whether transmitted in writing or preserved in memory by sages, mattered. When sages maintain, then, that prophecy through the Holy Spirit came to an end, the sense of that statement is simple. They took the position that all claims of writings directed to Israel with the claim of Heavenly authorship or sponsorship – and they were, as we know, very many indeed – were spurious.

That position, though, hardly provides a complete account of the view of the Judaic sages concerning divine communication with Israel. Quite to the contrary, they certainly recorded their conviction that God continued to set forth valid messages, the Torah continued to expand, and Israel remained in active, day-to-day and tangible communication with Heaven. If, then, prophecy and the Holy Spirit are set aside, that only calls attention to other media of communication, and these media, too, attest to the character of the Rabbinic Judaic system as a whole. Let us begin with the same context as has captured our interest.

The first medium of charismatic authority conferred by heavenly recognition was possession of the echo, which would confirm Heaven's approval of a mortal sage. In the analysis of a Tannaite formulation of matters now found in the Tosefta (Tosefta Sotah 3:13–14), hence *c.* 300–400 CE, that statement of matters, rejecting the claim of authenticity put forth by competing Judaisms, immediately comes under considerable revision. The purpose of the restatement of matters cannot be missed. It is to make explicit sages' claim that their group possessed media for direct communication with Heaven. These were two, one of which is not readily discerned from prophecy or the workings of the Holy Spirit, the other of which represents a distinctive and very particular means for communication with Heaven, one that defines the very character and essence of this Judaism. The former – the communication via the Holy Spirit and its surrogate, the echo – is expressed in the following, in the form in which the passage occurs at Bavli Sotah 48B. Italics represent Aramaic, bold face type, the Tosefta passage, plain type, the Hebrew of the Bavli:

[O] *Rather, said R. Nahman bar Isaac, "What is meant by 'former' prophets? It is used to distinguish Haggai, Zechariah, and Malachi, who are the latter prophets."*

[P] *For our rabbis have taught on Tannaite authority:*

[Q] **When the latter prophets died, that is, Haggai, Zechariah, and Malachi, then the Holy Spirit came to an end in Israel.**

[R] **But even so, they made use of an echo.**

[S] **Sages gathered together in the upper room of the house of Guria in Jericho, and a heavenly echo came forth and said to them, "There is a man among you who is worthy to receive the Holy Spirit, but his generation is unworthy of such an honor." They all set their eyes upon Hillel, the elder.**

[T] And when he died, they said about him, "Woe for the humble man, woe for the pious man, the disciple of Ezra" [T. Sot. 13:3].

[U] Then another time they were in session in Yabneh and heard an echo saying, "There is among you a man who is worthy to receive the Holy Spirit, but the generation is unworthy of such an honor."

[V] They all set their eyes upon Samuel the younger.

[W] At the time of his death what did they say? "Woe for the humble man, woe for the pious man, the disciple of Hillel the Elder!"

[X] Also: he said at the time of his death, "Simeon and Ishmael are destined to be put to death, and the rest of the associates will die by the sword, and the remainder of the people will be up for spoil. After this, the great disasters will fall."

[Y] Also concerning R. Judah b. Baba they ordained that they should say about him, "Woe for the humble man, woe for the pious man, disciple of Samuel the Small." But the times did not allow it [T. Sot. 13:4].

[Z] For they do not raise a lamentation for those who are put to death by the government.

How sages differentiated "the Holy Spirit" from the "echo" is not clear in the passage before us. The two serve the same purpose and with the same effect, and both are relied upon. The passage clearly affirms that while prophecy in a narrow sense may have ceased, Heavenly communication continued abundantly.

To be sure, the "the Holy Spirit" and "the echo" clearly are to be differentiated. The former presumably represents direct, the latter, indirect communication; the former provides an articulated Heavenly message, the latter one given through some indirect means, as in the case at hand, where the echo announces that the Heavenly Spirit is available, which, in context, means that prophecy remains viable, but the generation is unworthy to receive prophecy, even though persons of sufficient standing to serve as prophets, such as Hillel, were available. This is made explicit in the cited prophecy of Samuel, who predicts the coming events. That fact leaves no doubt that receiving the Holy Spirit and setting forth prophecy are not readily distinguished in the source before us. But it also opens the question of how else, besides prophecy or the Holy Spirit, Heaven conveys its messages.

When it came to setting norms of behavior, moreover, Rabbinic Judaism rarely admitted the Holy Spirit or the heavenly echo into the discussion conducted by the sages. Charisma found a cool welcome indeed when the definition of routine demanded rigorous and reasoned debate. Then sages' own rationality took over, the reasons and traditions they could muster decided matters, and a heavenly echo was explicitly dismissed as source of authority over the formation of the law. That view is stated explicitly in the famous story of the debate on the status, as to cultic cleanness of uncleanness, of the oven of Akhnai, an oven built in pieces joined by sand. The claim that it was subject to uncleanness rested on the view that the oven was complete, whole, and functioning, even though in form it was in pieces. The claim that it was not subject to uncleanness held that because the oven was broken down and not a complete utensil, it did not have the capacity to receive uncleanness. The course of the debate, not the law in particular, is what matters, and here is how the issue is represented. Two points are important. First, the echo may not intervene in the reasoned debate of sages, but, second, sages themselves possessed charismatic power, in the present context, the power to perform supernatural deeds themselves. So the sages are represented as holy men, able to do miracles, but the law is set forth by sages in their capacity as masters of tradition and reasoning concerning tradition. The passage occurs at the Talmud of Babylonia tractate Baba Mesia 59a–b:

[I.15 A] *There we have learned:* If one cut [a clay oven] into parts and put sand between the parts,

[B] R. Eliezer declares the oven broken-down and therefore insusceptible to uncleanness.

[C] And sages declare it susceptible.

[D] [59B] And this is what is meant by the oven of Akhnai [M. Kel. 5:10].

[E] *Why* the oven of Akhnai?

[F] Said R. Judah said Samuel, "It is because they surrounded it with argument as with a snake and proved it was insusceptible to uncleanness."

[G] *A Tannaite statement:*

[H] On that day R. Eliezer produced all of the arguments in the world, but they did not accept them from him. So he said to them, "If the law accords with my position, this carob tree will prove it."

78

[I] The carob was uprooted from its place by a hundred cubits — and some say, four hundred cubits.

[J] They said to him, "There is no proof from a carob tree."

[K] So he went and said to them, "If the law accords with my position, let the stream of water prove it."

[L] The stream of water reversed flow.

[M] They said to him, "There is no proof from a stream of water."

[N] So he went and said to them, "If the law accords with my position, let the walls of the school house prove it."

[O] The walls of the school house tilted toward falling.

[P] R. Joshua rebuked them, saying to them, "If disciples of sages are contending with one another in matters of law, what business do you have?"

[Q] They did not fall on account of the honor owing to R. Joshua, but they also did not straighten up on account of the honor owing to R. Eliezer, and to this day they are still tilted.

[R] So he went and said to them, "If the law accords with my position, let the Heaven prove it!"

[S] An echo came forth, saying, "What business have you with R. Eliezer, for the law accords with his position under all circumstances!"

[T] R. Joshua stood up on his feet and said, " 'It is not in heaven' (Deut. 30:12)."

[U] *What is the sense of,* " 'It is not in heaven' (Deut. 30:12)"?

[V] Said R. Jeremiah, "[The sense of Joshua's statement is this:] For the Torah has already been given from Mount Sinai, so we do not pay attention to echoes, since you have already written in the Torah at Mount Sinai, 'After the majority you are to incline' (Ex. 23:2)."

[W] *R. Nathan came upon Elijah and said to him, "What did the Holy One, blessed be he, do at that moment?"*

[X] *He said to him, "He laughed and said, 'My children have overcome me, my children have overcome me!' "*

[Y] They said:

[Z] On that day they brought all of the objects that R. Eliezer had declared insusceptible to uncleanness and burned them in fire [as though they were unclean beyond all purification].

[AA] They furthermore took a vote against him and cursed him.

[BB] They said, "Who will go and inform him?"

[CC] Said to them R. Aqiba, "I shall go and tell him, lest someone unworthy go and tell him, and he turn out to destroy the entire world [with his curse]."

[DD] What did R. Aqiba do? He put on black garments and cloaked himself in a black cloak and took his seat before him at a distance of four cubits.

[EE] Said to him R. Eliezer, "Aqiba, why is today different from all other days?"

[FF] He said to him, "My lord, it appears to me that your colleagues are keeping distance from you."

[GG] Then he too tore his garments and removed his shoes, moved his stool and sat down on the ground, with tears streaming from his eyes.

[HH] The world was blighted: a third olives, a third wheat, a third barley.

[II] And some say, also the dough in women's hands swelled up.

[JJ] *A Tannaite authority taught:*

[KK] There was a great disaster that day, for every place upon which R. Eliezer set his eyes was burned up.

[LL] And also Rabban Gamaliel was coming by ship. A big wave arose to drown him.

[MM] He said, "It appears to me that this is on account only of R. Eliezer b. Hyrcanus."

[NN] He stood upon his feet and said, "Lord of the world, it is perfectly obvious to you that it was not for my own honor that I have acted, nor for the honor of the house of my father have I acted, but it was for the honor owing to you, specifically, so that dissension should not become rife in Israel."

[OO] The sea subsided.

[PP] *Imma Shalom, the wife of R. Eliezer, was the sister of Rabban Gamaliel. From that time onward she never left R. Eliezer to fall on his face {in prayer}. {So great was the power of his prayer that if he were to recite certain prayers because of the injury done him, God would listen and destroy her brother.}*

[QQ] *One day, which was the day of the New Moon, she mistook, assuming that the month was a defective one; and others say, she was distracted by a poor man who came and stood at her door, and to whom she took out a piece of bread.*

[RR] *She found that her husband had fallen on his face, and she said to him, "Get up, for you have killed my brother."*

[SS] *Meanwhile the word came from the house of Rabban Gamaliel that he had died.*

[TT] *He said to her, "Then how did you know?"*

[UU] *She said to him,* "So do I have as a tradition from the household of the father of my father: 'All gates are locked, except for the gates that receive complaints against overreaching.' "

Clearly, the passage treats Eliezer as a holy man, who has remarkable power to pray, bless, and curse. People did indeed take account of those powers, but when it came to authority over the law, the acknowledged charismatic gifts were null.

Since sages maintained, as we see, that the Holy Spirit and prophecy no longer serve to convey to Israel Heaven's wishes on any given occasion, we have to ask ourselves what media did sages identify for the same purpose, that is, what served Israel in its diminished capacity – unworthy of having the Holy Spirit represented in its midst – for the delivery of Heaven's views. Let me explain how we shall find in the passage that follows the particular message that concerns us: the place of prophecy in Rabbinic Judaism.

To understand the importance of the passage, we have to recall that the Rabbinic documents, and in particular, the Talmud of Babylonia, set forth not only random sayings but also systematic expositions of matters of law and theology. A given topic will be subjected to a complete presentation, and that will form the locus classicus for the Oral Torah's presentation of its view on that matter. When we wish to investigate a problem of law or theology, the Talmud of Babylonia sets on display, in its own characteristic idiom, a systematic account of the subject. But we have to learn how to identify its messages, since they are to be located not only in what a given authority says in his own name, but how the authoritative document selects and arranges a variety of otherwise unrelated statements.

Now to return to our problem: here we shall review most of the treatment by the Talmud of M. Makkot 3:15, since it is characteristic of the document to set forth a systematic presentation of a fundamental theme by presenting a composite of distinct, free-standing compositions, which, placed into relationship with one another and juxtaposed, make a point that, on their own, the composites of which the composite is comprised do not convey.[2] It is the connections between one topic and another that the compiler brings to our attention through his selection and arrangement, in one order and not in some other, of a variety of distinct statements; then the compiler – that is, the anonymous voice of the Talmud – speaks through the collage that he has formulated. The premise of this analysis should be made explicit. How the whole of a complex composite of Talmudic materials – a set of free-standing statements or compositions – holds together at any one passage requires explanation. I maintain that in the principles of compilation – juxtaposition, arrangement of propositional compositions in one order rather than some other – the framers of the document make a statement on a large-scale topic. It is through the connections they make that they direct our minds to the conclusions they wish us to draw.

This we uncover through the inquiry into structure and system, in a given context. Questions of structure pertain to how the document is put together and is so framed as to convey its framers' messages in consistent forms. The coherent formal program contains ample indication of the character and purpose of any given detailed analytical discussion. Questions of system concern the points of emphasis and current stress, the agenda that comes to expression in whatever topic is subject to analysis. The framers of the composites that comprise the document pursue a uniform analytical program throughout. Here too, they never leave us in doubt as to what they wish to discover or demonstrate. So it does not suffice to cite a statement we deem relevant to our topic – for example, concerning the cessation of the Holy Spirit. We have to take a close look at what else sages say in the same context, how they say it, and the order in which they make their statements. With a mastery of not only their vocabulary, but also their grammar, we find ourselves able to discern the judgments that they wished to set forth and the message they wished to convey about a given topic.

In the case at hand, what we have is a remarkably coherent statement on the entire problem of prophecy and the Holy Spirit, then and now; on how sages themselves fit into the framework of divine revelation; and on the particular uses to which, in the age beyond the end of the Holy Spirit and prophecy, prophecy itself is to be put. We shall work our way through the bulk of the rather subtle and complex composite, noting as we proceed the messages that the compiler's juxtapositions prove to set forth. We start with the Mishnah-passage that forms the provocation and pretext for the analysis of our problem as to how God conveys messages to humanity:

[A] "All those who are liable to extirpation who have been flogged are exempt from their liability to extirpation,

[B] "as it is said, 'And your brother seems vile to you' (Deut. 25:3) –

[C] "once he has been flogged, lo, he is tantamount to your brother," the words of R. Hananiah b. Gamaliel.

[D] Said R. Hananiah b. Gamaliel, "Now if one who does a single transgression – [Heaven] takes his soul on that account, he who performs a single religious duty – how much the more so that his soul will be saved for [handed over to] him on that account!"

(M. Makkot 3:15A–D)

Now the statement attributed to Hananiah maintains that Heaven weighs in the balance a single transgression and a single religious duty. The latter saves the soul. Others, by contrast, require repentance. The discussion unfolds in the following; I underline the passage that is critical to my argument:

[I.1 A] [Said R. Hananiah b. Gamaliel, "Now if one who does a single transgression – Heaven takes his soul on that account, he who performs a single religious duty – how much the more so that his soul will be saved for him on that account!":] Said R. Yohanan, "R. Hananiah b. Gamaliel's colleagues [Aqiba and Ishmael, who insist upon repentance, not punishment, as the condition of avoiding extirpation] differed from him."

[B] *Said R. Adda bar Ahhah, "They say in the household of the master, 'We have learned in the Mishnah:* There is no difference between the Sabbath and the Day of Atonement except that deliberately violating this one is punishable at the hands of an earthly court, while deliberately violating that one is punishable through extirpation [M. Meg. 1:5C].' *Now if {Hananiah b. Gamaliel were right,} then both the one and the other should be punishable in the hands of an earthly court."*

[C] *R. Nahman bar Isaac says, "Lo, who is the authority behind this Mishnah-passage? It is R. Isaac, who has said, 'There is no flogging of those who are subject to the penalty of extirpation.' For it has been taught on Tannaite authority:*

[D] "R. Isaac says, 'All those violations of the law that are punishable by extirpation were subject to a single encompassing statement ['For whoever shall do any of these abominations – the persons that do them shall be cut off from among their people' (Lev. 18:29)], and why was the penalty of extirpation made explicit in particular in the case of his sister? It was to impose in that case the penalty of extirpation and not mere flogging.'"

[E] R. Ashi said, "You may even say the opinion accords with the view of rabbis. In the case of the Sabbath, the principal penalty is inflicted by the earthly court, in the case of the Day of Atonement, the principal penalty is inflicted by the heavenly court."

So far, the presentation represents a standard Rabbinic dispute on a point of law. The interesting initiative now takes place:

[2 A] Said R. Adda bar Ahbah said Rab, "The decided law is in accord with R. Hananiah b. Gamaliel."

[B] *Said R. Joseph, "Well, who has gone up to heaven and 'said' {that is, returned and made this definitive statement}?!"*

[C] *Said to him Abbayye, "But then, in line with what R. Joshua b. Levi said, 'Three rulings were made by the earthly court, and the court on high concurred with what they had done,' ask the same question — who has gone up to heaven and returned and 'said' {made this definitive statement}?! Rather, we expound verses of Scripture {to reach dependable conclusions}, and in this case, too, we expound verses of Scripture."*

For our purpose the interesting point comes at 2 [B], Joseph's (sarcastic) statement that he thinks it unlikely that sages possess direct knowledge of Heaven's will in a given point of law. Abbayye's reply in the name of Joshua b. Levi provides us with the key to the way in which, in this Judaism, people know Heaven's will: sages do not have to go to Heaven on consultations, because they have direct access to God's will as expressed in Scripture. The Holy Spirit, or prophecy, gives way to another medium for communication between Heaven and earth, although, as we shall see presently, prophecy retains a critical position for itself. The issue then becomes subtle: at what point does Heaven communicate for which purpose? The first part of the answer is that when it comes to the determination of law, it is by the correct exposition of Scripture that sages have an accurate and reliable picture of Heaven's will. The upshot, in so many words, and in the exact context at hand, is then simply stated: study of the Torah for sages has now replaced prophecy. For the age at which prophecy is no longer available, Torah-learning substitutes quite nicely. But that is only for the stated purpose and takes place only in the single context: the nature of norms and how they are determined. Here, masters of Torah enter into communion with Heaven through their knowledge of the Torah and its traditions, but also its logic.

The passage proceeds to expand on that claim by giving three examples of occasions on which the earthly court, that is, sages, made a ruling that was then confirmed by the corresponding court in Heaven. This view is expressed in the continuation of the foregoing passage. I indent secondary glosses and expansions of the primary discourse:

[3 A] *Reverting to the body of the foregoing:* "R. Joshua b. Levi said, 'Three rulings were made by the earthly court, and the court on high concurred with what they had done,' ask the same question:"

[B] And what were these?

[C] Reciting the scroll of Esther, greeting people with the divine name, and the presentation of the Levite's tithe to the Temple chamber.

[D] Reciting the scroll of Esther, as it is written, "They confirmed, and the Jews took upon them and their descendants" (Est. 9:27) —

[E] "they confirmed" above what they had "taken upon themselves" below.

[F] greeting people with the divine name: as it is written, "As it is said, 'And behold Boaz came from Bethlehem; and he said to the reapers, "The Lord be with you." And they answered, "The Lord bless you"' (Ruth 2:4). And Scripture says, 'The Lord is with you you mighty man of valor' (Judges 6:12)."

[G] *What is the point of the addition,* "The Lord is with you you mighty man of valor" (Judges 6:12)?

[H] *Lest you say that Boaz made this up on his own, and Heaven did not approve, come and note what follows:* "The Lord is with you you mighty man of valor" (Judges 6:12).

[I] and the presentation of the Levite's tithe to the Temple chamber: as it is written, "Bring the whole tithe to the store house that there may be food in my house and try me herewith, says the Lord of hosts, if I will not open for you the windows of heaven and pour out for you a blessing, until there be no enough" (Mal. 3:10).

[J] *What is the meaning of the phrase,* "until there be no enough" (Mal. 3:10)?

[K] Said Rami bar Rab, "Until your lips get tired of saying, 'Enough, enough.'"

85

What is striking in the same composite is a matching composition, inserted immediately after the allegation that sages below made decrees that Heaven accepted and confirmed. We are given three examples in which, in ancient times, the Holy Spirit did operate. Here again, the context is identical: rulings on norms of conduct, which people carried out and Heaven confirmed. So retrospectively, the Holy Spirit, which, as we saw, forms the counterpart to prophecy, is shown to have worked in the age of prophecy exactly as, and for the purpose for which, the Heavenly Court worked in the age after prophecy in confirming sages' gifts of the spirit. That is, sages through their right reasoning and exposition of the Torah now were accomplishing precisely what, in the age of prophecy, prophets did, as in the following case:

[4 A] Said R. Eleazar, "In three places the Holy Spirit made an appearance: at the court of Shem, at the court of Samuel in Ramah, and at the court of Solomon.

[B] "at the court of Shem: 'And Judah acknowledged them and said, she is right, it is from me' (Gen. 38:26).

[C] *"And how did he know for sure? Perhaps as he had come to her, so other men had come to her?*

[D] "But an echo came forth and said, 'She is right, these things have come about by my insistence.'

[E] "at the court of Samuel in Ramah: ' "Here I am, witness against me before the Lord and before his anointed: whose ox have I taken or whose ass?" And they said, "You have not defrauded us nor oppressed us, nor have you taken anything from anybody." And he said to them, "The Lord is witness against you and his anointed is witness this day that you have found nothing against me," and he said, "he is witness" ' (1 Sam. 12:3–5)."

[F] " 'And he said' should be, 'and they said,' But an echo came forth and said, 'I am witness in this matter.'

[G] "and at the court of Solomon: 'And the king answered and said, "Give her the living child and in no way kill it, she is his mother" ' (1 Kgs. 3:27).

[H] *"So how did he know for sure? Maybe she was just crafty?* But an echo came forth and said, 'She is his mother.' "

[5 A] *Said Raba, "But maybe Judah was able to calculate the months and days and found them to coincide?*

[B] "[And the answer is:] *Where we can see evidence, we may propose a hypothesis, but where there is no evidence to be discerned, there also is no hypothesis to be proposed!*

[C] *"Maybe Samuel referred to all Israel using a collective noun and a singular verb, in line with the usage here:* 'O Israel, you [sing.] are saved by the Lord with an everlasting salvation, you shall not be ashamed' (Is. 45:17)?

[D] *"And with Solomon too, could he reach such a conclusion merely because he saw that one woman was compassionate, the other not?*

[E] *"All of these conclusions, therefore, are tradition."*

To understand the upshot of the passage, we have to call to mind sages' name for Moses: "our rabbi," the archetypal sage and source of the Torah. When, then, sages speak of Moses, they address them-selves to the figure in Scripture with which they identify. Then when they allege that Moses made rulings that prophets nullified, they are prepared to credit prophecy with gifts that transcend even those given to the masters of the Torah in the model of Moses himself. When we realize precisely what prophecy could accomplish that Moses himself could not, we realize what is at stake. Moses gave laws, and the laws of the Torah, the five books of Moses, always take priority; the prophetic writings, we recall, do not provide suffi-cient evidence to sustain an opinion on a legal question.

But that is not the whole story. Prophecy in its received record retains its validity for precisely the purpose for which, to begin with, the prophecy set forth their divine messages, namely, to convey the meaning of historical events and to declare the future history of Israel. Now, when it comes to history, as we shall see, matters are reversed. Moses, hence the Torah, written and oral, steps aside. The prophets, and not Moses, the lawgiver and the greatest prophet of all, take priority, and sages celebrate the enduring authority of their historical predictions, which override those of Moses, the archetypal sage, himself:

[2 A] Said R. Yosé bar Hanina, "Four decrees did our lord, Moses, make against Israel. Four prophets came along and annulled them.

[B] "Moses said, 'And Israel dwells in safety alone at the fountain of Jacob' (Deut. 33:28). Amos came and annulled it: 'Then I said, O Lord God, stop, I ask you, how shall Jacob stand alone, for he is small,' and it goes on, 'The Lord repented concerning this: This also shall not be, says the Lord god' (Amos 7:5–6).

[C] "Moses said, 'And among those nations you shall have no repose' (Deut. 28:65). Jeremiah came and annulled it: 'Thus says the Lord, the people that were left of the sword have found grace in the wilderness, even Israel, when I go to provide him rest' (Jer. 31:1).

[D] "Moses said, 'The Lord...visits the sin of the fathers upon the children and upon the children's children to the third and to the fourth generation' (Ex. 34:7), but Ezekiel said, 'the soul that sins it shall die' (Ez. 18:3–4).

[E] "Moses said, 'And you shall perish among the nations' (Lev. 26:38), but Isaiah said, 'And it shall come to pass in that day that a great horn shall sound and they shall come who were lost in the land of Assyria' (Is. 27:13)."

Now the passage in its own terms presents the striking claim that the prophets brought Israel comfort when Moses, "our rabbi," troubled them with a fate they could not endure.

The passage just now cited does not end the discussion of the matter. It forms part of a larger composite, and only when we note the juxtapositions that are involved here, those effected by the compositor who assembled these free-standing compositions and placed them together, that we perceive the entire message at hand. For it is one that is set forth by the making of connections between one composition and another, the setting forth as a sequence of several completed thoughts, each independent, but all changed by reason of juxtaposition with other thoughts. Through the making of the connections among the compositions at hand, that is, through forming them into a continuous composite, the compiler makes a point of his own. To understand that point, let us note that, at I.2, we have had a discussion on the relationship of the decisions of the earthly court and those of the heavenly court; I.3 has expanded on that point, a secondary development of its principal, factual allegation. I.4, continuous with the foregoing, has then introduced the Holy Spirit, giving us instances in which the Holy Spirit intervened in Israel's history. Then comes a passage I need not cite verbatim, an elaborate exposition of a statement in the Mishnah-passage treated here, briefly given as follows:

**Therefore he gave them abundant Torah and numerous commandments:**

[B] R. Simelai expounded, "Six hundred and thirteen commandments were given to Moses, three hundred and sixty-five negative ones, corresponding to the number of the days of the

solar year, and two hundred and forty-eight positive commandments, corresponding to the parts of man's body."

This passage is elaborately expounded. Then comes the passage
cited just now, II.2, the decrees by Moses that the prophets nullified. And what follows at that point is a systematic resort to
prophecy, which is to say, what do the prophets reveal that study of
the Torah does not reveal? The answer is, as we have seen, Israel's
history and its meaning. Here is what the Holy Spirit should
convey, which is what the prophets do convey. And the passage
about the supersession effected by prophecy continues.

Its message is explicit. Jacob may stand alone; Israel will find
grace in the wilderness; the children will not suffer for the sins of
the fathers, and Israel will not perish among the nations. The apocalyptic visions of Deuteronomy 33 and Leviticus 26 are then
dispatched in favor of a benign message. If that were not sufficient
to show how sages affirmed the results of prophecy for the interpretation of history, the following makes that point in so many words:

[4 A]  Once upon a time Rabban Gamaliel, R. Eleazar b. Azariah, R.
Joshua, and R. Aqiba were walking along the way and heard
the roar of Rome all the way from Puteoli, at a distance of a
hundred and twenty miles. They began to cry, but R. Aqiba
brightened up.

[B]  They said to him, "Why so cheerful?"

[C]  He said to them, "Why so gloomy?"

[D]  They said to him, "These Cushites worship sticks and stones
and burn incense to idolatry but live in safety and comfort,
while as to us, the house that was the footstool for our God is
burned [24B] with fire! Why shouldn't we cry?!"

[E]  He said to them, "But that's precisely why I rejoice. If those
who violate his will have it so good, those who do his will all
the more so!"

[5 A]  Once again, they were going up to Jerusalem. When they got
to Mount Scopus, they tore their garments. When they reached
the Temple mount, they saw a fox emerge from the house of the
Holy of Holies. They began to cry, but R. Aqiba brightened up.

[B]  They said to him, "Why so cheerful?"

[C]  He said to them, "Why so gloomy?"

[D]  They said to him, "The place of which it once was said, 'And
the non-priest who draws near shall be put to death' (Num.
1:51) has become a fox hole, so shouldn't we weep?"

[E] He said to them, "But that's precisely why I rejoice. It is written, 'And I will take to me faithful witnesses to record, Uriah the priest and Zechariah son of Jeberechiah' (Is. 8:2). And what has Uriah the priest to do with Zechariah? Uriah lived during the first Temple, and Zechariah during the second, but Scripture had linked the prophecy of Zechariah to the prophecy of Uriah. In the case of Uriah: 'Therefore shall Zion for your sake be plowed as a field' (Mic. 3:12). Zechariah: 'Thus says the Lord of hosts, there shall yet old men and old women sit in the broad places of Jerusalem' (Zech. 8:4). Until the prophecy of Uriah was fulfilled, I was afraid that the prophecy of Zechariah might not be fulfilled. Now that the prophecy of Uriah has come about, we may be certain that the prophecy of Zechariah will be fulfilled word for word."

[F] They said to him, "Aqiba, you have given us comfort, Aqiba, you have given us comfort."

The position of Aqiba in the case at hand repeats the results of the general statement given earlier that the prophets may be relied upon for a clear picture of Israel's future history and its meaning. Not only have the prophets reshaped Moses' prophecy concerning Israel's future; they also have provided certain and reliable grounds for optimism about Israel's near-at-hand expectations. But, we recognize immediately, the reason that prophecy serves has little bearing on the possibility of divine revelation in the here and now of Aqiba's time. Aqiba finds a solution in prophecy because prophecy has defined a pattern, a paradigm or model, through which the present is to be interpreted and the future made known. So prophecy is converted into that rule-making, generalization-framing, logical mode of thought and inquiry that sages had formed of the Torah of Moses itself.

Here the paradigm that Aqiba finds in Scripture tells him what data require attention, and what do not. The prosperity of the idolaters matters only because the paradigm explains why to begin with we may take account of their situation. The destruction of the Temple matters also because it conforms to an intelligible paradigm. In both cases, we both select and also understand events by appeal to the pattern defined by the working of God's will. The data at hand then yield inferences of a particular order – the prosperity of idolaters, the disgrace of Israel in its very cult. We notice both facts because they complement one another and illustrate the workings of the model: validating prophecy, interpreting experience in light of its message.

The representation of prophecy in the authoritative writings of Rabbinic Judaism proves more complex than we had anticipated. Two familiar propositions turn out to require modification in context. The first, that Rabbinic Judaism rejects prophecy, and the second, that it substitutes Torah-learning for prophecy, prove necessary but not sufficient. Rabbinic Judaism affirms prophecy and recognizes the presence in the midst of its Israel of the Holy Spirit. It explicitly rejects the intervention of prophecy or the Holy Spirit in matters of the determination of law, because it maintains that these matters are resolved through the interplay of practical reason and applied logic, on the one side, and accurate tradition, on the other. The often-cited story about the debate between Eliezer and Joshua abut a matter of law, in which Heaven intervenes through *ad hoc* miracles, only to be rebuked by Joshua with the citation of the verse, "[The Torah} is not in Heaven," tells only part of the tale.

What changes matters is the complex composite, working its way through the logical components of the topic, that we have followed here. Beginning with the well-known allegation that the Holy Spirit ended with Haggai, Zechariah, and Malachi, we found that sages take the very opposite position. If the person of the Holy Spirit is not present, still, the workings of the Holy Spirit continue, through the echo from Heaven, which conveys Heaven's wishes just as reliably as did the Holy Spirit. So what, precisely, came to an end is not clear. That question becomes even more urgent when we recall how Samuel the Younger found himself able to predict the future, which is the result of receiving the Holy Spirit or the message through the echo.

This picture of matters is expressed in so many words in a striking passage, which represents the sage as a party to the discussions of not only the earthly, but also the Heavenly court. The sage now participates in that process of learning and practical reason that the study of the Torah inaugurates, and Heaven – engaged in the same issues, confirming above what sages declare below – now does more than (merely) reach the same conclusions that sages have reached. It finds itself unable – so sages present matters – to conduct its affairs without the participation of sages themselves.

The story that follows states in so many words that sages are required for Heaven to do its work of Torah-study. I take that statement to mean that prophecy ended in one form, continued in many forms, but found its true fulfillment in the mastery of the Torah that (some) sages accomplished. Not only so, but, as we saw in so many words, sages maintained that the court in Heaven confirmed precisely what sages' court on earth determined, on the basis of the correct exposition of the Torah, to be the law. Each time sages declared the decided law emerging from controversy, Joseph's remark pertains: "Who has gone to heaven," and Abbayye's reply comes into play: the earthly court made its rulings, the Heavenly court confirmed them. But sages went still further. They maintained that God in heaven studies the Torah just as they do, and that communication from heaven to earth takes place on that account. In so many words they specify that something very like prophecy takes place when the Torah is studied on earth as it is in heaven, and the following story is explicit in that regard. The passage occurs at Babylonian Talmud tractate Baba Mesia 86a.

[I.39 A] *Said R. Kahana, R. Hama, son of the daughter of Hassa, told me that Rabbah b. Nahmani died in a persecution. {And here is the story:}*

[B] *Snitches maligned him to the government, saying, "There is a man among the Jews who keeps twelve thousand Israelites from paying the royal poll-tax for a month in the summer and for a month in the winter."*

[C] *They sent a royal investigator {parastak} for him but he did not find him. He fled, going from Pumbedita to Aqra, from Aqra to Agma, from Agma to Shehin, from Shehin to Seripa, from Seripa to Ena Damim, from Ena Damim back to Pumbedita. In Pumbedita he found him.*

[D] *The royal investigator happened by the inn where Rabbah was located. They brought him two glasses of liquor and then took away the tray {and this excited the ill-will of demons}. His face was turned backward. They said to him, "What shall we do with him? He is the king's man."*

[E] *{Rabbah} said to them, "Bring him the tray again, and let him drink another cup, and then remove the tray, and he will get better."*

[F] *They did just that, and he got better.*

[G] *He said, "I am sure that the man whom I am hunting is here." He looked for him and found him.*

[H] *He said, "I'm leaving here. If I am killed, I won't reveal a thing, but if they torture me, I'm going to squeal."*

[I] *They brought him to him and he put him in a room and locked the door on him. But {Rabbah} sought mercy, the wall fell down, and he fled to Agma. He was in session on the trunk of a palm and studying.*

[J] *Now they were debating in the session in the firmament the following subject:* If the bright spot preceded the white hair, he is unclean, and if the white hair preceded the bright spot, he is clean. [The Mishnah-paragraph continues: and if it is a matter of doubt, he is unclean. And R. Joshua was in doubt] [M. Neg. 4:11F–H] –

[K] The Holy One, blessed be he, says, "It is clean."

[L] *And the entire session in the firmament say,* "Unclean."

[M] *They said, "Who is going to settle the question? It is Rabbah b. Nahmani."*

[N] For said Rabbah b. Nahmani, "I am absolutely unique in my knowledge of the marks of skin-disease that is unclean and in the rules of uncleanness having to do with the corpse in the tent."

[O] *They sent an angel for him, but the angel of death could not draw near to him, since his mouth did not desist from repeating his learning. But in the meanwhile a wind blew and caused a rustling in the bushes, so he thought it was a troop of soldiers. He said, "Let me die but not be handed over to the kingdom."*

[P] *When he was dying, he said, "It is clean, it is clean."* An echo came forth and said, "Happy are you, Rabbah bar Nahmani, that your body is clean, and your soul has come forth in cleanness."

[Q] *A note fell down from heaven in Pumbedita:* "Rabbah bar Nahmani has been invited to the session that is on high."

[R] *Abbayye, Raba, and all the rabbis came forth to tend to his corpse, but they did not know where he was located. They went to Agma and saw birds hovering over and overshadowing the corpse. "This proves that he is there."*

[S] *They mourned him for three days and three nights. A note fell down:* "Whoever refrains [from the mourning] will be excommunicated." *They mourned for him for seven days. A note fell down:* "Go to your homes in peace."

[T] *The day on which he died a strong wind lifted a Tai-Arab who was riding on a camel from one side of the Pappa canal and threw him down onto the other side. He said, "What is this?"*

[U] *They told him, "Rabbah bar Nahmani has died."*

[V] *He said before him, "Lord of the world, the whole world is yours, and Rabbah bar Nahmani is yours. You are Rabbah's, and Rabbah is yours. Why are you destroying the world on his account?" The wind subsided.*

It would be difficult to find more explicitly stated the view that God does communicate with sages, the communication is explicit and substantive, and the medium of communication, if not prophecy, is then comparable to prophecy: "the Lord spoke to..." is here replaced by a letter falling to earth.

The Torah, then, is the medium for communication from Heaven to earth, not only way back in the time of Moses, but also in the here and now of sages' own day. It is important to note, moreover, that the interplay of Heaven and earth takes place not only in matters of law, but also theology and the interpretation of events and prediction of the future, certainly critical matters in the conception of prophecy that sages set forth for themselves. When, moreover, the prophets – for so Solomon and Samuel and David are explicitly classified – made their rulings, the same media of heavenly confirmation that serves sages came into play. Since sages represent Solomon and David as sages, the point is clear: Heaven has a heavy stake in sages' deliberations, follows them, responds to them. In this context we recall the story of how Heaven calls up Rabbah bar Nahmani, requiring his knowledge of a matter of purity law!

Were we to close at this point, the resulting account would distort the actualities of Rabbinic Judaism. For they accorded recognition not only to the charisma accruing to mastery of the Torah, but also, and especially, to the gifts of the spirit attained by unlettered people, not only men but also women. Indeed, at the very heart and center of Rabbinic Judaism we find the systemic reversal – from Torah to ignorance, from man to woman – which places above sages' Torah-learning a remarkable gift of character and conscience, the gift of humility and self-sacrifice. That gift represents a spiritual power far above the power of the Torah. It is portrayed in a set of stories that scarcely require exposition, so unmediated is the power of the narrative.

The stories address the question of how simple folk are able to perform miracles that learned rabbis cannot carry out, and they deal with the conception of *zekhut,* the word that stands for the empowerment, of a supernatural character, that derives from the virtue of one's ancestry or from one's own virtuous deeds of a very particular order. If we wanted a single word to represent charismatic power and moral authority, that word for Rabbinic Judaism would have to serve. That moral authority is attained through acts of will consisting of submission, on one's own volition, to the will of Heaven. Such acts performed by the holy people endowed Israel with a lien and entitlement upon Heaven. When done by individuals, these same types of acts of omission or commission provoke Heaven to acts of special favor – prayers are answered, miracles are done. Here is moral authority signified by charismatic power, set forth in the purest sense: what we cannot by will impose, we can by will evoke. What we cannot accomplish through coercion, we can achieve through submission. God will do for us what we cannot do for ourselves, when we do for God what God cannot make us do. In a wholly concrete and tangible sense, love God with all the heart, the soul, the might, we have. Here is the clearest doctrine of charismatic authority that Rabbinic Judaism puts forth.

Even though a man was degraded, one action sufficed to win for him that heavenly glory to which rabbis in lives of Torah-study aspired. The mark of the system's integration around *zekhut* lies in its insistence that all Israelites, not only sages, could gain *zekhut* for themselves (and their descendants). A single remarkable deed, exemplary for its deep humanity, sufficed to win for an ordinary person the *zekhut* that elicits supernatural favor enjoyed by some rabbis on account of their Torah-study. The centrality of *zekhut* in the systemic structure, the critical importance of the heritage of virtue together with its supernatural entitlements therefore emerge in a striking claim. Even though a man was degraded, one action sufficed to win for him that heavenly glory to which rabbis in general aspired. The rabbinical story-teller whose writing we shall consider assuredly identifies with this lesson, since it is the point of his story and its climax.

In all three instances that follow, defining what the individual must do to gain *zekhut*, the point is that the deeds of the heroes of the story make them worthy of having their prayers answered, which is a mark of the working of *zekhut*. It is deeds beyond the strict requirements of the Torah, and even the limits of the law altogether, that transform the hero into a holy man, whose holiness served just like that of a sage marked as such by knowledge of the Torah. The following stories should not be understood as expressions of the mere sentimentality of the clerks concerning the lower orders, for they deny in favor of a single action of surpassing power sages' lifelong devotion to what the sages held to be the highest value, knowledge of the Torah:

*Y. Taanit 1:4.I.*

[F] A certain man came before one of the relatives of R. Yannai. He said to him, "Rabbi, attain *zekhut* through me [by giving me charity]."

[G] He said to him, "And didn't your father leave you money?"

[H] He said to him, "No."

[I] He said to him, "Go and collect what your father left in deposit with others."

[J] He said to him, "I have heard concerning property my father deposited with others that it was gained by violence [so I don't want it]."

[K] He said to him, "You are worthy of praying and having your prayers answered."

The point of [K], of course, is self-evidently a reference to the possession of entitlement to supernatural favor, and it is gained, we see, through deeds that the law of the Torah cannot require but must favor: what one does on one's own volition, beyond the measure of the law. Here I see the opposite of sin. A sin is what one has done by one's own volition beyond all limits of the law. So an act that generates *zekhut* for the individual is the counterpart and opposite: what one does by one's own volition that also is beyond all requirements of the law.

[L] A certain ass-driver appeared before the rabbis [the context requires: in a dream] and prayed, and rain came. The rabbis sent and brought him and said to him, "What is your trade?"

[M] He said to them, "I am an ass-driver."

[N] They said to him, "And how do you conduct your business?"

[O] He said to them, "One time I rented my ass to a certain woman, and she was weeping on the way, and I said to her, 'What's with you?' and she said to me, 'The husband of that woman [me] is in prison [for debt], and I wanted to see what I can do to free him.' So I sold my ass and I gave her the proceeds, and I said to her, 'Here is your money, free your husband, but do not sin [by becoming a prostitute to raise the necessary funds].'"

[P] They said to him, "You are worthy of praying and having your prayers answered."

The ass-driver clearly has a powerful lien on Heaven, so that his prayers are answered, even while those of others are not. What did he do to get that entitlement? He did what no law could demand: impoverished himself to save the woman from a "fate worse than death."

[Q] In a dream of R. Abbahu, Mr. Pentakaka ["Five sins"] appeared, who prayed that rain would come, and it rained. R. Abbahu sent and summoned him. He said to him, "What is your trade?"

[R] He said to him, "Five sins does that man [I] do every day, [for I am a pimp:] hiring whores, cleaning up the theater, bringing home their garments for washing, dancing, and performing before them."

[S] He said to him, "And what sort of decent thing have you ever done?"

[T] He said to him, "One day that man [I] was cleaning the theater, and a woman came and stood behind a pillar and cried. I said to her, 'What's with you?' And she said to me, 'That woman's [my] husband is in prison, and I wanted to see what I can do to free him,' so I sold my bed and cover, and I gave the proceeds to her. I said to her, 'Here is your money, free your husband, but do not sin.'"

[U] He said to him, "You are worthy of praying and having your prayers answered."

[Q] moves us still further, since the named man has done everything sinful that one can do, and, more to the point, he does it every day. So the singularity of the act of *zekhut*, which suffices if done only one time, encompasses its power to outweigh a life of sin – again, an act of *zekhut* as the mirror-image and opposite of sin. Here again, the single act of saving a woman from a "fate worse than death" has sufficed.

[V] A pious man from Kefar Imi appeared [in a dream] to the rabbis. He prayed for rain and it rained. The rabbis went up to him. His householders told them that he was sitting on a hill. They went out to him, saying to him, "Greetings," but he did not answer them.

[W] He was sitting and eating, and he did not say to them, "You break bread too."

[X] When he went back home, he made a bundle of faggots and put his cloak on top of the bundle [instead of on his shoulder].

[Y] When he came home, he said to his household [wife], "These rabbis are here [because] they want me to pray for rain. If I pray and it rains, it is a disgrace for them, and if not, it is a profanation of the Name of Heaven. But come, you and I will go up [to the roof] and pray. If it rains, we shall tell them, 'We are not worthy to pray and have our prayers answered.'"

[Z] They went up and prayed and it rained.

[AA] They came down to them [and asked], "Why have the rabbis troubled themselves to come here today?"

[BB] They said to him, "We wanted you to pray so that it would rain."

[CC] He said to them, "Now do you really need my prayers? Heaven already has done its miracle."

[DD] They said to him, "Why, when you were on the hill, did we say hello to you, and you did not reply?"

[EE] He said to them, "I was then doing my job. Should I then interrupt my concentration [on my work]?"

[FF] They said to him, "And why, when you sat down to eat, did you not say to us 'You break bread too'?"

[GG] He said to them, "Because I had only my small ration of bread. Why would I have invited you to eat by way of mere flattery [when I knew I could not give you anything at all]?"

[HH] They said to him, "And why when you came to go down, did you put your cloak on top of the bundle?"

[II] He said to them, "Because the cloak was not mine. It was borrowed for use at prayer. I did not want to tear it."

[JJ] They said to him, "And why, when you were on the hill, did your wife wear dirty clothes, but when you came down from the mountain, did she put on clean clothes?"

[KK] He said to them, "When I was on the hill, she put on dirty clothes, so that no one would gaze at her. But when I came home from the hill, she put on clean clothes, so that I would not gaze on any other woman."

[LL] They said to him, "It is well that you pray and have your prayers answered."

The pious man of [V], finally, enjoys the recognition of the sages by reason of his lien upon Heaven, able as he is to pray and bring rain. What has so endowed him with *zekhut*? Acts of punctiliousness of a moral order: concentrating on his work, avoiding an act of dissimulation, integrity in the disposition of a borrowed object, his wife's concern not to attract other men and her equal concern to make herself attractive to her husband. None of these stories refers explicitly to *zekhut*; all of them tell us about what it means to enjoy not an entitlement by inheritance but a lien accomplished by one's own supererogatory acts of restraint. In the end, it is not only, or mainly, Torah-study that endows a person with charismatic power. The principals of the story are not the men who can pray and have their prayers answered, but the women who are the heroines although, even in the stories, they take a secondary role.

To conclude: in the view of Rabbinic Judaism, nothing ended with the cessation of prophecy – not direct communication from Heaven to earth, not prediction of the future, not divine guidance for especially favored persons concerning the affairs of the day. Canonical prophecy ended, but the works of prophecy continued in other forms, both on Heaven's side with the Holy Spirit and later on with the echo, and on earth's side with sages joining in conversation with Heaven through the echo, on the one side, and through Torah-learning, on the other. But more important than prophecy as indication of charismatic authority, we see at the end, the superhuman acts of restraint, self-sacrifice, love beyond the requirements of the law – these form the source of the most remarkable charisma of all.

# 4

# CHARISMATA OF GUIDANCE IN PRIMITIVE AND EARLY CHRISTIANITY

## Gifts of the spirit and the myth of the apostolic succession of bishops

The way in which we come to use the word "charismatic" is itself instructive within a consideration of our topic. The term "charism" (from *kharisma* in Greek) refers simply to a gift or a favor bestowed; the word derives from *kharis*, the favor or grace which gives such a gift. Within the New Testament, of course, "grace" is a coordinated benefit: all *kharismata* (the plural of *kharisma*, "charism") come from God.[1] They are endowments of divine spirit. Once that equation was made in the cultures of the West, it was straightforward to think of the "charism" as a "spiritual gift."

That is just what happens in the well-known passage from 1 Corinthians in which Paul sets the stage for the Christian theory of charismatic guidance of the Church:

> But concerning the spiritual things, brothers, I do not want you to be ignorant. You know that when you were gentiles, you were carried away, as you were led, to dumb idols. So I make known to you that no one speaking by God's spirit says, Jesus is accursed. And no one is able to say, Jesus is Lord, except by Holy Spirit. But there are allotments of gifts (*kharismata*), but the same spirit. And there are allotments of services, and the same Lord. And there are allotments of activities, but the same God makes everything active in everything. But to each the manifestation of the spirit is given for what benefits. To one a word of wisdom is given through the spirit, and to another a word

of knowledge according to the same spirit, to yet another faith by the same spirit, to another gifts of healings by the one spirit, to another activities of powers, to another prophecy, to another discernments of spirits, to yet another generations of tongues, but to another interpretation of tongues. One and the same spirit makes all these things active, allotting to each by itself, just as it wishes.

(1 Corinthians 12:1–11)

This picture of the sovereign distribution of gifts by the spirit is so categorical, the term, *pneumatika* ("spiritual things," a neuter plural adjective) is commonly rendered "spiritual gifts."[2] The result is that the term "gifts" itself (*kharismata*) is taken in the same sense in common English, so that a charism is an endowment of spirit. By extension, someone possessed of "charisma" is spiritually endowed. By means of Max Weber, that typically Christian usage was elevated into a sociological theory of how people in communities come to recognize authority (and later to routinize it with reference to their usual activities).[3]

The specificity of that Christian vision of Paul's in 1 Corinthians 12 needs to be stressed, precisely because it has been globalized in modern discussion. When he explains in a classic manner in the same chapter how diverse members belong to a single body,[4] it comes immediately after he has treated of the spirit as we have seen, and after he has laid a foundation for the language of "body" in reference to the eucharist (in 1 Corinthians 11). In view of that eucharistic meaning, he puts forward the "body of Christ" as the principal definition of the Church:

For just as the body is one and has many members, and all the members of the body (being many) are one body, so is Christ. For in one spirit we were all baptized into one body – whether Jews or Greeks, slave or free – and we all were given to drink of one spirit.

(1 Corinthians 12:12–13)

By focusing on the "body" as the medium of eucharistic solidarity and then developing its corporate meaning, Paul turns the traditional, Petrine understanding of spirit (as received in baptism) into the single principle of Christian identity. His reply to any attempt to form discrete fellowships within the Church will now always be, "Is Christ divided?" (1 Corinthians 1:13).

The startling quality of the Pauline conception of "the body of Christ" does not derive from how the concept itself is developed within the letters written by Paul or later attributed to Paul. That trajectory is a relatively consistent product of the interaction between the eucharistic theology of solidarity with Christ, which was common within Hellenistic Christianity, and the quasi-Stoic language of incorporation into a body which Paul himself had learned in Tarsus, his home. The radical feature of Pauline usage is not to be found in the development of the concept, but rather in the claim that the Church is defined solely in respect of this "body." Whether Jew or Greek, only incorporation into Christ mattered to Paul (1 Corinthians 12:12–13), and that incorporation, of course, was by virtue of the very spirit (in baptism) whose operation Paul was at pains to spell out immediately before he spoke of Christ's body in this way. Indeed, the opening of chapter 12 (1 Corinthians 12:2–3) uncovers the central axiom of Paul's thought concerning the people of God: before they received God's spirit they were gentiles, and now they are Israel.[5]

The conviction that the Church is animated by the spirit of God, and is identifiable with the body of Christ, invites the thought that the actual organization of that community is articulated by God personally. Paul answers the invitation to that thought (still within chapter 12!), and marks out a paradigm of communal order:

> And you are Christ's body, and members every one, even those whom God appointed in the Church – first, apostles; second, prophets, third, teachers, then powers, then gifts of healings, helps, pilots, generations of tongues. Not all are apostles; not all are prophets; not all are teachers; not all are powers; not all have gifts of healings; not all speak in tongues; not all interpret!
>
> (1 Corinthians 12:27–30)

Although the communal emphasis of this model is manifest, it is scarcely a hierarchical list: it even seems to confuse the agents of authority with what such authorities do. But what may seem to be confusion from the point of view of setting out a neat hierarchy with clearly specified powers is a strength from Paul's point of view. After all, as we saw in Chapter 2 (pp.51–56), he understood the spirit of the apostle (his own spirit, in the case of 1 Corinthians 5) as joining with Jesus' power in this community, the body of Christ, in order to administer an ultimate discipline, conditioned only by the last judgment. As compared to apostolic authority as endowed by the spirit of God, everything else – including every other office – faded into conditionality.

Just that emphasis posed a difficulty within the early Church. Judged by the criterion of the spirit and *kharismata*, everything was weighed in the favor of apostolic authority and nothing explained the legitimacy of episcopal authority. Whether one defined apostles as sent by Jesus before his death or after, the fact of their being sent by him, and the fact of their spiritual endowment as a result of his resurrection, was manifest. The more obvious that was, the less obvious was the legitimacy of bishops.

The role of James as *mebaqqer* provided a vital precedent for what was to come, but his office could not continue long as he had defined it. Eusebius claims a direct succession of James' episcopal throne in Jerusalem (*Ecclesiastical History* 7.19), but he himself makes clear that the conditions caused by the revolts against Rome in fact destroyed any hope of continuity with Judaism in the Church in Jerusalem. As he puts it, when the second great revolt was put down, the episcopal succession of the circumcision ceased (*Ecclesiastical History* 4.5); after Hadrian renamed the city and banned Jewish residents there, the church in Aelia (as it was called, in the Emperor's honor) was gentile, as was its new bishop, Mark (*Ecclesiastical History* 4.6).

Even before that time, the principle of turning to a relation of Jesus for the leadership of the church in Jerusalem had been abandoned. Immediately after James' death, Symeon – an alleged cousin of Jesus' – was elected bishop (again, according to Eusebius, *Ecclesiastical History* 3.11, 22), but he was executed by the Romans (at the age of 120!) after persistent persecution, first under Vespasian and then under Trajan (*Ecclesiastical History* 3.11–12, 32).[6] In fact, in the wake of the revolt of 66–70 CE, the relatives of Jesus were subject to suspicion as of the family of David during the reign of Domitian (*Ecclesiastical History* 3.19–20),[7] and the third bishop of Jerusalem (Justus) is simply styled "a Jew" by Eusebius (*Ecclesiastical History* 3.35).

Because Symeon is portrayed as so long-lived, and as enjoying an unbroken tenure as bishop (despite the very disruptive conditions Eusebius himself relates), Eusebius' narrative effects an overlap between the direct succession from Jesus and apostolic leadership on one hand, and the authority of bishops on the other hand. He is at pains to stress that, after the death of James, the entire family of Jesus came together to establish Symeon as James' successor

(*Ecclesiastical History* 3.11). It is no coincidence that, immediately thereafter, Eusebius speaks of the episcopal succession in Rome: Linus, Anencletus (Linus' brother), and Clement, with Clement specified as Paul's colleague on the basis of Philippians 4:3 (*Ecclesiastical History* 3.13–16, citing the letter of Clement). So the reign of Domitian finds a relative of Jesus and a colleague of Paul's securely ensconced as bishops. By blood and by personal delegation, bishops are Jesus' representatives: the myth of apostolic succession is designed to reinforce that representation.

James and Paul are not the only ones who can claim such direct succession from Jesus. At the same time, Eusebius hastens to add, John "the apostle and evangelist" lived on in Patmos (*Ecclesiastical History* 3.18). So the apostle who stands behind the Fourth Gospel is identified with the seer of the Revelation (see Revelation 1:9), and both are equated with the "elder" (*presbuteros*) named John who lived until the time of Papias in the second century. Irenaeus (the second-century writer, citing Papias, in turn)[8] is Eusebius' authority in respect of John, much as Hegesippus is his authority for James and Symeon, and the letter of Clement is his authority for the bishops of Rome. Eusebius is not only using their information, but developing their theory of apostolic succession. That theory in its synthesized form has it that the episcopal authority of the second century enjoys the warrant of the original apostles ( John the apostle and seer and elder), Paul (by means of Clement), and the relatives of Jesus (above all, Symeon).

Eusebius himself later shows that he is aware that the theory is a myth, when he admits that John the apostle cannot be identified with the other John (*Ecclesiastical History* 3.39). The issue of the identity of the people concerned continues to be disputed,[9] but one thing stands out plainly: when Eusebius recounts the episcopal succession, using the data and the perspectives of the letter of Clement, Hegesippus, and Irenaeus, the controlling interest is not historical, but ecclesiological. The letter of Clement to the Corinthians in fact permits us to understand why the matter of succession had become so crucial from the close of the first century.

Clement's letter calmly sets out the myth which would become the basis of ecclesiastical authority within Catholic and Orthodox Christianity:[10]

> The Apostles were entrusted with the gospel for us from
> the Lord Jesus Christ; Jesus Christ was sent from God.
> Christ, therefore, is from God and the Apostles from

Christ. Both, accordingly, came in proper order by the will of God. Receiving their orders, therefore, and being filled with confidence because of the resurrection of the Lord Jesus Christ, and completely assured by the word of God, with full assurance of the holy spirit, they went forth announcing the gospel, the kingdom of God that was about to come. Preaching, accordingly, throughout countries and cities, they appointed their first-fruits, after testing them by the spirit, to be bishops and deacons of those who were about to believe.

(1 Clement 42:1–4)

That Clement can have written in such terms to Corinth, some forty years after Paul's correspondence, is remarkable. Gone is the Pauline pleading on the basis of Paul's own apostolic authority and the reception of the spirit by his hearers through that ministry (compare 1 Corinthians 1:1 – 2:16), gone is the emphasis on the diffusion of the spirit through the whole congregation (1 Corinthians 12:1–11), gone is the confusing delight in the multiplicity of spiritual *charismata* of leadership (1 Corinthians 12:27–30). In their place there is wonderful simplicity and linear order: the spirit of God proceeds by a straight line through Christ, the apostles, and bishops and deacons.

Clement insists that the office of bishop should be conferred on mature persons and that – to avoid contention – appointment should be for life; he claimed general apostolic warrant for that practice (1 Clement 44:1–3). To depose a bishop without cause is held to be sinful, and Clement holds the Corinthians to account for just that behavior (44:4–6). The need to assert discipline in Corinth will come as no surprise to readers of Paul's correspondence with that city, but – in addition to the new importance placed on the episcopacy – Clement needs to explain how the focus of the Holy Spirit can be construed as so narrow.

In order to forward both explanations, Clement relies on the Pastoral Epistles. In them, as we have seen, the episcopal office – and even the apostolic succession of episcopacy, through Timothy – is clearly set out. Moreover, Clement assumes that the model set up by the Pastoral Epistles (see Chapter 2, pp. 56–63) reflects the activity of the apostles generally. In the next section, we will see how that generalizing of the Pastorals' episcopal model of ministry was achieved. Moreover, the Pastorals insist that bishops exercise their authority on the basis of mature expertise in the Scriptures (see

Chapter 2, pp. 59–69). When Clement addresses the issue of why the authority of the spirit should be exercised by bishops, he in fact argues that this arrangement accords with Scripture, and is not an innovation. In an extended comparison (chapter 43), he speaks of Moses' establishment of Aaron's priesthood in Numbers 17, by having the heads of all the tribes put their staffs in the sanctuary on what Clement calls "the table of God" (43:2).[11] Because Aaron's rod alone was found to have blossomed and to be bearing fruit, his "tribe" was designated as alone worthy of priesthood.

Clement's exegesis of Numbers 17 is a matter of the straightforward application of Scripture to the situation of the Church. In that application, Clement is both less complicated and more prescriptive than Paul.[12] Clement attests, in that respect, a distinctive approach to the interpretation of Scripture, in both style and substance, when it concerns issues of the order of the Church. As we will see in Chapter 6 of the present study, the idiom of intellectual discourse changes within classic Christianity when one shifts from theological to ecclesiological issues and concerns. For the present purpose, however, we wish to focus on just one feature of what 1 Clement says: bishops and deacons were established by the apostles themselves in the power of the Holy Spirit, and that establishment is warranted by Scripture.

The term "deacon" simply means "servant" in Greek (*diakonos*), and was already applied by Paul to the ministers of the gospel of Jesus generally, as we have seen in Chapter 2 in the discussion of 2 Corinthians 11:23–33 (see pp. 51–56). In fact, "service" or ministry (*diakonia*) expressed for Paul the authoritative agency of human beings to convey what God would have people understand:

> And we have such confidence in regard to God through Christ, not that we are worthy of ourselves to consider anything as from ourselves: but our worth is from God, who also made us worthy to be servants of a new covenant, not of letter but of spirit. For the letter kills, but the spirit makes alive. But if the service of death, carved in stone letters, was in glory, so that the sons of Israel were not able to behold the face of Moses, for the fading glory of his face, how much more shall the service of the spirit be in glory?
>
> (2 Corinthians 3:4–8)

In what follows, Paul pursues that comparison to brilliant effect; the present point is that it is not the effect which the comparison with Moses in 1 Clement seeks. Where Paul seeks contrast with Moses, 1 Clement insists on continuity. By the same token, the definition of *diakonos* shifts as we move from Paul to Clement. The generic reference of Paul, such that *diakonos* may serve him to compare himself with Apollos (see 1 Corinthians 3:5; pp. 55–56) becomes in Clement a particular reference to an order of ministry below that of the bishop (a "deacon" within an ordered – and carefully ordained – ministry). That is possible because between Paul and Clement there lies a swift evolution of the myth that the spirit of God as conveyed for the purposes of authoritative discipline is mediated only by the laying on of hands as practiced by the apostles and their successors.

## Laying hands on deacons, priests (and others)

The book of Acts, written just before the time of 1 Clement, is instructive in this regard (see Acts 6:1–6). There, the choice of the original seven deacons by the twelve apostles is provided with a utilitarian motivation. A problem emerges within the community: in the daily ministry (which included the provision of food), Greek-speakers were being overlooked in comparison to Aramaic-speakers. But the apostles decide that they personally should not "leave the word of God to serve tables" (Acts 6:2). As a result, seven men are chosen (corresponding to 70, the traditional number of the nations in Judaism[13]), attested to be full of spirit and wisdom, and the apostles lay hands on them in prayer for their ministry.

What follows immediately in Acts falsifies the theory that the authority of the seven was restricted to the administration of food, leaving preaching to the twelve apostles. In the narrative, Stephen goes on to perform miracles and signs, and his preaching and consequent martyrdom result in a programmatic (but, as it turns out, providential) persecution of the Church (Acts 6:8 – 8:3). The pivot of the opposition to Stephen is that he preaches against the Temple and the law (so Acts 6:11–15), and he directly speaks of both the Temple and the execution of Jesus as primary instances of resistance to the Holy Spirit (Acts 7:44–53). His vision, when he himself is described as full of the Holy Spirit, of Jesus as the Son of Man at God's right, provokes his stoning (Acts 7:54–60). In the tension between Stephen's identity as directly endowed with God's spirit and as an ancillary worker for the apostles, it is obvious that the spiritual designation is prior and more powerful.

In fact, however, the point of the apostolic laying on of hands is rooted in the understanding of its association with the spirit of God. Laying on of hands is well established within the Hebrew Bible as a gesture of sacrifice: the assignment of what is shown to be one's own to the holy, the realm of God.[14] In the case of Jesus' activity, however, the laying on of hands is particularly associated with the ability to purify, and therefore to produce healing. In Mark 5:21–43 Jesus enters into contact with the two primary sources of impurity, blood and death, and purifies them both. The association of the two stories – and their two media of impurity – cannot be coincidental, because the narrative of the woman with a flow of blood is sandwiched within the story of the raising of Yair's daughter:

> And one of the leaders of the synagogues came, named Yair. He saw him and fell at his feet, and implored him a lot, saying, "My little daughter is at her end, so come lay hands on her, so she might be saved and live." And he went after him, and a big crowd followed him and pressed in on him.
>
> And a woman who had a flow of blood twelve years (and had suffered a lot from many physicians and had spent everything she had and was no better but rather got worse) heard concerning Jesus. She came in the crowd from behind, and touched his garment. For she said, "If I touch even his garments, I will be saved." And at once the fountain of her blood dried up, and she knew in her body that she was healed of her illness.
>
> Jesus at once recognized in himself the power gone out of him, turned in the crowd, and said, "Who touched me?" And his students said to him, "You see the crowd pressing in on you, and you ask, 'Who touched me?'" And he looked around to see the woman who had done it. But the woman was afraid and trembling: she knew what had happened to her. She came and worshiped him and told him the whole truth. But he said to her, "Daughter, your faith has saved you; depart in peace and be healed from your illness."
>
> While he was still speaking, they came from the leader of the synagogue, saying, "Your little daughter is dead: why do you still bother the teacher?" But Jesus overheard the word spoken, and said to the leader of the synagogue, "Do not be afraid; only believe." And he did not let anyone follow along with him except Rock [Peter] and Yakob and

Yohanan the brother of Yakob. And they came into the house of the leader of the synagogue, and he saw a disturbance, both weeping and much wailing, and he entered and said to them, "Why are you distressed and weeping? The child is not dead, but sleeps." And they ridiculed him. But he put everyone out, took the father of the child and the mother and those with him and went into where the child was. He grasped the hand of the child and he said to her, "*Talitha kuoum*", which is translated: "Girl, I say to you, arise." And at once the girl arose and walked around, for she was twelve years old. And they were at once beside themselves with great excitement. And he admonished them a lot so that no one should know this, and he said to give her something to eat.

(Mark 5:22–43)

In addition to the fact that one story is sandwiched within the other,[15] the woman had the flow of blood for twelve years, Yair's daughter was twelve years old, they are both called "daughter," and – of course – they are both women. It would be difficult to construct a story more pointed towards the issue of purity, and the relationship to the issue of healing is manifest.

The intensity of focus on purity is also clear in the relationship between the two types of uncleanness involved. Yair's daughter is thought to be dead, and a corpse is a primary source of contagious uncleanness: it is the way a being is not created by God. In the book of Haggai, the prophet asks the question of the priests, whether contact with a holy thing makes a thing holy, and permits it to communicate holiness further. They answer "No," but they readily agree that contact with a corpse makes whatever touches it unclean, and also that uncleanness by indirect contact results (Haggai 2:11–13). Haggai underscores, then, the intense conviction that corpses communicate uncleanness. The woman in the story, however, is a source of blood; the uncleanness associated with her is of a different order. Blood does not belong to the realm of human contact because "the blood is the life" (Leviticus 17:10–14; Deuteronomy 12:23), and contact with menstruating women or women with irregular bleeding is a matter of systematic control (Leviticus 15:19–30). Death and blood are the longitude and latitude of Israel's map of purity, and these two stories together seek to redraw that map.

The task of mapping purity and impurity is, of course, also taken up in the Mishnah, which devotes a tractate to observing how corpse-uncleanness (as well as other impurities) may be determined, and how far it extends (Ohalot), and a tractate to the questions of flows such as the woman had (Zabim), and – for that matter – a tractate to how to diagnose and treat "outbreak" on the skin (Negaim). What is stunning about the stories in Mark within the context of Judaism is not the fact that impurity is recognized, but its treatment. How we are to account for the flow of blood stopping and the girl reviving is not explained, except on the confidence that Jesus' purification amounts to healing. Contagious purity is also healing purity.

The direction of purity then, from the inside out, is consistent as one compares such stories with Jesus' distinctive teaching (see Mark 7:15).[16] Mention has already been made of the question posed by the prophet Haggai, whose point is that – normally speaking – it is uncleanness that is contagious, not sanctity. But the larger point is that, because God's spirit is active within Israel (Haggai 2:5), despite the current state of uncleanness, the Temple can be sanctified, blessing will come, the line of David is continued (Haggai 2:14–23). Jesus' point is similar, but it is directed to the body of Israel rather than to the body of the Temple. Moreover, he holds that healing purification may be generalized, to the extent that he sends some of his disciples to heal in the name of the kingdom of God (Matthew 10:7–8; Mark 6:13; Luke 9:6, 10:9).

Along with other such stories,[17] the double narrative of the daughter of Yair and the hemorrhagic woman establishes a pattern in which Jesus' contact by laying on hands (and/or being touched) purifies and heals. The basis of this power is Jesus' endowment by the spirit in baptism. This endowment is both in the sense that Jesus comes into relationship with the spirit, so that contact with him conveys purity, and in the sense that – after the resurrection – he endows others with that same spirit. The story in the Synoptic Gospels of Jesus' immersion by John is a model of the primitive experience of Christian baptism as it came to be practiced after the resurrection.[18] That marked the moment Jesus' movement stressed the availability of the spirit in order to fulfill the covenant of Israel, and its preaching became increasingly international, and predominantly Greek. Rabbi Yeshua became Jesus; his movement became Christianity. The Christian catechumen, prepared by a year-long catechesis such as the Gospel according to Mark represents, enters the water, and is able to call on God as Father under the inspiration of the Holy Spirit, which is Jesus' own spirit (Galatians 4:4–6). The believer can call God Father because the same spirit informs the believer that he is God's son (as in Mark 1:11). The dialectics of the spirit, such that it is poured out to enable the relationship between Father and Son as the truth of the covenant, was what permitted Christianity to thrive as a religious movement despite its lack of the usual resources (material, social, and historical) which make for the emergence of a major religion.

Acts may be said to be the story after the resurrection of the outward-moving impact of the spirit from its center in Jerusalem. Stephen marks the point at which the persecution of Christianity in the vicinity of Jerusalem results in its acceptance elsewhere, especially by non-Jews. Once the inclusion of non-Jews is effected, those who are associated with Paul and Barnabas in Antioch (named as Symeon called Niger, Lucius of Cyrene, and Manaen, an associate of Herod Antipas[19]), as well as those apostles themselves, are said to be directed by the spirit (Acts 13:1–4, 16:6–10, 20:28). Barnabas and Paul are sent to move further into untried territory, after fasting, prayer, and laying on of hands (Acts 13:3).

Paul becomes the principal agent of baptism and the spirit, once the field of mission is far from Antioch, and it is from his perspective that the story of Apollos' ministry in Ephesus and Corinth is told (Acts 18:24 – 19:7). Apollos teaches only what is called the baptism of John, although Priscilla and Aquila correct him. But the definitive correction occurs when Paul comes to Ephesus, and those who had been baptized into John's baptism are now baptized into Jesus' name, and receive the Holy Spirit when Paul lays his hands on them.

The followers of Jesus act by laying on hands principally to heal at first, as in the case of Peter and John and the lame man in the Temple (Acts 3:7). But the apostolic Church is clear that this is a matter of God himself "stretching forth a hand so that healing and signs and powers are done by the name of your holy child Jesus" (Acts 4:30). Just as healing had been possible in the case of Jesus because the spirit of God was identified with him in an unprecedented way, so healing among the apostles is occasioned by the unprecedented outpouring of that spirit after the resurrection. Peter's speech in the house of Cornelius is precisely instructive of the ideology of the apostolic Church in this case: God is said to have anointed Jesus "by the Holy Spirit and power" (Acts 10:38), and then that same spirit "fell upon all those hearing the word" of Jesus' resurrection (10:44). The Holy Spirit, the same spirit initially active in the case of Jesus, becomes contagiously available from the apostles.

Just as the Holy Spirit is understood to be available by means of the apostles, so the range of its activity is every bit as broad – and indeed broader – than the example of Jesus would lead one to expect. Laying on of hands, associated with the Holy Spirit, designates the seven deacons who have special responsibilities for the Greek-speaking disciples in Jerusalem (Acts 6:6), as well as Barnabas and Saul as delegates of the church in Antioch (13:2–3). That gesture is unequivocally associated with the coming of the spirit when Peter and John travel to Samaria in order to ensure that those baptized into Jesus' name by Philip should also receive the Holy Spirit (Acts 8:17–19). That story, together with the much-discussed incident involving Apollos (Acts 19:6), establishes that the circle of Peter was especially responsible for primitive Christian teaching in regard to the spirit, and that Paul was in that sense a member of the Petrine circle. By the time of Hebrews, baptism and laying on of hands were associated closely, because they referred to a commonly accepted pairing of immersion into Jesus' name and reception of the spirit of God (Hebrews 6:2).

Since, in particular, apostolic ministry was not limited to the twelve in Jerusalem (as we have seen in Chapter 2), and also since the spirit which was communicated by that ministry was explicitly understood to come to all who were baptized, the limitation of the spirit to certain, designated leaders when it concerned the discipline of the Church did not come as a matter of course. Acts shows us the way toward that limitation in 13:1–4, already referred to, but even more precisely in Paul's speech to the elders in Miletus (20:17–38). "Elder" (in Greek *presbuteros*) is simply the continuation of the Israelite institution of the *zaken*, the local head of a given family.[20] That was a natural institution to influence the Church, whether in a Palestinian or a Hellenistic phase, because the constitution of the household church was so prevalent.[21]

The naturalness of the institution of the *zaken/presbuteros* for the early Church is intimated by the first letter of Peter, in which the putative author (as Peter, rightly considered an apostle on any theory of the apostolate reflected in the New Testament) speaks of himself as "fellow elder" (1 Peter 5:1). Here is another indication, along with Acts and 1 Clement, that the Church by the time of the 90s had articulated itself in a new institutional language, which incorporated the apostolate's authority within a new structure. But the actual moment of that articulation is attributed by Acts to Paul. Having sent from Miletus (where he stayed, on the way to Jerusalem) to the elders of Ephesus, he gave them parting instructions, in the midst of which he indicates the grounds of their authority:

> Take heed, then, for yourselves and for all the flock, in which the Holy Spirit has appointed you overseers (*episkopous*) to shepherd the Church of God, which he purchased through his own blood.
>
> (Acts 20:28)

The same spirit of God by which Jesus healed, and which is conveyed to all believers after the resurrection by means of the apostolic ministry, here becomes the principle of a particular ordering of the Church. Indeed, Acts prepares the way for the articulation of this principle, because Paul and Barnabas have already been described as personally selecting elders, church by church, observing the practice of prayer and fasting by which they themselves had been chosen (Acts 14:23, with Acts 13:1–3).

We have already seen in Chapter 2 (pp. 60–61) that the laying on of hands is attested in the Pastoral Epistles, as well as Acts, as the medium of this authorization of the Holy Spirit for ministry. We cited 1 Timothy 4:13–16, 5:22, to which we may now add 2 Timothy, which emphasizes that Paul's own hands were laid on Timothy for the reception of his charism (2 Timothy 1:6), while 1 Timothy 4:14 is equally clear that Timothy's authority came "through prophecy with laying on of hands by the eldership." Two features of the evolution of Christian polity become plain in this eloquent difference. First, the restriction of the laying on of hands to apostles in their choice of bishops is a myth which required time to develop and become accepted. It is an obvious attempt to circumscribe the conception of who might be empowered to exercise the charism of leadership within the Church. Second and relatedly, "elders" were progressively displaced from a position of relative pre-eminence to being under episcopal authority. They had been interchangeable with bishops in Acts 20:17 and 28, and even with apostles in the instance of the laying on of hands in Timothy's case (1 Timothy 4:14). Now, in 2 Timothy, they find no mention.

What is going on here is an attempt to coordinate policy in a hierarchical way within the myth that the charism of leadership is an endowment of the Holy Spirit through the apostles, and by that means alone. Already within 1 Timothy, Timothy's authorization expressly includes the discipline of other leaders within his church: elders, both male and female,[22] and widows (1 Timothy 5:1–21).

Obviously, that arrangement is circular, if Timothy's authority is understood to derive from the eldership (as in 1 Timothy 4:14). That is just the anomaly which 2 Timothy resolves: now Timothy is the recipient of God's charism by the laying on of Paul's hands. It is no coincidence that, within the development of the practice of the Church, healing by contact was increasingly referred to as anointing (see Mark 6:13; James 5:14–15), rather than laying on of hands: healing and ordination are now quite distinct, and its human agents are distinct.

2 Timothy not only develops the motif of apostolic succession; it also directly links that succession to the validity of what Timothy teaches:

> Hold to the paradigm of healthy words which you heard from me in faith and in the love in Jesus Christ: guard the good treasure which dwells in us through Holy Spirit.
> (2 Timothy 1:13–14)

In two respects, this is an advance beyond the position marked out in 1 Timothy.[23] First, the basis of teaching is now no longer simply the Scripture correctly interpreted[24] (see 1 Timothy 1:3–8, and the discussion on pp. 59–61); rather, the teaching of the apostles is now to be transmitted along the lines of paradigms or models proper to it. Because 2 Timothy was composed in the period just after all three Synoptic Gospels began first to be circulated, this may be taken as an endorsement of the use of such sources of tradition as authoritative. Second, the treasure of the charism endowed by the spirit, a spirit held in common by both Paul and Timothy, is here mentioned in the same breath with "the paradigm of healthy words" which came from Paul. The utility of the Pauline letters is therefore endorsed, and endorsed as a source of spiritually authorized teaching, when applied by those who exercise a charism like Paul's. The bishop now stands proxy for the apostle in spiritual and intellectual terms.

Still, for the myth of the apostolic succession to work, it was necessary also to make it clear that elders did not represent a line of authority separate from that of bishops. That aim is attained in the letter to Titus, the last of the Pastoral Epistles. Here, the picture of Paul laying hands on Timothy (which 2 Timothy had used to replace the laying on of hands by elders) is filled out considerably:

> For this I left you in Crete: so that you might set right
> what remains, and appoint elders by city, as I directed you,
> if one is blameless, husband of one wife, having faithful
> children, not under accusation of dissipation or indisci-
> pline.
>
> (Titus 1:5–6)

This profile of leadership confirms the social constituency envisaged
by the Pastorals in the analysis of David Verner[25]: "The leaders of
the church were a group that consisted in large part of prosperous
householders. They tended to be older men, although young men
may have occasionally entered their ranks." The challenge the
Pastorals face is to coordinate these various households in a given
city, and from city to city, within the authority of a given bishop.

That role is undertaken by Titus himself, with Paul's direct
authorization. Immediately after he is told to appoint elders, Titus
is reminded what a bishop must be:

> For it is necessary for a bishop to be blameless as God's
> manager, not willful, not wrathful, not drunken, no bully,
> no money-grubber, but hospitable, loving good, sober, just,
> devout, self-controlled, holding fast to the faithful word
> according to the doctrine, so that he might be able also by
> the sound doctrine to summon and confute those who
> contradict.
>
> (Titus 1:7–9)

This emphasis upon the personal qualities of the bishop, such that
he orders the ideal household which the Church has become in the
minds of its leaders, is anticipated, as we have seen, in 1 Timothy
(3:1–7, and the discussion above, pp. 59–61). What the letter to
Titus achieves by this repetition is to align Titus with the example
of Timothy, and to insist that they are both – along with similar
figures – to be understood as the agents of episcopal authority
among elders (that is, presbyters, priests[26]) wherever the model of
household churches in urban communities is realized. And that
agency comes down to their ability to enforce what is not only
correct interpretation of Scripture (1 Timothy) or a paradigm of
healthy words (2 Timothy), but now healthy doctrine, an emerging
standard of correct, apostolic, theology. The doctrinal and institutional progression as one reads through the Pastoral Epistles is
palpable, and that progression reinforces at every turn the recourse

to apostolic succession. By the time of Titus (*c.* 100 CE), in fact, the New Testament is on the cusp of considering Judaism an alien religion:[27] Titus is warned to keep his people away from "Jewish myths" (Titus 1:14), because the myth of apostolic succession is now complete and sufficient as an institutional description of the people of God.

## The persistent problem of prophecy

One of the teachers ("from the circumcision," Titus 1:10–11) opposed by the letter of Titus is apparently styled a prophet: "One of them, their very own prophet, said, 'Cretans are always liars, evil beasts, lazy gluttons'" (Titus 1:12). Such are affairs in Crete that the author of Titus actually agrees, "This testimony is true" (1:13)! Aside from being among the most politically incorrect statements in the New Testament, the reference to the Jewish prophet in Crete is remarkable for several reasons. It was said of Hillel, Jesus' contemporary, that he was worthy to have the Holy Spirit rest on him; but that his generation was unworthy (see Sotah 48b). So how could a person be acclaimed a prophet among Jews in Crete?

That question cannot be answered simply by remarking that Rabbinic literature is generally speaking later than the New Testament. In 1 Maccabees 4:42–6, the priests loyal to the revolt store the desecrated stones of the Temple which had been defiled in 167 BCE until a prophet should arise to explain what should be done with them. So there was a sense, at least in some circles (and highly official, influential circles) that classical prophecy had come to an end. Still, Josephus reports the movements of prophetic pretenders, who claimed divine inspiration for their efforts to free the land of the Romans (*Jewish War* 2.258–65, 7.437–46). Prophecy continued as a movement (or movements) within both Judaism and Christianity in the first century, and proved to be a disrupting influence.

On the Christian side, the passage from Titus shows that Judaic prophecy in Crete had a particular profile: anti-local (1:12), insistent upon circumcision (1:10), skilled in myths as well as the Torah (1:14), dedicated to issues of purity (1:15). It seems to bother the author especially that this prophetic enterprise is profitable (1:11). The prophets are competing in the Hellenistic market-place of ideas,[28] while the elders of the Church are seeking to colonize the household structure of the Graeco-Roman world.

Prophetic itineracy, which had been a major strength within the practice of Jesus, was seen soon after the destruction of the Temple to be a threat to the stability of the household church. That is shown not only by the letter to Titus, but in the warning against "false prophets" in what is known as the "little apocalypse" in the Synoptic Gospels (Matthew 24–5; Mark 13). This is an eschatological prediction based upon the events of the disastrous siege of Jerusalem which resulted in the burning of the Temple, and part of that disaster – and particularly to be avoided in the understanding of this apocalypse – are the false prophets and false christs (Matthew 24:24; Mark 13:22).

Between the little apocalypse and the letter to Titus, we are provided with a trajectory of the development of prophecy in the last third of the first century. It begins as an itinerant, apocalyptic movement, and develops into an increasingly cosmopolitan drive to secure Judaism and its customs a place in the Hellenistic world. Christianity was susceptible to the influence of Judaic prophecy, since Christians also – fundamentally, as a matter of their baptism – acknowledge the revived and continuing power of the Holy Spirit.

Luke and Acts, together with the Pastoral Epistles, permit us to see how Christianity attempted to meet the challenge of fresh prophetic activity, loyal to Judaism. It is notable that Luke's version of the little apocalypse (Luke 21:5–36) does not mention the false prophets and false christs, although there is a warning about not being led astray (Luke 21:8). The reason for that is that Luke claims that Judaic prophecy – in its recent and/or contemporary form – actually attests the truth of Christ. The spirit of God, it is frequently remarked, is portrayed as being as active at the beginning of Luke as it is at the beginning of Acts. And that portrayal in the Gospel results in Zechariah the father of John the Baptist (1:67), and Simeon (2:25–6), and Anna (2:36–7) all being identified in prophetic terms. Instead of denigrating false prophets, the Gospel according to Luke co-opts Judaic prophecy, along with the Judaic Scriptures, to attest the coming of Christ.

The reason this Gospel can depart from the policy of Matthew and Mark, and embrace prophecy, is that some prophets are understood to act in the interests of Jesus' movement. That is the case even when their actual identification with the movement is uncertain. Anna, for example, is simply said to give thanks and to speak "concerning him" to all who were awaiting the redemption of Jerusalem (2:38). Although "concerning him" (*peri autou*) apparently refers to Jesus, without the sequencing which places the prophecy of

Simeon beforehand, little the Gospel says would seem to make of Anna a prophetess of Christ. The situation is sometimes much the same in the book of Acts, where the prophet Agabus predicts a famine and the arrest of Paul, but his relation to the apostles as a whole remains unclear (Acts 11:27–30,[29] 21:10–11). On the other hand, Acts is quite clear about both the prophetic and the Christian identity of Judas and Silas (Acts 15:22–33) and the daughters of Philip (Acts 21:8–9), as well as the group in Antioch (Acts 13:1–3).

By the time of Luke, it appears, Christians in Antioch were confident about their ability to provide true prophecy with a home. Indeed, Syrian Christianity as a whole was to develop a psalmic tradition of song and praise by means of the Holy Spirit (see the *Odes of Solomon*),[30] and the opening of Luke – with its songs of Mary and Zechariah and Simeon – provides what are probably the earliest texts of this prophetic form of worship. Part of that incorporation of prophetic worship is that the leaders of the Church, the bishops who emerge in the Pastoral Epistles as the successors of the apostles with the Holy Spirit available to them, are conceived to be endowed "through prophecy with laying on of hands by the eldership" (1 Timothy 4:14, cited more fully and discussed in Chapter 2, pp. 60–61).

But the settlement regarding prophecy worked out in the environment of Luke's Antioch and in the ideal set up by the Pastoral Epistles was not effective everywhere. Indeed, the alacrity of Luke and Acts to embrace prophecy which is not identifiably Christian suggests that Antioch was unusual in this regard. Even in Crete, as Titus 1:12 has shown us, "prophets" were more often in competition with elders and bishops than they were ancillary witnesses to the apostolic succession. Such a problem is also reflected in the *Didache* (see chapters 11 and 15), where prophets and even apostles are subjected to a degree of local control.[31] The control is effected in two steps. First, apostles and prophets who seek to stay more than a few days in a community, or ask for money, are condemned as false prophets (so *Didache* 11). Then, the election of bishops and deacons is enjoined, with the assurance that they "are honored among you with the prophets and teachers" (so *Didache* 15). Once the myth of the apostolic succession was accepted, it maintained an institution of spirit which did not brook competition with those who claimed personally spiritual authority.

But competition was inevitable, inasmuch as Christianity's fundamental dedication to the reception of the Holy Spirit was systemic. The greatest challenge on the basis of prophetic inspiration to Christianity during its classical period[32] originated in Asia Minor. That is not surprising, since with the close of the canon the region around Ephesus had been a seedbed of Christian prophecy, most eloquently attested by the Revelation of John (c. 100 CE).[33] Around 157 CE,[34] a native of Phrygia named Montanus claimed that he was filled by the spirit, and had come as the comforter promised in the Gospel according to John to come after Jesus (John 14:26, 16:7). Associated with two prophetesses, Prisca and Maximilla, Montanism's "new prophecy" became extremely influential, reaching far beyond Asia Minor despite the resistance of leaders such as Apollinarius, Bishop of Hierapolis.[35] Its most famous convert was Tertullian, the great writer of North Africa, who became a Montanist in 207. In the environment of persecution which Tertullian addressed, the rigorism of the Montanists, which derived from their conviction that each believer was a vessel of the Holy Spirit, attracted him. Compromise is the first victim of persecution, and Montanism offered the prospect of continuing guidance directly from the spirit during a period in which the viability of the Church as a well-ordered household was seriously brought into question by the policy of the Romans.[36]

What was demanded by the conditions of the second century and later was an additional legitimation of the episcopate as the authentic instrument of the Holy Spirit in the Church. The myth of apostolic succession, which began to be articulated as the period of the New Testament came to a close, served an episcopate originally called into being by James but which thrived with the emergence of household churches living in concert. The storm clouds of persecution were gathering during the 90s under the Emperor Domitian, just as the Pastoral Epistles and 1 Clement and Acts were making their plea for a settled Church with a well-ordered authority. To continue its ascendancy, the episcopate needed to be articulated to meet the needs of a Church in the midst of martyrdom; it found just that articulation in Ignatius of Antioch.

## A charismatic and vicarious episcopate as the instrument of unity

Ignatius was bishop of Antioch, and exercised considerable influence from that city, much as Clement did from Rome. In his person, however, Ignatius magnified the role of the episcopate to the point where it has frequently been called monarchial, although he himself said that "it is better for me to die for Jesus Christ, than to reign as king over the ends of the earth" (*To the Romans* 6:1). The language of monarchy did not come naturally to him as a description of his authority. As he understood the ground of his own authority, he could not command in the way that Peter and Paul did, as apostles, but by imitating Jesus' suffering in his own person he could claim to represent Jesus, as a freedman represents the master who has released him from servitude (*To the Romans* 4:2–3). As will become clear shortly, Ignatius' ideal episcopate was the vicarious representation of God in Christ. What he gave up in apostolic authority he more than made up in the direct charism of embodying God among the faithful.

Ignatius countered many of the same tendencies of Judaic (and/or quasi-Judaic)[37] prophecy in the shape of complicated myths and millenarian schemes with which the Pastoral Epistles also engaged.[38] The fact that he did so in letters to Asia Minor, where Montanism also later emerged, put Ignatius in a position to articulate an episcopal principal in precisely the place and precisely the time where it needed to be enhanced in order to survive and predominate.

Ignatius' death as a martyr *c.* 107 CE did much to enhance the office he distinguished while he was alive. Eusebius, writing in the fourth century (324–5), says that Ignatius is still remembered, and gives a brief account of his heroism:

> Word has it that he was dispatched from Syria to the city of the Romans to become food for beasts in witness to Christ. And through Asia he made his conduct with a most careful watch of guards; in every city he stayed in, he was a strength to the parishes with words of instruction and exhortation. First and most of all he warned them to guard themselves against the heresies which were then first emerging, urging them to hold tight to the tradition of the apostles, which he – already a witness – thought necessary for accuracy to commit to writing. So when he was in Smyrna, where Polycarp was, he wrote one letter to the church in Ephesus, mentioning its pastor Onesimus, another to the church in Magnesia on the Meander, where again he made mention of Bishop Damas, another to the other church in Tralles, of which he relates Polybius was then ruler. In addition he wrote to the church in the city of the Romans, to which also he put out an appeal that they

not beseech him to deprive himself of the yearned-for martyrdom.

*(Ecclesiastical History* 3.36)

In his *Letter to the Romans* (6:2) Ignatius in fact insisted, "The pains of birth are upon me. Bear with me, brothers. Do not hinder me from living: do not wish me to die."

Ignatius' martyrdom did more than enhance his reputation: he actually incorporated the imitation of Christ within the definition of episcopal authority. In this, he developed and combined themes in the First Letter of Peter in the New Testament. 1 Peter, written around 90 CE and also directed to congregations in Asia Minor, had provided a classic statement of how suffering innocently put one in the position of truly following Christ (1 Peter 2:18–25). Owing to that careful statement, Ignatius can say more simply, "Permit me to be an imitator of the passion of my God" *(To the Romans* 6:3).

At the close of the passage in 1 Peter, the author speaks of how following this example leads to restoration: "For you were wandering like sheep, but now you are returned to the shepherd and overseer *(episkopos)* of your souls" (1 Peter 2:25). Does 1 Peter imply that God is, in effect, a bishop *(episkopos* in the institutional sense)? Contextually, it seems far more likely that "overseer" is used in the sense of the manager of a household here. But the passage does combine the key terms, pastoral and managerial, which came to be associated with the episcopate by the time of Ignatius. It is precisely for that reason that, when Ignatius envisages himself as dead, he can say that the church in Syria "uses God for a pastor, instead of me; Jesus Christ, along with your love, will be its only bishop" *(To the Romans* 9:1).

The readiness of the bishop for martyrdom, in the sense of comprehensive testimony to Jesus Christ, provided Ignatius in his own mind with the true charism of leadership. He self-consciously writes to the churches "in the apostolic fashion"[39] *(To the Trallians,* preface), and Eusebius is right to portray him as a deliberate exponent of the apostolic tradition. But in that same letter, he develops a telling hierarchy of obedience which in fact relativizes even apostolic authority in favor of the episcopate. He says first *(To the Trallians* 2:1–2) that his readers should obey the bishop as they would Jesus Christ, and priests as they would apostles. He then slightly revises that scheme to include deacons:[40] "Similarly, all should have regard for the deacons as Jesus Christ, just as the bishop is a type of the Father, and the priests as God's council and apostles' college" (*To the Trallians* 3:1). A threefold ministry – of bishops, priests, and deacons – clearly emerges here, with deacons aligned with bishops as having a most direct claim upon the loyalty of believers. The ground of that claim is not only apostolic succession (which here in fact figures more in the depiction of priests), but in the competence of bishops to stand in place of God within the Church. Each bishop is a vicarious representative of God himself, so that the readiness of Bishop Ignatius to follow the passion of God was inherent in his vocation to institutional ministry.

# Part 3

# SCRIPTURAL AUTHORITY

# 5

# THE COMMANDING VOICE OF SCRIPTURE IN RABBINIC JUDAISM

The Torah, the Pentateuch in particular within ancient Israelite Scripture, received as God's word in God's own wording, formed the highest authority of all in Rabbinic Judaism. Demonstration of a proposition by appeal to Scripture, properly interpreted, would therefore settle all questions. More broadly still, the great issues of the formative age tended to work themselves out in conflict over the meaning of ancient Israelite Scripture. Hence when we understand the paramount authority of Scripture and tradition, we uncover the deepest layers of authority to which the kindred religions appeal. But how matters worked themselves out – at issue then is how the sages of Scripture identified the message set forth by the commanding voice of Scripture – defines the governing question. Precisely what told them those passages of Scripture, among many candidates, that would definitively settle questions, overcome schism and set holy Israel upon the right path? Bitter disputes on just these matters marked every initiative in Scripture and its interpretation.

The character of the first document of Rabbinic Judaism hardly conforms to the description just now given, since recognizing the priority of the written Torah as authority for Rabbinic Judaism, we should anticipate systematic demonstration out of Scripture for the propositions of behavior and belief that the Mishnah sets forth, but we find no such sustained effort. Only episodically, as in the following uncommon instance, do framers of compositions cite Scripture to prove their points:

## *Mishnah-tractate Sotah 8:1*

[A] The anointed for battle, when he speaks to the people, in the Holy Language did he speak,

[B] As it is said, And it shall come to pass when you draw near to the battle, that the priest shall approach (this is the priest anointed for battle) and shall speak to the people (in the Holy Language) and shall say to them, Hear, 0 Israel you draw near to battle this day (Deut. 20:2–3) –

[C] Against your enemies (Deut. 20:3) – and not against your brothers,

[D] Not Judah against Simeon, nor Simeon against Benjamin.

[E] For if you fall into their [Israelites'] hand, they will have mercy for you,

[F] as it is said, And the men which have been called by name rose up and took the captives and with the spoil clothed all that were naked among them and arrayed them and put shoes on their feet and gave them food to eat and something to drink and carried all the feeble of them upon asses and brought them to Jericho, the city of palm trees, unto their brethren. Then they returned to Samaria (2 Chron. 28:15).

[G] Against your enemies do you go forth.

[H] For if you fall into their hand, they will not have mercy upon you.

[I] Let not your heart be faint, fear not, nor tremble, neither be afraid (Deut. 20:3).

[J] Let not your heart be faint – on account of the neighing of the horses and the flashing of the swords.

[K] Fear not – at the clashing of shields and the rushing of the tramping shoes.

[L] Nor tremble – at the sound of the trumpets.

[M] Neither be afraid – at the sound of the shouting.

[N] For the Lord your God is with you (Deut. 20:4) –

[O] they come with the power of mortal man, but you come with the power of the Omnipresent.

This passage shows us what the Mishnah would have looked like, had appeal to Scripture formed the ultimate source of authority. The law is teased out of the language of Scripture, and it is validated by appeal to exegesis of Scripture. Scripture supplies not only facts, but the conclusions drawn from those facts – that is the clear claim of the exegete, who has formed the law out of verses of Scripture.

But that is not the way in which the Mishnah pursues its formulation and presentation of the law. For the Mishnah, Scripture – like nature and history, as we explained in *The Intellectual Foundations of Christian and Jewish Discourse: The Philosophy of Religious Argument* – is a source of irrefutable facts, but not much more. Rather, the Mishnah conducts its discourse through logic, in particular the logic of comparison and contrast: something is either like something else and so follows the rule governing that to which it is similar, or it is unlike something else and follows the opposite of the rule governing that to which it is dissimilar. The Mishnah's framers make up lists of things that bear the same indicative traits, and these lists then are shown to follow a single rule or produce a uniform consequence. The premise of the list is that the objects can be classified by appeal to their indicative qualities, and once classified, will conform to a single norm. In such a philosophical analysis guided by the principles of natural history, Scripture plays no role. The rule of logic governing Rabbinic thought in the Mishnah and related documents throughout is the simple principle of philosophy: "Something that is true of a particular case is true also of a similar case."[1] Once we explore the implications of that logic, we can account for the bulk of the disputes that predominate in the Mishnah, and, more important, the debates that clarify and purify the disputes throughout the normative writing. For faced with a situation the governing rule of which is unknown, we turn immediately to the appropriate likeness, and the dispute will take shape when two parties announce conflicting opinion on the governing simile. The debate that follows will allow each party to differentiate the other's simile from the case.

The working of the logic for normative law is clear. If we wish to discover the rule that governs a particular case, we shall have to find out that to which the case is similar (or even identical). When we know to what the unknown is to be compared, we also know the rule that governs the unknown. That simple rule of logic dictates the conduct of the dispute in the Rabbinic canon and determines the course of debate and the suitability and relevance of evidence adduced by all parties to a debate. And that generative logic spins out the entire fabric of discourse. For the engagement in analysis and argument will take the form of an examination of the facts of the case: is B really similar to A? Is it similar in the way that matters in context, or merely in general? If it is similar, is the similarity best explained through the consequence that is proposed, or is some other explanation going to make better sense of the similarity? And, finally, if it is alleged to be similar but shown to be different, then what conclusions are we to draw from the difference?

While science and philosophy dealt with the natural world and abstractions of social relationships, sages covered that middle ground of the concrete that also involved the social order. In the Rabbinic documents in general, we may characterize the paramount modes of thought and, consequently, also the lines of argument, in a simple way: (1) through similarity we make connections; (2) through the examination of difference, we then draw conclusions.

In challenging the allegation of similarity (all the more so, identity), and in differentiating what appear to be alike, we conduct the substance of argument. Modes of thought and analysis, media of the formulation of the same, and methods of explanation – these focus upon the work of analogy, comparison and contrast. Similar traits connect one thing to another but not to a third; differences distinguish one from another; like follows like, unlike follows the opposite rule.

To assess the role of Scripture and its authority in such an analytical, philosophical process of discovering the law, it suffices to consider a single case. In what follows Scripture supplies governing facts, so that when we identify the verse of Scripture that pertains, we also know the fact that must emerge. But Scripture provides only inert facts, not the active power of governing logic. That is the point at which analogy and contrast come into play, for the relevance of one verse of Scripture over another depends upon the appropriate comparison. In the following case, the governing analogy is the same, but the trait of the governing analogy that applies to the problem at hand is subject to dispute.

The facts of the case present no complexities. We deal with the sacrificial cult in the Temple in Jerusalem, in which sacrificial meat and other materials were placed on altar fires and burned up. What happens, however, when something is put on the altar that for one reason or another does not constitute a valid offering? Scripture is clear on that point – whatever touches the altar is sanctified by it, therefore may not be removed from it, no matter what it is that has touched the altar: "Whatever touches the altar shall become consecrated" (Exodus 29:37). The Mishnah's rule begins with the question: but what if what touches the altar is not suitable for consecration to begin with? Does the altar affect what is unsuitable *ex opere operato,* or does the rule of Scripture pertain only to what can have been legitimately placed upon the altar to begin with? The operative analogy derives from an offering that is wholly consumed on the altar fire, which is the burnt offering. In the dispute, the first of the two authorities invokes that analogy and maintains that, just as that offering, once placed on the altar, is not removed for any reason, so anything else that has been set on the altar must be left there. The operative trait of the burnt offering is that it is thrown into the fire, so whatever can be affected by the fire – whatever is appropriate for the altar fire – is left on the altar, but other things are removed. The second opinion addresses the same analogy, the burnt offering, but finds the operative trait the matter of being put on the altar to begin with. Whatever can be put on the altar is left there. Then what is at stake in the debate is whether the operative trait of the burnt offering is the altar fire ("burnt") or being put on the altar to begin with ("offering"). Joshua, in what follows, focuses upon the fire, Gamaliel on the altar, and the dispute then works itself out in terms of the governing analogy and the reading of the verse of Scripture that provides the analogy

### Mishnah-tractate Zebahim 9:1

[A] The altar sanctifies that which is appropriate to it. [If something is placed on the altar that is suitable for the altar, it is not to be removed.]

[B] R. Joshua says, "Whatever is appropriate to [not the altar but] the altar fires, if it has gone up [onto the fires], should not go down, since it is said, 'This is the burnt offering – that which goes up on the hearth on the altar' (Lev. 6:9): just as the burnt offering, which is appropriate to the altar fires, if it has gone up, should not go down, so whatever is appropriate to the altar fires, if it has gone up, should not go down."

[C] Rabban Gamaliel says, "Whatever is appropriate to the altar, if it has gone up, should not go down, as it is said, 'This is the burnt offering on the hearth on the altar' (Lev. 6:2): just as the burnt offering, which is appropriate to the altar, if it has gone up, should not go down, so whatever is appropriate to the altar, if it has gone up, should not go down."

[D] The difference between the opinion of Rabban Gamaliel and the opinion of R. Joshua is only the blood and the drink offerings.

[E] For Rabban Gamaliel says, "They should not [having been placed on the altar] go down."

129

[F] And R. Joshua says, "They should go down."

The exchange of disputed opinion in principle, [B]–[C], is followed up with the exchange of opinion on a concrete case, [E]–[F]. Implicit is the point of the dispute, which is the salient trait of the governing analogy. Then the logic of argument, shared by both parties, conforms to that analysis through comparison and contrast (analogy and polarity) that philosophy valued.

A still better articulation of the problem of analogical reasoning presents itself when the acknowledged facts are placed on display, followed by the dispute and the debate. In our second case drawn from the Mishnah, the facts are set forth as an axiom, then the dispute replaces what we should have expected in the form of a theorem (prove this, prove that, out of the axiom). At stake, as is common in the Mishnah, is how we classify a mixture of substances, each belonging to its own taxon. In the case at hand, we deal with blood of sacrificial animals. Depending upon the character of the offering – the animal and the purpose its sacrifice is meant to serve – the blood may require four acts of tossing upon the corner of the altar or only one; and it may require tossing to a point on the upper side of the altar wall or to one on the lower side of the wall, differentiated by a red line around the center of the altar wall. The issue, which is to be predicted on the basis of the facts at hand, is how we are to toss a bowl of blood that is to be tossed in a single act of tossing that has been confused with a bowl of blood that is to be tossed in four such acts:

*Mishnah Zebahim 8:10–11*

[A] [Blood] which is to be tossed in a single act of tossing which was mixed up with [blood] which is to be tossed in a single act of tossing –
[B] let them be tossed in a single act of tossing [below the red line].
[C] [Blood] which is to be tossed in four acts of tossing [which was mixed up with] blood which is to be tossed in four acts of tossing –
[D] let them be tossed in four acts of tossing [below the red line].
[E] [Blood] which is to be tossed in four acts of tossing [which was mixed up] with blood which is to be tossed in one act of tossing –
[F] R. Eliezer says, "Let them be tossed in four acts of tossing."
[G] R. Joshua says, "Let them be tossed in a single act of tossing."

[H] Said to him R. Eliezer, "And lo, he transgresses the rule against diminishing [the required acts of tossing, so Deut. 4:2]."

[I] Said to him R. Joshua, "And lo, he transgresses the rule against adding [to the required acts of tossing – Deut. 4:2]."

[J] Said to him R. Eliezer, "The prohibition against adding is stated only in connection with the act in itself."

[K] Said to him R. Joshua, "The prohibition against diminishing is stated only in connection with the act in itself."

[L] And further did R. Joshua say, "When you placed [the blood four times], you transgressed the prohibition against adding, and you did the deed with your own hand, and when you did not sprinkle [four times], you transgressed against the prohibition against diminishing, but [at least] you did not do the deed with your own hand."

The issue is joined at [E], with the dispute exposed at [F]–[G]. Then at [H] we invoke the governing verse of Scripture, counterpart to the governing analogy: "You shall not add anything to what I command you or take anything away from it" (Deuteronomy 4:2). If blood that is to be tossed four times is tossed only once, that represents an act of diminution; if blood that is to be tossed one time is tossed four times, it is an act of addition. Then the analogy itself is subjected to analysis, [J]–[L]. Here is where the dispute and its evidence gives way to argument. Eliezer rejects Joshua's reading of the relevant verse, since, he maintains, the prohibition against adding to what the Torah requires concerns the act in itself, which is done as it should be done – four times – and not the blood that is to be tossed only once. Joshua employs the same reasoning with the opposite result, [K]: one should not diminish the action, but as to the blood, that is another matter. So each party reasons in precisely the terms and manner of the other. At the end, Joshua introduces the point of differentiation: whether the deed that, of necessity, violates the principle of not diminishing or augmenting is done by the priest or not. If one does the deed four times, he himself is responsible by reason of an affirmative action. If one does not sprinkle four times blood that is to be sprinkled four times, that is an act of omission, not of commission. And, implicitly, that is to be preferred.

So far we have not seen a point at which the governing criterion of the appropriate analogy is made explicit. Our understanding of the way in which the Mishnah carries on its work, in essential autonomy and not in a relationship of dependence upon Scripture, will be complete when we see how the Tosefta, a compilation of complementary material for the Mishnah, presents us with a striking case in which the governing analogy is introduced in an explicit manner. Here a more philosophical mode of argument comes to full articulation. What we see is how argument by analogy and contrast works. The case concerns the disposition of what is subject to doubt – along with mixtures, a favorite theme of the framers of the Mishnah. In the following case, what we do not know is the status of objects immersed in an immersion-pool that, at a given point in time, is found to be lacking in the requisite volume of water and so unable to effect the purification of what is immersed. Specifically, how do we dispose of those objects immersed in the time from the last point at which it was known that the pool had a valid volume of water?

### Tosefta Miqvaot 1:16–19

[A] An immersion-pool which was measured and found lacking – all the acts requiring cleanness which were carried out depending upon it

[B] whether this immersion-pool is in the private domain, or whether this immersion-pool is in the public domain – [Supply: ] objects that have been immersed are unclean.]

[C] R. Simeon says, "In the private domain, it is unclean. In the public domain, it is clean."

Thus far we have the statement of the case. Now comes the dispute and debate:

[D] Said R. Simeon, "There was the case of the water-reservoir of Disqus in Yabneh was measured and found lacking.

[E] "And R. Tarfon did declare clean, and R. Aqiba unclean.

[F] "Said R. Tarfon, 'Since this immersion-pool is in the assumption of being clean, it remains perpetually in this presumption of cleanness until it will be known for sure that it is made unclean.'

[G] "Said R. Aqiba, 'Since this immersion-pool is in the assumption of being unclean, it perpetually remains in the presumption of uncleanness until it will be known for sure that it is clean.'"

The principle is, do we focus upon the prevailing assumption as to the status of the pool, and confirm that status, or do we declare the governing analogy to be the status of the unclean object that was immersed in the pool, and confirm that status? The former status is confirmed as valid, since we have assumed the pool was valid until we discovered that it was lacking in the requisite volume of valid water; the latter status is confirmed as unclean, since we assume objects that have been declared unclean remain so until they are validly purified. Now at stake is, which is the governing analogy?

[H]  "Said R. Tarfon, 'To what is the matter to be likened? To one who was standing and offering [a sacrifice] at the altar, and it became known that he is a son of a divorcee or the son of a woman who has undergone the rite of removing the shoe,
[I]  " 'for his service is valid.'
[J]  "Said R. Aqiba, 'To what is the matter to be likened?
[K]  " 'To one who was standing and offering [a sacrifice] at the altar, and it became known that he is disqualified by reason of a blemish –
[L]  " 'for his service is invalid.' "

Thus far we have the conflict between relevant analogies. Now how is the argument articulated? It is through the challenge of each party to the pertinence of the analogy introduced by the other:

[M]  "Said R. Tarfon to him, 'You draw an analogy to one who is blemished. I draw an analogy to the son of a divorcee or to the son of a woman who has undergone the rite of removing the shoe [and is invalid for marriage into the priesthood].
[N]  " 'Let us now see to what the matter is appropriately likened.
[O]  " 'If it is analogous to a blemished priest, let us learn the law from the case of the blemished priest. If it is analogous to the son of a divorcee or to the son of a woman who has undergone the rite of removing the shoe, let us learn the law from the case of the son of the divorcee or the son of a woman who has undergone the rite of removing the shoe.' "

In fact, as we shall now see, Tarfon's statement of the issue of which analogy governs proves to set matters up to allow Aqiba to settle the question. He does so by differentiating the analogical cases, showing where the true point of similarity – now, he insists, not mere similarity but identity! – is to be located.

[P] "R. Aqiba says, 'The unfitness affecting an immersion-pool affects the immersion-pool itself, and the unfit aspect of the blemished priest affects the blemished priest himself.

[Q] "'But let not the case of the son of a divorcee or the son of a woman who has undergone the rite of removing the shoe prove the matter, for his matter of unfitness depends upon others.

[R] "'A ritual pool's unfitness [depends] on one only, and the unfitness of a blemished priest [depends] on an individual only, but let not the son of a divorcee or the son of a woman who has undergone the rite of removing the shoe prove the matter, for the unfitness of this one depends upon ancestry.'

[S] "They took a vote concerning the case and declared it unclean."

[T] "Said R. Tarfon to R. Aqiba, 'He who departs from you is like one who perishes.'"

Aqiba finds no difficulty in acknowledging the similarity, but he criticizes the use of the analogy by differentiating, in the manner of Socrates, between similarity and identity. He is able to differentiate ("divide") the analogy into its operative components, and, in doing so, he shows that the analogy as he proposes to apply it sustains his position. Now, we must ask ourselves, what authority has Scripture exercised in these massive analytical exercises? The answer is, very little!

Had the formation of Rabbinic Judaism concluded, then, with the Mishnah and the Tosefta, any account of the authority of Scripture in that Judaism would suffice with a single sentence: Scripture supplied facts, the Mishnah, everything else. But nearly the entirety of the subsequent literature contradicts that conclusion. Much of it is shaped in the form of the exegesis of Scripture, and to begin with, at every passage of the Mishnah on which they contribute an interpretation, the two Talmuds form their commentaries upon the Mishnah around the question, what is the source of this rule? to which the answer invariably follows, "as it is said...," or "as it is written...," with a verse of Scripture following. We may therefore state that one fundamental motif of the formation of Rabbinic Judaism was to mediate the authority of Scripture, not merely its facticity, into the mainstream of that Judaism that the Mishnah had inaugurated.

Why, to begin with, did the sages have to address the question of the primacy of Scriptural authority in the law of the Mishnah? Because, when, in *c.* 200 CE, the Mishnah reached closure and was received and adopted as law by the state-sanctioned Jewish governments in both the Roman empire, in the land of Israel, and Iran, in Babylonia, respectively, the function and character of the document precipitated a considerable crisis. Politically and theologically presented as the foundation for the everyday administration of the affairs of Jewry, the Mishnah ignored the politics of the sponsoring regimes. Essentially ahistorical, the code hardly identified as authoritative any known political institution, let alone the patriarchate in the land of Israel, or the exilarchate in Babylonia. True, that political–institutional flaw (from the viewpoint of the sponsoring authorities) scarcely can have proved critical.

But the silence of the authorship of the Mishnah on the theological call for their document presented not a chronic but an acute problem. Since Jews generally accepted the authority of Moses at Sinai, failure to claim for the document a clear and explicit relationship to the Torah of Moses defined that acute issue. Why should people accept as authoritative the rulings of this piece of writing? Omitting reference to a theological, as much as to a political, myth, the authorship of the Mishnah also failed to signal the relationship between their document and Scripture. Since, for all Judaisms, Hebrew Scriptures in general, and the Pentateuch in particular, represented God's will for Israel, silence on that matter provoked considerable response. Let me now spell out in some detail the political, theological, and literary difficulties presented by the Mishnah to any theory that the Mishnah formed part of God's revelation to Moses at Sinai.

Laws issued to define what people were supposed to do could not stand by themselves; they had to receive the imprimatur of Heaven, that is, they had to be given the status of revelation. Accordingly, to make its way in Israelite life, the Mishnah as a constitution and code demanded for itself a theory of beginnings at (or in relation to) Sinai, with Moses, from God. The character of the Mishnah itself hardly won confidence that, on the face of it, the document formed part of, or derived from, Sinai. It was originally published through oral formulation and oral transmission, that is, in the medium of memorization. But it had been in the medium of writing that, in the view of all of Israel until about 200 CE, God had been understood to reveal the divine word and will. The Torah was a written book. People who claimed to receive further messages from God usually wrote them down. They had three choices in securing acceptance of their account. All three involved linking the new to the old.

In claiming to hand on revelation, they could, first, sign their books with the names of biblical heroes. Second, they could imitate the style of biblical Hebrew. Third, they could present an exegesis of existing written verses, validating their ideas by supplying proof-texts for them. From the closure of the Torah literature in the time of Ezra, *c.* 450 CE, to the time of the Mishnah, nearly seven hundred years later, we do not have a single book alleged to be holy and at the same time standing wholly out of relationship to the Holy Scriptures of ancient Israel. The pseudepigraphic writings fall into the first category, the Essene writings at Qumran into the second and third. We may point also to the Gospels, which take as a principal problem the demonstration of how Jesus had fulfilled the prophetic promises of the Old Testament and in other ways carried forward and even embodied Israel's Scripture.

Insofar as a piece of Jewish writing did not find a place in rela-tionship to Scripture, its author laid no claim to present a holy book. The contrast between Jubilees and the Testaments of the Patriarchs, with their constant and close harping on biblical matters, and the several books of Maccabees, shows the differences. The former claim to present God's revealed truth, the latter, history. So a book was holy because in style, in authorship, or in (alleged) origin it continued Scripture, finding a place therefore (at least in the author's mind) within the canon, or because it provided an exposition on Scripture's meaning. But the Mishnah made no such claim. It entirely ignored the style of biblical Hebrew, speaking in a quite different kind of Hebrew altogether. It is silent on its author-ship through sixty-two of the sixty-three tractates (the claims of tractate Abot to the Mishnah's origin in an oral tradition from Sinai are *post facto*). In any event, nowhere does the Mishnah contain the claim that God had inspired the authors of the document. These are not given biblical names and certainly are not alleged to have been biblical saints. Most of the book's named authorities flourished within the same century as its anonymous arrangers and redactors, not in remote antiquity. Above all, the Mishnah contains scarcely a handful of exegeses of Scripture. These, where they occur, play a trivial and tangential role. This then is the problem of the Mishnah: different from Scripture in language and style, indifferent to the claim of authorship by a biblical hero or divine inspiration, stun-ningly aloof from allusion to verses of Scripture for nearly the whole of its discourse – yet authoritative for Israel.

It was not therefore a statement of theory alone, telling only how things will be in the eschaton. Nor was it a wholly sectarian docu-ment, reporting the view of a group without standing or influence in the larger life of Israel. True, in some measure it bears both of these traits of eschatology and sectarian provenance. But the Mishnah was (and is) law for Israel. It entered the government and courts of the Jewish people, both in the motherland and also overseas, as the authoritative constitution of the courts of Judaism. The advent of the Mishnah therefore marked a turning in the life of the nation–religion. The document demanded explanation and apology. And the one thing one could not do, as a Jew in third-century Tiberias, Sepphoris, Caesarea, or Beth Shearim, in Galilee, was ignore the thing. True, one might refer solely to ancient Scripture and tradition and live life out within the inherited patterns of the familiar Israelite religion–culture. But as soon as one dealt with the Jewish government in charge of everyday life – went to court over the damages done to a crop by a neighbor's ox, for instance – one came up against a law in addition to the law of Scripture, a document the principles of which governed and settled all matters. Thus the Mishnah rapidly came to confront the life of Israel. The people who knew the Mishnah, the rabbis or sages, came to dominate that life. And their claim, in accord with the Mishnah, to exercise authority and the right to impose heavenly sanction came to perplex. Now the crisis is fully exposed.

One response was represented by the claim that the authorities of the Mishnah stood in a chain of tradition that extended back to Sinai; stated explicitly in the Mishnah's first apologetic, tractate Abot, which circulated from approximately a generation beyond the promulgation of the Mishnah itself, that view required amplification and concrete demonstration. This approach treated the word *torah* as a common noun, as the word that spoke of a status or classification of sayings. A saying was *torah*, that is, enjoyed the status of torah or fell into the classification of *torah*, if it stood in the line of tradition from Sinai.

A second and distinct response took the same view of *torah* as a common noun. This response was to treat the Mishnah as subordinate to, and dependent upon, Scripture. Then *torah* was what fell into the classification of the revelation of *Torah* by God to Moses at Sinai. The way of providing what was needed within that theory was to link statements of the Mishnah to statements ("proof-texts") of Scripture. The Tosefta, *c.* 300, a compilation of citations of and comments upon the Mishnah, together with some autonomous materials that may have reached closure in the period in which the work of redaction of the Mishnah was going on, as well as the Talmud of the Land of Israel, *c.* 400, fairly systematically did just that.

The former solution treated Torah with a small 't', that is to say, as a generic classification, and identified the Mishnah with the Torah revealed to Moses at Sinai by claiming a place for the Mishnah's authorities in the process of tradition and transmission that brought torah – no longer, the Torah, the specific writing comprising the Five Books of Moses – to contemporary Israel, the Jewish people. It was a theological solution, expressed through ideas, attitudes, implicit claims, but not through sustained rewriting of either Scripture or the Mishnah.

The latter solution, by contrast, concerned the specific and concrete statements of the Mishnah and required a literary, not merely a theological, statement, one precise and specific to passages of the Mishnah, one after the other. What was demanded by the claim that the Mishnah depended upon, but therefore enjoyed the standing of, Scripture, was a line-by-line commentary upon the Mishnah in light of Scripture. But this too, we stress, treated *torah* as a common noun.

The third way would set aside the two solutions, the theological and the literary, and explore the much more profound issues of the fundamental and generative structure of right thought, yielding, as a matter of fact, both Scripture and the Mishnah. This approach insisted that *torah* was always a proper noun. There was, and is, only The Torah. But this – The Torah – demanded expansion and vast amplification. When we know the principles of logical structure and especially those of hierarchical classification that animate The Torah, we can undertake part of the task of expansion and amplification, that is, join in the processes of thought that, in the mind of God, yielded The Torah. For when we know how God thought in giving The Torah to Moses at Sinai and so accounting for the classifications and their ordering in the very creation of the world, we can ourselves enter into The Torah and participate in its processes. That is the approach taken by the compilers of Sifra, upon whose work we shall concentrate.

To begin with, the authority of Scripture would have to be founded upon that same logical structure that sustained the Mishnah itself. And that required two exercises, first, a systematic critique of the logic of the Mishnah, and second, a reconstitution of the presentation of the Mishnah's rules themselves within the framework of Scripture. That work was done in a document that cites and criticizes the presentation of the law of the Mishnah, Sifra, a systematic exegetical reading of the book of Leviticus, which probably reached closure sometime toward the end of the third century. The authorship of Sifra composed the one (and the only truly successful) document to accomplish the union of the two Torahs, Scripture, or the written Torah, and the Mishnah, or the oral Torah. This was achieved not merely formally but through the interior structure of thought. It was by means of the critique of practical logic and the rehabilitation of the probative logic of hierarchical classification (*Listenwissenschaft*) in particular that the authorship of Sifra accomplished this remarkable feat of intellect. That authorship achieved the (re-)union of the two Torahs into a single cogent statement within the framework of the written Torah by penetrating into the deep composition of logic that underlay the creation of the world in its correct components, rightly classified, and in its right order, as portrayed by the Torah.

Specifically, by systematically demolishing the logic that sustains an autonomous Mishnah and by equally thoroughly demonstrating the dependency, for the identification of the correct classification of things, not upon the traits of things viewed in the abstract, but upon the classification of things by Scripture in particular, the framers of Sifra recast the two parts of the Torah into a single coherent statement through unitary and cogent discourse. At stake, therefore, for our authorship is the dependency of the Mishnah upon Scripture, at least for the encompassing case of the book of Leviticus. So in choosing, as to form, the base-text of Scripture, the authorship of Sifra made its entire statement *in nuce.* Then by composing a document that for very long stretches cannot have been put together without the Mishnah and at the same time subjecting the generative logical principles of the Mishnah to devastating critique, that same authorship took up its mediating position. The destruction of the Mishnah as an autonomous and free-standing statement, based upon its own logic, is followed by the reconstruction of large tracts of the Mishnah as a statement wholly within, and in accord with, the logic and program of the written Torah in Leviticus. we therefore represent as a triumph of intellect the work of the authorship of Sifra, as we now know it in its recurrent and fixed forms of rhetoric and logic and equally permanent protocol of relationships with other documents, particularly Scripture and Mishnah (with Tosefta).

Sifra's authorship attempted to set forth the dual Torah as a single, cogent statement, doing so by reading the Mishnah into Scripture not merely for proposition but for expression of proposition. On the surface that decision represented a literary, not merely a theological, judgment. But within the deep structure of thought, it was far more than a mere matter of how to select and organize propositions. Presenting the two Torahs in a single statement constituted an experiment in logic, that logic, in particular, which made cogent thought possible, and which transformed facts into propositions, and propositions into judgments of the more, or the less, consequential. It will take many pages of the shank of this book to demonstrate the profound layers of thought upon which the authorship of Sifra erected its remarkable writing. At this point, it suffices to warn that our authorship did something no one else in Judaic antiquity even imagined attempting to do, and that was, to state the dual Torah in a single, coherent, cogent piece of writing, a piece of writing in which new thought came to expression in a very particular medium indeed.

While the Mishnah's other apologists wrote the written Torah into the Mishnah, Sifra's authorship wrote the oral Torah into Scripture. That is to say, the other of the two approaches to the problem of the Mishnah, the one of Sifra, claimed to begin with to demonstrate that the Mishnah found its correct place within the written Torah itself. Instead of citing verses of Scripture in the context of the Mishnah, the authorship of Sifra cited passages of the Mishnah in the context of Scripture, Leviticus in particular. Let us concentrate on the other solution, the one that characterized authorities from Abot and the Tosefta through the Bavli, which we may call "the appeal to the Torah for a solution to the problem of the Mishnah."

Sifra's authorship's position is that the Mishnah is authoritative not because it is *torah* in the generic sense, but because it simply amplifies or depends upon the Torah, in the particular sense of the Five Books of Moses. The earliest exegetical strata of the two Talmuds and the legal–exegetical writings produced in the two hundred years after the closure of the Mishnah took the position that the Mishnah is wholly dependent upon Scripture and authoritative, in the status (but not the classification!) of the Torah, because of that dependency. Whatever is of worth in the Mishnah can be shown to derive directly from Scripture. So the Mishnah was represented as deemed distinct from, and subordinate to, Scripture. This position is expressed in an obvious way. Once the Talmuds cite a Mishnah-pericope, they commonly ask, "What is the source of these words?" And the answer invariably is, "As it is said in Scripture." This constitutes not only a powerful defense for the revealed truth of the Mishnah. It presents, also, a stunning judgment upon the standing (and, as a matter of fact, the classification) of the Mishnah. For when the exegetes find themselves constrained to add proof-texts, they admit the need to acknowledge that the Mishnah is not (part of) The Torah but only a secondary expression or amplification of The Torah.

That judgment upon the Mishnah forms part of the polemic of Sifra's authorship – but only part of it. Sifra's authorship conducts a sustained polemic against the failure of the Mishnah to cite Scripture very much or systematically to link its ideas to Scripture through the medium of formal demonstration by exegesis. Sifra's rhetorical exegesis follows a standard redactional form. Scripture will be cited. Then a statement will be made about its meaning, or a statement of law correlative to that Scripture will be given. That statement sometimes cites the Mishnah, often verbatim. Finally, the author of Sifra invariably states, "Now is that not (merely) logical?" And the point of that statement will be, "Can this position not be gained through the working of mere logic, based upon facts supplied (to be sure) by Scripture?"

The polemical power of Sifra lies in its repetitive demonstration that the stated position, citation of a Mishnah-pericope, is not only not the product of logic, but is, and only can be, the product of exegesis of Scripture. That is only part of the matter, as we shall explain, but that component of the larger judgment of Sifra's authorship does make the point that the Mishnah is subordinated to Scripture and validated only through Scripture. In that regard, the authorship of Sifra stands at one with the position of the authorships of the other successor-writings, even though Sifra's writers carried to a much more profound level of thought the critique of the Mishnah. They did so by rethinking the logical foundations of the entire Torah.

We recall that, for the framers of the Mishnah, to show something to be true, one has to demonstrate that, in logic, it conforms to the regularity and order that form the guarantee of truth. Analysis is meant to discover order: the rule that covers diverse, by nature disorderly, things, the shared trait, the general and prevailing principle of regularity. And to discover the prevailing rule, one has to know how to classify things that seem to be each *sui generis*, how to find the rule that governs diverse things. And that explains the centrality in the system of the Mishnah of the classification of things. At issue between the framers of the Mishnah and the authorship of Sifra is the correct source of classification. The framers of the Mishnah effect their taxonomy through the traits of things.

Let us now examine one sustained example of how Sifra's authorship rejects the principles of the logic of hierarchical classification as these are worked out by the framers of the Mishnah. We emphasize that the critique applies to the way in which a shared logic is worked out by the other authorship. For it is not the principle that like things follow the same rule, unlike things, the opposite rule, that is at stake. Nor is the principle of hierarchical classification embodied in the argument *a fortiori* at issue. What our authorship disputes is that we can classify things on our own by appeal to their traits or indicative characteristics, that is, utterly without reference to Scripture. The argument is simple. On our own, we cannot classify species into genera. Everything is different from everything else in some way. But Scripture tells us what things are like what other things for what purposes, hence it is Scripture that imposes on things the definitive classifications, not traits we discern in the things themselves. When we see the nature of the critique, we shall have a clear picture of what is at stake when we examine, in some detail, precisely how the Mishnah's logic does its work. That is why at the outset we present a complete composition in which Sifra's authorship tests the modes of classification characteristic of the Mishnah, resting as they do on the traits of things viewed out of the context of Scripture's categories of things.

### 5. Parashat Vayyiqra Dibura Denedabah Parashah 3

[V:I.1 A] "[If his offering is] a burnt offering [from the herd, he shall offer a male without blemish; he shall offer it at the door of the tent of meeting, that he may be accepted before the Lord; he shall lay his hand upon the head of the burnt offering, and it shall be accepted for him to make atonement for him]" (Lev. 1:2):

[B] Why does Scripture refer to a burnt offering in particular?

[C] For one might have taken the view that all of the specified grounds for the invalidation of an offering should apply only to the burnt offering that is brought as a free will offering.

[D] But how should we know that the same grounds for invalidation apply also to a burnt offering that is brought in fulfillment of an obligation [for instance, the burnt offering that is brought for a leper who is going through a rite of purification, or the bird brought by a woman who has given birth as part of her purification rite, Lev. 14 and 12, respectively]?

[E] It is a matter of logic.

[F] Bringing a burnt offering as a free will offering and bringing a burnt offering in fulfillment of an obligation [are parallel to one another and fall into the same classification].

[G] Just as a burnt offering that is brought as a free will offering is subject to all of the specified grounds for invalidation, so to a burnt offering brought in fulfillment of an obligation, all the same grounds for invalidation should apply.

[H] No, [that reasoning is not compelling. For the two species of the genus, burnt offering, are not wholly identical and can be distinguished, on which basis we may also maintain that the grounds for invalidation that pertain to the one do not necessarily apply to the other. Specifically:] if you have taken that position with respect to the burnt offering brought as a free will offering, for which there is no equivalent, will you take the same position with regard to the burnt offering brought in fulfillment of an obligation, for which there is an equivalent? [For if one is obligated to bring a burnt offering by reason of obligation and cannot afford a beast, one may bring birds, as at Lev. 14:22, but if one is bringing a free will offering, a less expensive form of the offering may not serve.]

[I] Accordingly, since there is the possibility in the case of the burnt offering brought in fulfillment of an obligation, in which case there is an acceptable equivalent [to the more expensive beast, through the less expensive birds], all of the specified grounds for invalidation [which apply to the in any case more expensive burnt offering brought as a free will offering] should not apply at all.

[J] That is why in the present passage, Scripture refers simply to "burnt offering," [and without further specification, the meaning is then simple:] all the same are the burnt offering brought in fulfillment of an obligation and a burnt offering brought as a free will offering in that all of the same grounds for invalidation of the beast that pertain to the one pertain also to the other.

[2 A] And how do we know that the same rules of invalidation of a blemished beast apply also in the case of a beast that is designated in substitution of a beast sanctified for an offering [in line with Lev. 27:10, so that, if one states that a given, unconsecrated beast is to take the place of a beast that has already been consecrated, the already consecrated beast remains in its holy status, and the beast to which reference is made also becomes consecrated]?

[B] The matter of bringing a burnt offering and the matter of bringing a substituted beast fall into the same classification [since both are offerings that in the present instance will be consumed upon the altar, and, consequently, they fall under the same rule as to invalidating blemishes].

[C] Just as the entire protocol of blemishes apply to the one, so in the case of the beast that is designated as a substitute, the same invalidating blemishes pertain.

[D] No, if you have invoked that rule in the case of the burnt offering, in which case no status of sanctification applies should the beast that is designated as a burnt offering be blemished in some permanent way, will you make the same statement in the case of a beast that is designated as a substitute? For in the case of a substituted beast, the status of sanctification applies even though the beast bears a permanent blemish! [So the two do not fall into the same classification after all, since to begin with one cannot sanctify a permanently blemished beast, which beast can never enter the status of sanctification, but through an act of substitution, a permanent blemished beast can be placed into the status of sanctification.]

[E] Since the status of sanctification applies [to a substituted beast] even though the beast bears a permanent blemish, all of the specified grounds for invalidation as a matter of logic should not apply to it.

[F] That is why in the present passage, Scripture refers simply to "burnt offering," [and without further specification, the meaning is then simple:] all the same are the burnt offering brought in fulfillment of an obligation and a burnt offering brought as a substitute for an animal designated as holy, in that all of the same grounds for invalidation of the beast that pertain to the one pertain also to the other.

[3 A] And how do we know [that the protocol of blemishes that apply to the burnt offering brought as a free will offering apply also to] animals that are subject to the rule of a sacrifice as a peace offering?

[B] It is a matter of logic. The matter of bringing a burnt offering and the matter of bringing animals that are subject to the rule of a sacrifice as a peace offering fall into the same classification [since both are offerings and, consequently, under the same rule as to invalidating blemishes].

144

[C] Just as the entire protocol of blemishes apply to the one, so in the case of animals that are subject to the rule of a sacrifice as a peace offering, the same invalidating blemishes pertain.

[D] And it is furthermore a matter of an argument *a fortiori,* as follows:

[E] If to a burnt offering is valid when in the form of a bird, [which is inexpensive], the protocol of invalidating blemishes apply, to peace offerings, which are not valid when brought in the form of a bird, surely the same protocol of invalidating blemishes should also apply!

[F] No, if you have applied that rule to a burnt offering, in which case females are not valid for the offering as male beasts are, will you say the same of peace offerings? For female beasts as much as male beasts may be brought for sacrifice in the status of the peace offering. [The two species may be distinguished from one another].

[G] Since it is the case that female beasts as much as male beasts may be brought for sacrifice in the status of the peace offering, the protocol of invalidating blemishes should not apply to a beast designated for use as peace offerings.

[H] That is why in the present passage, Scripture refers simply to "burnt offering," [and without further specification, the meaning is then simple:] all the same are the burnt offering brought in fulfillment of an obligation and an animal designated under the rule of peace offerings, in that all of the same grounds for invalidation of the beast that pertain to the one pertain also to the other.

The systematic exercise proves for beasts that serve in three classifications of offerings, burnt offerings, substitutes, and peace offerings, that the same rules of invalidation apply throughout. The comparison of the two kinds of burnt offerings, voluntary and obligatory, shows that they are sufficiently different from one another that as a matter of logic, what pertains to the one need not apply to the other. Then come the differences between an animal that is consecrated and one that is designated as a substitute for one that is consecrated. Finally we distinguish between the applicable rules of the sacrifice; a burnt offering yields no meat for the person in behalf of whom the offering is made, while one sacrificed under the rule of peace offerings does. What is satisfying, therefore, is that we run the changes on three fundamentally different differences and show that in each case, the differences between like things are greater than the similarities. We cannot imagine a more perfect exercise in the applied and practical logic of comparison and contrast.

The authorship of Sifra concurs in the fundamental principle that sanctification consists in calling things by their rightful name, or, in philosophical language, discovering the classification of things and determining the rule that governs diverse things. Where that authorship differs from the view held by the Mishnah concerns – we emphasize – the origins of taxa: how do we know what diverse things form a single classification of things? Taxa originate in Scripture. Accordingly, at stake in the critique of the Mishnah is not the principle of logic necessary for understanding the construction and inner structure of creation. All parties among sages concurred that the inner structure set forth by a logic of classification alone could sustain the system of ordering all things in proper place and under the proper rule. The like belongs with the like and conforms to the rule governing the like, the unlike goes over to the opposite and conforms to the opposite rule. When we make lists of the like, we also know the rule governing all the items on those lists, respectively. We know that and one other thing, namely, the opposite rule, governing all items sufficiently like to belong on those lists, but sufficiently unlike to be placed on other lists. That rigorously philosophical logic of analysis, comparison and contrast, served because it was the only logic that could serve a system that proposed to make the statement concerning order and right array. Let us first show how the logic of proving propositions worked, then review Sifra's authorship's systematic critique of the way in which the Mishnah's framers applied that logic, specifically, proposed to identify classifications.

The thrust of Sifra's authorship's attack on the Mishnah's taxonomic logic is readily discerned. Time and again, we can easily demonstrate, things have so many and such diverse and contradictory indicative traits that, comparing one thing to something else, we can always distinguish one species from another. Even though we find something in common, we also can discern some other trait characteristic of one thing but not the other. Consequently, we also can show that the hierarchical logic on which we rely, the argument *a fortiori* or *qol vehomer*, will not serve. For if on the basis of one set of traits which yield a given classification, we place into hierarchical order two or more items, on the basis of a different set of traits, we have either a different classification altogether, or, much more commonly, simply a different hierarchy. So the attack on the way in which the Mishnah's authorship has done its work appeals not merely to the limitations of classification solely on the basis of traits of things. The more telling argument addresses what is, to Listenwissenschaft, the source of power and compelling proof: hierarchization. That is why, throughout, we must designate the Mishnah's mode of *Listenwissenschaft* a logic of hierarchical classification. Things are not merely like or unlike, therefore following one rule or its opposite. Things also are weightier or less weighty, and that particular point of likeness of difference generates the logical force of *Listenwissenschaft*.

Sifra's authorship demonstrates that *Listenwissenschaft* is a self-evidently valid mode of demonstrating the truth of propositions. But the sole source of the correct classification of things is Scripture and only Scripture. Without Scripture's intervention into the taxonomy of the world, we should have no knowledge at all of which things fall into which classifications and therefore are governed by which rules. How then do we appeal to Scripture to designate the operative classifications? Here is a simple example of the alternative mode of classification, one that does not appeal to the traits of things but to the utilization of names by Scripture. What we see is how by naming things in one way, rather than in another, Scripture orders all things, classifying and, in the nature of things, also hierarchizing them. Here is one example among many of how our authorship conceives the right way of logical thought to proceed:

### 7. *Parashat Vayyiqra Dibura Denedabah Parashah 4*

[VII:V.1 A] "…and Aaron's sons the priests shall present the blood and throw the blood [round about against the altar that is at the door of the tent of meeting]:"

[B] Why does Scripture make use of the word "blood" twice [instead of using a pronoun]?

[C] [It is for the following purpose:] How on the basis of Scripture do you know that if blood deriving from one burnt offering was confused with blood deriving from another burnt offering, blood deriving from one burnt offering with blood deriving from a beast that has been substituted therefor, blood deriving from a burnt offering with blood deriving from an unconsecrated beast, the mixture should nonetheless be presented?

[D] It is because Scripture makes use of the word "blood" twice [instead of using a pronoun].

147

[2 A] Is it possible to suppose that while if blood deriving from beasts in the specified classifications, it is to be presented, for the simple reason that if the several beasts while alive had been confused with one another, they might be offered up,

[B] but how do we know that even if the blood of a burnt offering were confused with that of a beast killed as a guilt offering, [it is to be offered up]

[C] I shall concede the case of the mixture of the blood of a burnt offering confused with that of a beast killed as a guilt offering, it is to be presented, for both this one and that one fall into the classification of Most Holy Things.

[D] But how do I know that if the blood of a burnt offering were confused with the blood of a beast slaughtered in the classification of peace offerings or of a thanksgiving offering, [it is to be presented]?

[E] I shall concede the case of the mixture of the blood of a burnt offering confused with that of a beast slaughtered in the classification of peace offerings or of a thanksgiving offering, [it is to be presented], because the beasts in both classifications produce blood that has to be sprinkled four times.

[F] But how do I know that if the blood of a burnt offering were confused with the blood of a beast slaughtered in the classification of a firstling or a beast that was counted as tenth or of a beast designated as a passover, [it is to be presented]?

[G] I shall concede the case of the mixture of the blood of a burnt offering confused with that of a beast slaughtered in the classification of firstling or a beast that was counted as tenth or of a beast designated as a passover, [it is to be presented], because Scripture uses the word "blood" two times.

[H] Then while I may make that concession, might I also suppose that if the blood of a burnt offering was confused with the blood of beasts that had suffered an invalidation, it also may be offered up?

[I] Scripture says, "…its blood," [thus excluding such a case].

[J] Then I shall concede the case of a mixture of the blood of a valid burnt offering with the blood of beasts that had suffered an invalidation, which blood is not valid to be presented at all.

[K] But how do I know that if such blood were mixed with the blood deriving from beasts set aside as sin offerings to be offered on the inner altar, [it is not to be offered up]?

[L] I can concede that the blood of a burnt offering that has been mixed with the blood deriving from beasts set aside as sin offerings to be offered on the inner altar is not to be offered up, for the one is offered on the inner altar, and the other on the outer altar [the burnt offering brought as a free will offering, under discussion here, is slaughtered at the altar "...that is at the door of the tent of meeting," not at the inner altar].

[M] But how do I know that even if the blood of a burnt offering was confused with the blood of sin offerings that are to be slaughtered at the outer altar, it is not to be offered up?

[N] Scripture says, "...its blood," [thus excluding such a case].

In place of the rejecting of arguments resting on classifying species into a common genus, we now demonstrate how classification really is to be carried on. It is through the imposition upon data of the categories dictated by Scripture: Scripture's use of language. That is the force of this powerful exercise. Section 1 of our passage sets the stage, simply pointing out that the use of the word "blood" twice encompasses a case in which blood in two distinct classifications is somehow confused in the process of the conduct of the cult. In such a case it is quite proper to pour out the mixture of blood deriving from distinct sources, for example, beasts that have served different, but comparable, purposes. We then systemically work out the limits of that rule, showing how comparability works, then pointing to cases in which comparability is set aside. Throughout the exposition, at the crucial point we invoke the formulation of Scripture, subordinating logic or in our instance the process of classification of like species to the dictation of Scripture.

The reason for Scripture's unique power of classification is the possibility of polythetic classification that only Scripture makes possible. Because of Scripture's provision of taxa, we are able to undertake the science of *Listenwissenschaft,* including hierarchical classification, in the right way. What can we do because we appeal to Scripture, which we cannot do if we do not rely on Scripture? It is to establish the possibility that we can appeal to shared traits of otherwise distinct taxa and so transform species into a common genus for a given purpose. Only Scripture makes that initiative feasible, so our authorship maintains.

What is at stake? It is the possibility of doing precisely what the framers of the Mishnah wish to do. That is to join together masses of diverse data into a single, encompassing statement, to show the rule that inheres in diverse cases. In what follows, we shall see an enormous, coherent, and beautifully articulated exercise in the comparison and contrast of many things of a single genus. The

whole holds together, because Scripture makes possible the statement of all things within a single rule. That is, as we have noted,
precisely what the framers of the Mishnah proposed to accomplish.
Our authorship maintains that only by appeal to The Torah is this
feat of learning possible. If, then, we wish to understand all things
all together and all at once under a single encompassing rule, we
had best revert to The Torah, with its account of the rightful names,
positions, and order, imputed to all things.

## 22. Parashat Vayyiqra Dibura Denedabah Parashah 11

[XXII:I.1 A] [With reference to M. Men. 5:5:] There are those
[offerings which require bringing near but do not require
waving, waving but not bringing near, waving and
bringing near, neither waving nor bringing near: These
are offerings which require bringing near but do not
require waving: the meal offering of fine flour and the
meal offering prepared in the baking pan and the meal
offering prepared in the frying pan, and the meal offering
of cakes and the meal offering of wafers, and the meal
offering of priests, and the meal offering of an anointed
priest, and the meal offering of gentiles, and the meal
offering of women, and the meal offering of a sinner. R.
Simeon says, "The meal offering of priests and of the
anointed priest – bringing near does not apply to them,
because the taking of a handful does not apply to
them. And whatever is not subject to the taking of a
handful is not subject to bringing near,"] [Scripture] says,
"When you present to the Lord a meal offering that is made in
any of these ways, it shall be brought [to the priest who shall
take it up to the altar]:"

[B] What requires bringing near is only the handful alone. How do
I know that I should encompass under the rule of bringing near
the meal offering?

[C] Scripture says explicitly, "meal offering."

[D] How do I know that I should encompass all meal offerings?

[E] Scripture says, using the accusative particle, "the meal
offering."

[2 A] I might propose that what requires bringing near is solely the
meal offering brought as a free will offering.

[B] How do I know that the rule encompasses an obligatory meal
offering?

[C] It is a matter of logic.

[D] Bringing a meal offering as a free will offering and bringing a meal offering as a matter of obligation form a single classification. Just as a meal offering presented as a free will offering requires bringing near, so the same rule applies to a meal offering of a sinner [brought as a matter of obligation], which should likewise require bringing near.

[E] No, if you have stated that rule governing bringing near in the case of a free will offering, on which oil and frankincense have to be added, will you say the same of the meal offering of a sinner [Lev. 5:11], which does not require oil and frankincense?

[F] The meal offering brought by a wife accused of adultery will prove to the contrary, for it does not require oil and frankincense, but it does require bringing near [as is stated explicitly at Num. 5:15].

[G] No, if you have applied the requirement of bringing near to the meal offering brought by a wife accused of adultery, which also requires waving, will you say the same of the meal offering of a sinner, which does not have to be waved?

[H] Lo, you must therefore reason by appeal to a polythetic analogy [in which not all traits pertain to all components of the category, but some traits apply to them all in common]:

[I] the meal offering brought as a free will offering, which requires oil and frankincense, does not in all respects conform to the traits of the meal offering of a wife accused of adultery, which does not require oil and frankincense, and the meal offering of the wife accused of adultery, which requires waving, does not in all respects conform to the traits of a meal offering brought as a free will offering, which does not require waving.

[J] But what they have in common is that they are alike in requiring the taking up of a handful and they are also alike in that they require bringing near.

[K] I shall then introduce into the same classification the meal offering of a sinner, which is equivalent to them as to the matter of the taking up of a handful, and also should be equivalent to them as to the requirement of being drawn near.

[L] But might one not argue that the trait that all have in common is that all of them may be brought equally by a rich and a poor person and require drawing near, which then excludes from the common classification the meal offering of a sinner, which does not conform to the rule that it may be brought equally by a rich and a poor person, [but may be brought only by a poor person,] and such an offering also should not require being brought near!

[M] [The fact that the polythetic classification yields indeterminate results means failure once more, and, accordingly,] Scripture states, "meal offering,"

[N] with this meaning: all the same are the meal offering brought as a free will offering and the meal offering of a sinner, both this and that require being brought near.

The elegant exercise draws together the various types of meal offerings and shows that they cannot form a classification of either a monothetic or a polythetic character. Consequently, Scripture must be invoked to supply the proof for the classification of the discrete items. The important language is at [H]–[J]: these differ from those, and those from these, but what they have in common is.... Then we demonstrate, with our appeal to Scripture, the sole valid source of polythetic classification, [M]. And this is constant throughout Sifra.

While setting forth its critique of the Mishnah's utilization of the logic of comparison and contrast in hierarchical classification, the authorship of Sifra is careful not to criticize the Mishnah. Its position favors restating the Mishnah within the context of Scripture, not rejecting its conclusions, let alone its authority. Consequently, when we find a critique of applied reason divorced from Scripture, we rarely uncover an explicit critique of the Mishnah, and when we find a citation of the Mishnah, we rarely uncover linkage to the ubiquitous principle that Scripture forms the source of all classification and hierarchy. When the Mishnah is cited by our authorship, it will be presented as part of the factual substrate of the Torah. When the logic operative throughout the Mishnah is subjected to criticism, the language of the Mishnah will rarely, if ever, be cited in context. The operative language in dealing with the critique of the applied logic of *Listenwissenschaft* as represented by the framers of the Mishnah ordinarily is, "is it not a matter of logic?" Then the sorts of arguments against taxonomy pursued outside of the framework of Scripture's classifications will follow. When, by contrast, the authorship of Sifra wishes to introduce into the context it has already established a verbatim passage of the Mishnah, it will ordinarily, though not always, use *mikan amru* which, in context, means, "in this connection [sages] have said." It is a simple fact that when the intent is to demolish improper reasoning, the Mishnah's rules in the Mishnah's language rarely, if ever, occur. When the authorship of Sifra wishes to incorporate paragraphs of the Mishnah into their re-presentation of The Torah, they will do so either without fanfare, as in the passage at hand, or by the neutral joining-language "in this connection [sages] have said."

The authorship of Sifra never called into question the self-evident validity of taxonomic logic. Its critique is addressed only to how the Mishnah's framers identify the origins of, and delineate, taxa. But that critique proves fundamental to the case that that authorship proposed to make. For, intending to demonstrate that *The Torah* was a proper noun, and that everything that was valid came to expression in the single, cogent statement of The Torah, the authorship at hand identified the fundamental issue. It is the debate over the way we know things. In insisting, in agreement with the framers of the Mishnah, that there are not only cases but also rules, not only species but also genera, the authorship of Sifra also made its case in behalf of the case for The Torah as a proper noun. This carries us to the theological foundation for Sifra's authorship's sustained critique of applied reason.

In appealing to the principle, for taxonomy, of *sola Scriptura,* we mean to set forth what we conceive really to be at stake. It is the character of The Torah and what it is, in The Torah, the thing that we wish to discern. And the answer to that question requires theological, not merely literary and philosophical, reflection on our part. For we maintain that in their delineation of correct hierarchical logic, our authorship uncovered, within The Torah (hence by definition, written and oral components of The Torah alike) an adumbration of the working of the mind of God. That is because the premise of all discourse is that The Torah was written by God and dictated by God to Moses at Sinai. And that will in the end explain why our authorship for its part has entered into The Torah long passages of not merely clarification but active intrusion, making itself a component of the interlocutorial process. To what end we know: it was to unite the dual Torah. But on what basis?

In their analysis of the deepest structures of intellect of the Torah, that is, God's word in God's own wording, the authorship of Sifra supposed to enter into the mind of God, showing how God's mind worked when God formed the Torah, written and oral alike. And there, in the intellect of God, in their judgment humanity gained access to the only means of uniting the Torah, because that is where the Torah originated. But in discerning how God's mind worked, the intellectuals who created Sifra claimed for themselves a place in that very process of thought that had given birth to The Torah. Our authorship could rewrite the Torah because, knowing how The Torah originally was written, they too could write (though not reveal) The Torah.

This sages stated in so many words, in a story that underscores the foundations of Rabbinic Judaism: God is always Lord, even of the Torah, and God alone is the ultimate authority:

*Talmud of Babylonia Menahot 29b*

[5 A] Said R. Judah said Rab, "At the time that Moses went up on high, he found the Holy One in session, affixing crowns to the letters [of the words of the Torah]. He said to him, 'Lord of the universe, who is stopping you [from regarding the document as perfect without these additional crowns on the letters]?'

[B] "He said to him, 'There is a man who is going to arrive at the end of many generations, and Aqiba b. Joseph is his name, who is going to interpret on the basis of each point of the crowns heaps and heaps of laws.'

[C] "He said to him, 'Lord of the Universe, show him to me.'

[D] "He said to him, 'Turn around.'

[E] "He went and took a seat at the end of eight rows, but he could not grasp what the people were saying. He felt faint. But when the discourse reached a certain matter, and the disciples said, 'My lord, how do you know this?' and he answered, 'It is a law given to Moses from Sinai,' he regained his composure.

[F] "He went and came before the Holy One. He said before him, 'Lord of the Universe, How come you have someone like that and yet you give the Torah through me?'

[G] "He said to him, 'Silence! That is how the thought came to me.'

[H] "He said to him, 'Lord of the Universe, you have shown me his Torah, now show me his reward.'

[I] "He said to him, 'Turn around.'

[J] "He turned around and saw his flesh being weighed out at the butcher-stalls in the market.

[K] "He said to him, 'Lord of the Universe, Such is Torah, such is the reward?'

[L] "He said to him, 'Silence! That is how the thought came to me.' "

# 6

# THE CONCILIAR VOICE
# OF SCRIPTURE IN
# CHRISTIANITY

Chapter 2 (pp. 62–69) permitted us to see the extraordinary power of James within the presentation of Acts. His position, requiring that non-Jewish Christians accept basic requirements of purity, was first articulated on his own authority, and then accepted by those present at the meeting in Jerusalem. The result is a letter sent by the meeting, as from the apostles and elders with the congregation as a whole, and under the express authority of the Holy Spirit, to the effect that baptized gentiles in Antioch, Syria, and Cilicia are to be required to abstain from food sacrificed to gods, from blood and strangled animals, and from fornication (so Acts 15:22–9).

The particulars of James' position have already been assessed, especially in reference to his development of an halakhic interpretation of Scripture which is reminiscent of the *pesherim* at Qumran, and to his authoritative role as the *mebaqqer* or *episkopos* in Christian Jerusalem. But the presentation in Acts permits us to see even more. Acts reflects (1) a particular context of consultation in which James' halakhic interpretation becomes normative, and (2) the establishment of a policy and style of argument which substantially refutes Paul's own, even as it embraces a view of circumcision which he can only have accepted. In both respects, Acts articulates what would become governing structures of Catholic, Orthodox Christianity, apart from which the evolution of the Church in late antiquity can not be understood.

## The conciliar context

In Acts 15, James speaks within a specific context, not only in Jerusalem, but within international Christianity as it then existed. A controversy erupts because "some had come down from Judea, who were teaching the brothers, If you do not circumcise by the

155

custom of Moses, you are not able to be saved" (15:1). The result is a dispute with Paul and Barnabas, which is not surprising, since they have just returned to Antioch after a successful completion of the work which the prophets and teachers there, by the direction of the Holy Spirit, had sent them out to do (Acts 13:1 – 14:28; see 13:3 and 14:26 for the framing of the section in terms of the "work" they completed). They announce that, by means of their ministry God has "opened a door of faith for the gentiles" (Acts 14:27).

That, of course, is the most positive way of relating their experience of preaching in Asia Minor. In the same section of Acts, a pattern is developed in which Paul and Barnabas announce that they "turn to the gentiles" because they have been rejected, even persecuted, by Jews (see Acts 13:46, and the whole of 13:42–51, 14:1–5, 14:19). Indeed, that is the providential pattern of the whole of Luke–Acts, in which even Jesus is rejected by his own – to the point of being prepared for stoning – and speaks of the extension of the work of the prophets to those outside of Israel as a consequence of that rejection (so Luke 4:14–30).[1] It is frequently and rightly maintained that the rejection of Jesus and his message by the Jews is a pivotal motif in Luke–Acts, in that it permits of the transition in the narrative to the emphasis upon the gentiles which is a signature concern.[2] But the relationship between Israel and the gentiles in Acts is actually more than a matter of the apologetic explanation of how gentiles came to predominate in the Church. The mention of the issue of circumcision in Acts 15, and the emphasis that the council in Jerusalem met to address that issue first of all, reflects a profoundly theological awareness that the very identity of the Church in respect of Israel is at stake.

Because the question of circumcision has already been dealt with in Acts 11, as a consequence of Peter's baptisms in the house of Cornelius, the mention of the issue in Acts 15 can only be read as taking up a deliberate resumption of what was a genuinely contentious concern within primitive Christianity. The extensive narrative in Acts 10 has already confirmed, by vision and the coming of the Holy Spirit upon those in that house, that non-Jews are indeed to be baptized, and Peter in Acts 11 personally rehearses those events for "the apostles and brothers who were in Judea" (11:1). Having heard his response to "those of the circumcision" in Jerusalem, who taxed Peter for visiting and eating with those who were foreskinned (11:2–3), Peter's hearers are reported to accept that "God has granted even the gentiles repentance for life" (11:18).

In *Judaism in the New Testament*,[3] we have already referred to the "romanticized" quality of Acts 15, in which the issues of both circumcision and the purity to be required of gentiles are taken up in a single meeting. We cited Paul's account of his relations with those in Jerusalem in Galatians 2 in order to support our observation. But now we can observe that the account in Acts is not only romanticized, but that it is self-consciously so. The council will simply confirm the earlier finding in regard to circumcision, on the precedent of Peter's baptisms in the house of Cornelius, and then proceed to the question of the regulations of purity which baptized non-Jews are to uphold.

By dealing with these issues together, Acts conflates not only the particular topics, but the leaders who settle both questions. The representative function of Paul and Barnabas (along with others) for the church in Antioch is underlined, because they bring news of the conversion of the gentiles to Phoenicia and Samaria on their way to Jerusalem, to the "great joy" of all (Acts 15:3). These "apostles" of Antioch (see the discussion in Chapter 2, pp. 51–56) are then received by both "the apostles and the elders" of the church in Jerusalem (Acts 15:4). When the gathering gets down to business, apostles and elders are again named as the participants (Acts 15:6). So the usual reference to this meeting as "the Apostolic Council of Jerusalem" is amply warranted.[4] In fact, it would be better to speak of the Council "in" Jerusalem, since apostles from other places are included. In addition, the "elders" are emphatically a part of proceedings, in a document in which elders and bishops together are understood to function within the apostolic succession (see Chapter 4, pp.107–116, and especially Acts 14:23, 20:28). The Council is both apostolic and episcopal, and the latter aspect is especially reinforced by the later appearance of James, the *mebaqqer/episkopos*.

So the two major strands of power, apostolic and episcopal (the latter in the shape of James, its generative authority), are concentrated in the Council, and the first issue of concern is circumcision. Believers who are named as Pharisees insist that "it is necessary both to circumcise them (that is, believing gentiles) and to command them to keep the law of Moses" (15:5). That sets the stage for conflict, not only with Paul and Barnabas, but with Peter. And it is Peter who, in the midst of great controversy, rehearses what happened in the house of Cornelius yet again (15:7–11). Peter comes to what is not only a Pauline expression, but more particularly an expression of the Pauline school, that "through the grace of the Lord Jesus we believe to be saved, in the manner they also shall be" (Acts 15:11; see

Ephesians 2:8). For that reason, it seems natural for the reference to Barnabas and Paul to follow (15:12), and in that order: after all, Barnabas is much better known and appreciated in Jerusalem.

After this point, any version of Paulinism is difficult to discern in the decision of the Council, as we shall see in the next section. For the moment, it is pertinent simply to observe how the Petrine settlement regarding circumcision and baptism is accepted by James (15:13–18), and how the final disposition of the matter is under the signature of "the apostles and elders with the whole Church," including Paul and Barnabas as emissaries with Judas Barsabbaas and Silas (15:22–3). The Council explicitly declares that the Holy Spirit warrants the position of James, and that no other requirement as coming from Jerusalem is to be credited (15:24–9). The characterization of Judas and Silas remaining in Antioch in their role as prophets, together with Paul and Barnabas, reinforces the unanimity of the letter (*homothumadon*, 15:25),[5] and by the authority of the Holy Spirit (15:28). Every charism of leadership in the Church is involved in this decision, Paul's included, under the guidance of the Holy Spirit: how much more striking, then, that vital characteristics of Paul's position are rejected in their substance.

## The refutation of Pauline dialectics

What is confirmed here of Paul's activity among gentiles and his theological vocabulary of grace can hardly conceal what is implicitly denied: there is no assertion of Paul's characteristic claim, that all believers become sons of Abraham, and therefore Israel, by baptism. Even in Paul's own speech in the synagogue in Pisidian Antioch, the showcase of his theology in the Lukan account, although he imagines that "everyone who believes in him is justified" from what you cannot be justified from by Torah (13:38–9, a properly Paul formulation), he addresses these words to "sons of the family of Abraham, and those who fear God" (13:26; see also 13:17).[6] In other words, Acts 13 has him make the very distinction he argues against in Galatians, much as in Acts 15 he delivers a letter whose policy he at least partially rejects in Corinthians and Romans (as we shall see below). Acts is very plain: whatever may be acceptable of Paul's theology, his claim that believers become Israel without remainder[7] is jettisoned in favor of James' conviction, that gentile belief is meant to restore the fortunes of the family of David,[8] consonant with the prophecy of Amos (Acts 15:16–21, discussed in Chapter 2, pp. 62–69).

To understand the position which is evolved in Acts, and which is woven into the fabric of apostolic–episcopal authority, we must again refer to James' position, in this case in regard to circumcision. Acts 15:14–15 is explicit: James accepts Peter's account of how "God first visited, to take a people from gentiles for his name" (15:14). That "first" is notable, because it confirms the suggestion in Chapter 2 (pp. 47–56) that the Pentecostal theology of the Petrine school occasioned a new understanding of the horizon of God's spirit. Moreover, James here acknowledges that Peter's experience amounts to a precedent, which he personally accepts. Gentiles who believe in Jesus are not to be required to circumcise.

Recently, that picture in Acts has been vigorously denied by Robert Eisenman:[9]

> Whenever Acts comes to issues relating to James or Jesus' brothers and family members generally, it equivocates and dissimulates, trailing off finally into disinformation, sometimes even in the form of childish fantasy. Though sometimes humorous, especially when one is aware of what the parameters of the disputes in this period really were, this is almost always with uncharitable intent.

Almost all scholars of the literature would agree that this is an exaggerated finding.[10] One of the reasons for the freighted rhetoric is that Eisenman is concerned to insist, in the face of good indications to the contrary, that James required all believers to be circumcised.[11]

In his concern, he illustrates why there has been confusion in this regard. Galatians reflects the obvious dispute between Paul and the circle of James, and at one point Paul accuses Peter and Barnabas of "fearing those of the circumcision" (Galatians 2:12). Eisenman then links that statement with the characterization of James in the Pseudo-Clementine *Homilies*, where James warns Peter not to communicate with those who are unworthy. Both of those alleged supports in fact demonstrate the extraordinary weakness of his assertion (which may explain why it is fitted out with so much rhetoric).

When Paul uses the noun "circumcision" (*peritome*), he does so as a metonym for ancestral Judaism. So, for example, in the same chapter of Galatians, he refers to himself as entrusted with the gospel of uncircumcision and Peter as of circumcision, one predominantly for gentiles and the other predominantly for Jews (Galatians 2:7–8). Moreover, James and John are specifically included in this arrangement with Peter, on the side of circumcision, with Paul and Barnabas on the other side in mutually recognized ministry of the gospel (Galatians 2:9). To give the term "circumcision" a new sense, the sense of those who compel circumcision, is entirely unnatural within the logic of Galatians 2. Within the logic of the letter as a whole, it is even more unnatural: Paul makes a very clear distinction between his disagreement with the circle of James over the question of purity at meals (Galatians 2:11–21) and his open, crudely expressed contempt for those who are attempting to gentile circumcise converts to Christianity (Galatians 5:1–12). When Peter and Barnabas fall in with the policy of James in regard to purity, Paul calls that hypocrisy (Galatians 2:11–13); when unnamed teachers urge circumcision on the Galatians, Paul tells them to cut their genitals off (Galatians 5:1–12). In substance and tone, his attitude is different, because James – following Peter's lead – accepted that circumcision could not be required, while the anonymous disturbers in Galatians 5:12 most emphatically did not. Acts itself recognizes the existence of such teachers, and attests their implicit claim to represent the church in Jerusalem (15:24). The presence in Jerusalem of teachers whom Acts styles as believing Pharisees would suggest that they are the source of the simple conviction that the Torah, in this case Genesis 17:10–14, was to be upheld in the preaching of Jesus. Straightforward as that claim is, Acts attests just as emphatically that James is not its source: rather, he sees a place for gentiles as gentiles, in a role of support for an essentially Davidic revelation.

That picture of a place for the gentiles within Christian preaching is actually confirmed by the pseudo-Clementine literature which Eisenman cites in support of his argument. That literature is particularly pointed against Paul (whom it refers to as *homo inimicus*) and in favor of James. Indeed, the *Recognitions* (I.43–71) even relate that, prior to his conversion to Christianity, Saul assaulted James in the Temple. Martin Hengel refers to this presentation as an apostolic novel (*Apostelroman*), deeply influenced by the perspective of the Ebionites, and probably to be dated within the third and fourth centuries.[12] The ordering of Peter under James is clearly a part of that perspective, as Hengel shows, and much earlier Joseph Lightfoot found that the alleged correspondence between Clement and James was a later addition to the Pseudo-Clementine corpus.[13] But even if the Pseudo-Clementines are taken at face value, they undermine Eisenman's view:[14] they portray James as the standard for how Hellenistic Christians are to teach (see *Recognitions* 11.35.3).[15]

In a sense there is nothing surprising about that portrayal, in that Paul himself – writing in Galatians, where he has every interest in diminishing any sense that he is dependent upon his predecessors in Jerusalem – describes himself as laying out his gospel for the gentiles for apostolic scrutiny, "lest I were running or had been running in vain" (Galatians 2:1–2). He had earlier framed his gospel in discussion with Peter, and had also met James, whom he describes as an apostle at that point (around the year 35 CE; see Galatians 1:18–19). Then, fourteen years later (or around 49 CE), it is before three "pillars" of the Church – James and Peter and John, in that order – that Paul lays out his case, and receives authorization to continue among the gentiles (Galatians 2:3–10).

In his description of James' circle, Irenaeus (around 180 CE) refers to their permitting activity among the gentiles, while they themselves preserved their proper customs (*pristinis observantionibus*, *Against Heresies* 3.12.15). As Hengel points out, most of the sources regarding James do not involve him in disputes concerning the law, and when the Pseudo-Clementines target such disputes, they do so by way of an attack on Paul.[16] Epiphanius reports the legend among the Ebionites that Paul accepted circumcision in the first place only to marry the daughter of the high priest, and then – disappointed in his design – attacked circumcision and the law (*Panarion* 30.16). In other words, the Ebionite case against Paul is made, not by claiming that James required circumcision, but by asserting that Paul accepted and then opposed circumcision for the worst of motives, whether theological or personal. Implicitly, the sources are in agreement that James did not require circumcision of gentile converts to Christianity.

Where Eisenman and the Tübingen school have erred is, not in imputing controversy to the Christian movement in its earliest stages, but in imputing the same controversy to every division. Paul disagreed with James, Peter, and sometimes with Barnabas, but not over the issue of whether circumcision should be required. Believing Pharisees did, on the other hand, disagree with all of those named apostles. Where James and Paul went their separate ways, ways between which Peter and Barnabas hesitated, was in the identification of non-Jewish believers. For Paul, they were Israel; for James, they were not.

The key to James' position in this regard was brilliantly provided by Kirsopp Lake in his study of the Council in Jerusalem. Scholarship since his time has provided a striking confirmation of his suggestion. Lake uses the proscriptions James insisted upon – of food sacrificed to idols, blood, things strangled, and fornication – as a way of describing how James and the Council would identify believing gentiles in relation to Israel. He observes the affinity with the rules in Leviticus 17 regarding non-Israelites who reside in the land: they are to desist from offerings to other gods and from the usage of any altar but in the Temple (Leviticus 17:7–9), they are to abstain from blood (Leviticus 17:10–13), and to avoid the sexual relations described in chapter 18 (Leviticus 18:24–30). By the time of the Talmud (Sanhedrin 56b), such prohibitions were elaborated into the so-called Noachic commandments, binding upon humanity generally, but Lake rightly observes they are formulated too late to have influenced Acts.[17]

The position of James in regard to the book of Leviticus, however, cannot be set aside simply by observing the date of the Talmud. We have already seen in Chapter 2 (pp. 67–68) that just the section of Leviticus in which chapters 17 and 18 are included (that is chapters 16–19) was particularly resonant with James' view of how the Torah was to be upheld in respect of gentiles. Lake is correct to point out that the regulations in Leviticus are for non-Israelite residents in the land, not abroad, and that fact needs to be taken into account. Nonetheless, there is nothing intrinsically improbable with the hypothesis that James' stipulations with regard to non-Jewish believers were framed with their compatibility with worship in the Temple in mind.

In any case, Lake also called attention to the requirements made of Gentiles within a work of Hellenistic Judaism, the fourth book of the *Sibylline Oracles* (4:24–34):[18]

> Happy will be those of earthly men who will cherish the great God, blessing before eating, drinking and having confidence in piety. They will deny all temples and altars they see: purposeless transports of dumb stones, defiled by animates' blood and sacrifices of four-footed animals. But they will behold the great renown of the one God, neither breaking into reckless murder, nor transacting what is stolen for gain, which are cold happenings. They do not have shameful desire for another's bed, nor hateful and repulsive abuse of a male.

What is especially striking about this prophecy is that it is directed to the people of Asia and Europe (*Sibylline Oracles* 4:1) through the mouth of the Sibyl (*Sibylline Oracles* 4:22–3), the legendary oracle of mantic counsel. Her utterance here is explicitly backed up by the threat of eschatological judgment for all (*Sibylline Oracles* 4:40–8).

A growing body of opinion has found that the emphasis upon prophecy in Luke–Acts accords with the perspectives of Hellenistic historians such as Diodorus Siculus and Dionysius of Halicarnassus.[19] The place of Sibylline prophecies, deriving from a prophetess whose origin "was already lost in the mist of legend by the fifth century" BCE,[20] is prominent in both. But while Luke–Acts invokes the motif of prophecy (literary and contemporary), the Sibyl makes no appearance in a work which is, after all, the largest in the New Testament. That suggests that the way for the synthesis of Hellenistic oracles and Hebrew prophecy had been prepared, especially by works such as the *Sibylline Oracles* of Hellenistic Judaism, but then that Luke–Acts insists upon the attestation of Jesus' coming (directly or indirectly) as an indispensable criterion of true prophecy (see the discussion in Chapter 4, pp.116–119).

The development of ethical requirements for gentiles in view of eschatological judgment was therefore part of the ethos of Hellenistic Judaism at the time Luke–Acts was composed. The demands cited by Lake in the fourth book of the *Sibylline Oracles*[21] comport well with the requirements set out in Acts 15, except for the specific proscription of blood. Still, reciting a blessing prior to eating might suggest that what is eaten is to be pure, and immersion is mentioned later in the *Sibylline Oracles* (4:165), so the issue is scarcely outside the range of concerns of Hellenistic Judaism.

Indeed, that concern is inherent in the third book of the *Sibylline Oracles*, which Collins dates within the period 163–145 BCE.[22] There, the Sibyl is portrayed as Noah's daughter-in-law (*Sibylline Oracles* 3:823–9), and it was Noah whom God instructed with the commandment not to consume blood or to shed human blood (Genesis 9:4–6). Noah receives cognate treatment in books 1 and 2 of the *Sibylline Oracles*. The dates of that part of the corpus are uncertain, and the Christian additions are evident, but Collins seems on secure ground in his argument that the Judaic redaction was completed before 70 CE in Phrygia.[23] Noah is here made an articulate preacher of repentance to all peoples (*Sibylline Oracles* 1:128–9) in an elegant expansion of the biblical story (*Sibylline Oracles* 1:125–282) which has the ark make land in Phrygia (*Sibylline Oracles* 1:262). The persistence of such an association between Noah and Asia Minor is intimated by 1 Peter 3:20, where the number of those in the ark (eight) is stressed, as in the *Sibylline Oracles* 1:282, in comparison to the number of those who were punished.

Within the context of Hellenistic Judaism as reflected in the *Sibylline Oracles*, then, a prohibition of blood to gentiles seems quite natural. If it is anachronistic to speak at this point of Noachic commandments, we may at least refer to the motif of Noah's instruction of all humanity as well established by the first century CE. Unfortunately, the *Genesis Apocryphon* from Qumran is fragmentary just as it speaks of Noah, but it is notable that Noah is told there that he is to rule over the earth and the seas and that "you shall not eat any blood" (*Genesis Apocryphon* 7.1, 11:17). Both those statements are more emphatic than what is said in the corresponding text of Genesis in Hebrew (Genesis 9:2, 4).

The possible connection between the motif in the *Sibylline Oracles* and the treatment of Noah in the *Genesis Apocryphon* is intriguing. The third book of the *Sibylline Oracles* is associated with the priestly family of the Oniads, which had been pushed out of Jerusalem prior to the Maccabean revolt.[24] They eventually settled in Egypt and enjoyed protection under the Ptolemies there, which is why Collins dates that book of the *Sibylline Oracles* between 163 and 145 CE. They were responsible for building the Temple at Leontopolis, in evident protest against the settlement in Jerusalem (Josephus, *Jewish War* 1.33; 7.420–32). Prior to settling in Egypt, however, Syria had been the Oniads' base.[25] The cultic protest of the Oniads, their chronology, and their association with Syria have all led to the inference that they were connected with the rise of the Essenes, and Philo's reference to Essenes in Egypt would support that inference.[26] To this we may add Josephus' observation that the Essenes were noted for their prophecy (for example, in *Jewish War* 2.159):[27] prophecy is a connecting link among the Essenes, the *Sibylline Oracles*, the emissaries of James and the Council who were prophets, and the ethos of Luke–Acts.

James' interpretation of Scripture (as we have seen in Chapter 2, pp. 68–69) shows similarities to the interpretation instanced at Qumran. His halakhic approach comports with an emphasis upon the necessity for all people, even gentiles, to keep a high degree of purity out of regard for the Torah. The evidence of the *Sibylline Oracles* reinforces the impression of James' Essene orientation, and shows how that perspective could be developed within a field well prepared by Hellenistic Judaism.

But what James' circle prepared on that field was a particular devotion to the Temple in Jerusalem. The ideal of Christian devotion which James has in mind is represented in Acts 21. There, Paul and his companion arrive in Jerusalem and are confronted by James and the elders, who tell them that Paul's reputation in Jerusalem is of teaching Jews in the Diaspora to forsake Moses, and especially to stop circumcising their children (Acts 21:17–21). Paul is then told to shoulder the expense of four men who had taken a vow, and to enter the Temple with them to offer sacrifice (Acts 21:22–6).

The nature of the vow seems quite clear. It will be fulfilled when the men shave their heads (Acts 21:24). We are evidently dealing with a Nazirite vow.[28] As set out in Numbers 6, a Nazirite was to let his hair and beard grow for the time of his vow, abstain completely from grapes, and avoid approaching any dead body. At the close of the period of the vow, he was to shave his head, and offer his hair in proximity to the altar (Numbers 6:18). The end of this time of being holy, the Lord's property, is marked by enabling the Nazirite to drink wine again (6:20).

Just such practices of holiness are attributed by Hegesippus (as cited by Eusebius, *Ecclesiastical History* 2.23) to James. The additional notice, that he avoided oil and avoided frequent bathing, is consistent with the especial concern for purity among Nazirites. They were to avoid any contact with death (Numbers 6:6–12), and the avoidance of all uncleanness – which is incompatible with sanctity – follows naturally. The avoidance of oil is also attributed by Josephus to the Essenes (*Jewish War* 2.123), and the reason seems plain: oil, as a fluid pressed from fruit, was considered to absorb impurity to such an extent that extreme care in its preparation was vital.[29] In the absence of complete assurance, abstinence was a wise policy. James' vegetarianism also comports with a concern to avoid contact with any kind of corpse, so that frequent immersion would become unnecessary. Finally, although Hegesippus' assertion that James could actually enter the sanctuary seems exaggerated, his acceptance of a Nazirite regime, such as Acts 21 explicitly associates him with, would account for such a remembrance of him, in that Nazirites were to be presented in the vicinity of the sanctuary.

As it turned out, James' advice proved disastrous for Paul. Paul's entry into the Temple caused a riot, because it was supposed he was bringing non-Jews in. As a result, he was arrested by a Roman officer (Acts 21:27 – 28:21), and so began the long legal contention which resulted ultimately in his death. The extent to which James might have anticipated such a result cannot be known, but it does seem obvious that his commitment to a Nazirite ideology blinded him to the political dangers which threatened the movement of which he was the nearest thing to the head.

The particular concern of James for practice in the Temple has left its mark on teaching attributed to Jesus. In Mark 7:15, Jesus set down a radical principle of purity: "There is nothing outside a person, entering in that can defile, but what comes out of a person is what defiles a person." That principle establishes that those in Israel were to be accepted as pure, so that fellowship at meals with them, as was characteristic in Jesus' movement from the beginning, was possible. Their usual customs of purity, together with their generosity in sharing and their willingness to receive and accept forgiveness, readied them to celebrate the fellowship of the kingdom of God.[30] His program was not as suited to Nazirites as it was to those his opponents called "tax agents and sinners;" to them Jesus seemed a drunk and a glutton (see Matthew 11:19; Luke 7:34).

But within this same chapter of Mark in which Jesus' principle is clearly stated, a syllogism is developed to attack a particular practice in the Temple:

> But he said to them, "Duly Isaiah prophesied about you frauds, as it is written, 'This people honors me with lips, But their heart is far distant from me. In vain they worship me, teaching men's commandments as doctrines.' Leaving the commandment of God, you adhere to men's tradition."
>
> And he was saying to them, "Duly you annul the commandment of God, so that you establish your tradition. For Moses said, 'Honor your father and your mother', and, 'Let the one who curses father or mother die the death.' But you say, 'If a person says to father or mother, Whatever you were owed from me is Qorban [that is, gift]', you no longer let him do anything for father or mother, voiding the word of God by your tradition. And you do many such things."
>
> (Mark 7:6–13)

Two features of this argument are striking. It assumes familiarity with the vow of *qorbana*, which does indeed mean "gift" in Aramaic. One could, in effect, shelter one's use of property by dedicating it to the Temple at one's death, continuing to use it during one's life.[31] Mishnah envisages a man saying, "Qorban be any benefit my wife gets from me, for she stole my purse" (Nedarim 3:2). The simple complaint about the practice in vv. 11–12 may indeed reflect Jesus' position, since his objection to commercial arrangements involving worship is well attested. But that only focuses our attention all the more on the syllogistic nature of the argument, which is unlike what we elsewhere find attributed to Jesus.

The argument as a whole is framed in Mark 7:6–7 by means of a reference to the book of Isaiah (29:13): the people claim to honor God, but their heart is as far from him as their vain worship, rooted in human commandments. That statement is then related to the custom of *qorban*, which is said to invalidate the plain sense of Moses' prescription to honor parents.[32] The simple and inevitable conclusion is that the tradition violates the command of God (see Mark 7:8–9, 13).

The logic of the syllogism is not complicated, and it can easily be structured in a different way.[33] The association of similar Scriptures is reminiscent of the rabbinic rule of interpretation, that a principle expressed in a text may be related to another text, without identity of wording between the two passages (*kayyoṣe bo bemaqom 'aḥer*).[34] But the scriptural syllogism by no means requires the invocation of any such formal principle. The fundamental argument is that the Law and the Prophets are antithetical to the practice of authorities in the Temple.

The rhetoric of the syllogism turns on the necessity of honoring Moses, as in the interpretation attributed to James in Acts 15 (see Acts 15:21). Moreover, the principle inherent here is that Scripture is that which is actually implemented in the case of Jesus' movement. Finally, the centrality of the Temple is manifest throughout.

The stance of James as concerns purity and the Temple, as well as his interpretation of Scripture, comports well with Hegesippus' description of his particular practices. The evidence in aggregate suggests that James understood his brother as offering an access to God through the Temple, such that Israel could and should offer God the Nazirites with their vows, such as Moses provided for. It has been argued that Jesus himself adhered to such a position,[35] but that seems to put a strain on his usual practice of fellowship at meals.[36]

Indeed, our suggestion that James was a Nazirite,[37] and saw his brother's movement as focused on producing more Nazirites, enables us to address an old and as yet unsolved problem of research. Jesus, bearing a common name, is sometimes referred to as "of Nazareth" in the Gospels, and that reflects how he was specified in his own time. There is no doubt but that a geographical reference is involved (see John 1:45–6).[38] But more is going on here. Actually, Jesus is rarely called "of Nazareth" or "from Nazareth," although he was probably known to come from there. He is usually called "Nazoraean" or "Nazarene." Why the adjective, and why the uncertainty in spelling? The Septuagint shows us that there were many different transliterations of "Nazirite:" that reflects uncertainty as to how to convey the term in Greek. (That uncertainty is not in the least surprising, since even the Mishnah refers to differing pronunciations [see Nazir 1:1].) Some of the variants are in fact very close to what we find used to describe Jesus in the Gospels.

In the Gospel according to Mark, the first usage is in the mouth of a demon, who says to Jesus (Mark 1:24): "We have nothing for you, Nazarene Jesus! Have you come to destroy us? I know who you are – the holy one of God!" In this usage, "Nazarene" in the first line clearly parallels "the holy one of God" in the last line. The demon knows Jesus' true identity, but those in the synagogue where the exorcism occurs do not. And they do not hear the demons, because Jesus silences them (so Mark 1:25). This is part of the well-known theme of the "Messianic secret" in Mark.[39]

For James and those who were associated with him, Jesus' true identity was his status as a Nazirite. The demons saw what others did not, and after the resurrection the knowledge of the holy one of God could be openly acknowledged and practiced. That practice could include men, women, and slaves, in accordance with the Mishnah (Nazir 9:1). In the Christian movement, the custom was apparently widespread. In Acts 18:18, it is said that even Paul "had his head shorn in Kenkhraea, because he had a vow." Such vows in regard to hair alone were held in Mishnah to equate to a Nazirite vow (Nazir 1:1), so that whatever Paul thought of his vow from his own perspective, many would have seen him as falling in with the program of James, the brother of Jesus. Under the influence of James, they might have said, even Paul was concerned with getting it right.

Where Paul got it precisely wrong, from the point of view of the Council, was in his assertion that food sacrificed to idols could be consumed, provided only it did not mislead anyone into a belief in the actuality of any god behind the idol. His mature articulation of his principle in this regard would involve at most grudging respect for the letter sent from the Council to Antioch:

> I know and I am convinced in the Lord Jesus that nothing is impure in itself, but to one who considers something to be impure, it is impure for him. If your brother is aggrieved on account of food, you are no longer walking by love: do not ruin with food that one for whom Christ died.
>
> (Romans 14:14–15)

The whole of chapter 14 is devoted to this issue, so that it is plain that the controversy is significant in Rome, as it had been in Corinth (see 1 Corinthians 8).

At the end of the day, it might be argued that the application of Paul's principle would lead to an acquiescence with the ruling of the Council, but his stance is hardly a ringing endorsement. For that reason, it is a bit difficult to imagine Paul – as Acts 15 clearly portrays him – delivering the Council's letter with Barnabas and Judas and Silas (Acts 15:22). After all, for the Council and for James there is something intrinsically impure in what is specified, and believing gentiles are to avoid it, as a matter of loyalty to the Torah. Paul is not in complete opposition to the policy, and he shows (as has been discussed in Chapter 2, pp. 54–55) that in matters of sexuality there are impure relations which are to be avoided at the peril of one's eschatological judgment. But to imagine him as complicit in the letter and delivering it in Antioch strains credulity. It is more likely that the meeting in respect of circumcision and the meeting in respect of impurity were distinct events.[40] For that reason, Christians continued to be divided over the question of whether the meat of animals notionally sacrificed to gods could be eaten.[41]

The Council of Luke–Acts controverts Pauline principle not only in substance, but also in style. Gone are the dialectics of discovering one element in Scripture in opposition to another, in order to discover which of them accords with the gospel of Jesus. Gone are the long arguments which explain how the triumphant element in Scripture can have been obscured by others, and how the unity of divine revelation may be maintained nonetheless. Gone is the elevation of that method to the point where it offers a way of understanding all human relations with God. Indeed, Paul himself, in Romans 14 and 1 Corinthians 8, is providing an example of how different from the Lukan James is his own take on what to do with a principle under active discussion within Christianity. Whether or not Paul knows James articulated the principle that food sacrificed to idols is not to be eaten, he obviously knows it is a serious principle, ardently maintained by some Christians. But instead of simply finding for or against the policy, Paul measures each and every act of eating against one's evaluation of the conscience one is eating with. Pauline dialectics are deployed as much in ethics as they are in Scripture.

All of that is set aside by the Council. The food not to be eaten, the behavior not to be indulged is stated, on the assertion that the

Holy Spirit and the Council, in accordance with the words of the prophet Amos as cited by James, make that the rule to be followed. Argument is beside the point. Once the consensus of the Council agrees with Scripture, that conciliar interpretation becomes normative. Because the Council in question is both apostolic and episcopal, Luke–Acts here provides a normative model of ecclesiastical authority, as well as a normative ruling.

## The authoritative council, and the creedal definition of Catholic Orthodoxy

The model of conciliar interpretation in Acts, leading up to the finding of normative ruling, was developed on a world-wide basis (for the *oikoumene* in its original sense, "the inhabited world") from the time of Constantine. In *The Intellectual Foundations of Christian and Jewish Discourse*, we have already seen how Eusebius, Bishop of Caesarea, established the precedent of political theory and the generation of global history within the Church, by directly comparing Constantine and Christ.[42] Because only the language of apocalypse could do justice to the sudden appearance of a ruler who bore the very image of God in Christ, the sequence of events leading up to that moment bore a new significance: history now bore the stamp of God's restoration of the world to its proper order[43] and substance.[44] After Eusebius, Augustine would work out a general historiography of providence, in his theory of the two Cities, and also work history out in properly global terms, but the intellectual contribution of Eusebius himself is frequently overlooked.

That contribution also reached into the practical realm, owing largely to his closeness to Constantine. In fact, we will shortly see that his friendship influenced the creedal formation of the Church. It was Eusebius more than anyone else who both shaped and reported the Council of Nicea, which provided the classic paradigm of christology. To be sure, that Council was not the first since the Apostolic Council, and it was not even Constantine's first foray into ordering the Church. It was, however, the first council which was ecumenical in its conception (despite its disproportionately Asian attendance), and shaped Christianity forever after.

Constantine's victory over Maxentius at the Milvian bridge in 312 gave him control of the western part of the Empire, with Licinius in control of the eastern part. The edict of Milan (issued in 313), which provided for the restoration of the Church's properties, was their joint work (see Eusebius, *Ecclesiastical History* 10.5.1–14).[45] That settlement raised a deeply divisive question in North Africa. During persecutions there, some clergy, both bishops and priests, were charged with being *traditores*: they had handed over, when required to do so, sacred books to the authorities. Led by Donatus of Casae Nigrae, those who argued that only more complete resistance was compatible with the faith accused the Bishop of Carthage of having been consecrated by *traditores*, and they chose a rival bishop.[46]

So to which bishop was the restoration of property to be made? Constantine directed restoration and gifts of support, both monetary and financial, to the Catholic Church as governed by Caecilian, the bishop to whom the Donatists objected (*Ecclesiastical History* 10.5–7). But the correspondence Eusebius cites also shows that the Emperor was disquieted by the controversy, about which he heard through the proconsul of Africa. He therefore summoned Caecilian to Rome, to appear before a meeting of bishops there in 313, with ten bishops who opposed him and ten who supported him. Constantine's explicit wish was to avoid schism (*skhisma*) in the Catholic Church: unity was the purpose to be realized.

When the Donatists lost in that meeting, they pursued their complaint, and Constantine convened another, larger, and more broadly based assembly of bishops and other clergy at Arles in 314. The condemnation of the Donatists, which was the result, did not end the Donatist schism by any means; it went on for another century. But the conciliar method had been established. In 316, the schismatics (as they were now being styled by Catholics) elected another leader named Donatus as their bishop, who directed a resistance to the councils of bishops – even imperial edicts – which often included violence and aggression. This, the more famous, Donatus asked rhetorically, "What has the Emperor to do with the Church?" (Optatus 3.3, *Contra Parmenianum Donatistam*).[47] Despite the vigor of his resistance, despite the appeal of the Donatists as the legitimate continuation of the Church of the martyrs,[48] that question was to prove moot.

The Donatists emerged at the stage at which the Church could face the basic issues which persecution had long posed, and which are well represented, for example, in Tertullian's *Apology*[49] from the second century: when one's life is at stake, is any cooperation to be construed as collaboration, any compromise as apostasy, and are leaders to be held to a higher standard than others? Persecution makes such questions inevitable and painful, but they can only be addressed at all fully after persecution has ended, much as in the case of France after the defeat of the Third Reich. But also as in such cases of national renewal after occupation, the virtues of the local independent cell, which are necessary for survival during persecution, can contradict the virtues of the whole to which the cells belong, which are necessary for any kind of larger coherence. Forgiving does not always involve forgetting, but the two are nearly identical, when the aim is social coherence after a period of fierce persecution. And broad coherence, indeed catholic (that is, universal) coherence in the definition of the Church is just what Constantine and his theological apologists, like Eusebius, had committed themselves to. The unity of the Church and the unity of the Empire had already been defined as mutually reinforcing, and the Emperor in Rome as much as the bishop in Carthage was seen to be the vicarious image of Christ. Ten years later, the Emperor would even be described as a theologian.

Constantine defeated his old ally Licinius in battle in 324, to become master of both halves of the Roman world. What he inherited from the Christian part of that world was a schism much more generally represented and only slightly less intense than that with which the Donatists had already furnished him in Africa. The Arian controversy is conventionally and understandably described as intellectual in origin, but – from first to last – the issues involved were far more basic, and even visceral. Only thus can the violence and persistence of the controversy be explained. Arius had sought, within the Trinitarian discussion which already had a long history by the time he wrote,[50] to distinguish between the Father and the Son by observing that only the Father had not been begotten (that is, he was *agennetos*). As the word of God, the Son may even be described as created, as in Proverbs 8:22.[51] The result was that Arius was excommunicated by a council convened by the bishop of Alexandria. But Arius, following to some extent the precedent of Origen,[52] took his case to Palestine, where he received the support of none other than Eusebius of Caesarea, who was then emerging as the principal apologist of the Constantinian settlement in theological terms. So councils in Bithynia and Palestine opposed the decision of the council in Alexandria; and after that factionalism was as endemic as it was destructive.

Constantine's resolve to call an ecumenical council, the first in history, therefore grew naturally out of an enormously complex political situation. The council was called for Nicea in Asia Minor, and therefore drew bishops from that region most of all. (Rome's bishop, for example, did not attend, but was represented by two priests.[53] Christians living under the Sassanids, of course, enjoyed no participation; the "inhabited world" in mind was strictly Graeco-Roman.) At the suggestion of Eusebius of Caesarea himself, the council proceeded on the basis of an already traditional creed, which they also elaborated to express belief in:

> one Lord Jesus Christ, the Son of God, begotten from the Father, God from God, light from light, true God from true God, begotten not made, of one essence with the Father, through whom all things came into being…

Robert Grant quotes J.N.D. Kelly (who in turn quotes C.H. Turner), "The old creeds were creeds for catechumens, the new creed was a creed for bishops;" and then explains how "every word of this formulation needs exegesis."[54]

But readers of *The Intellectual Foundations of Christian and Jewish Discourse* will recall this understanding, including the eternal generation of the Son from the Father, the Son's role in creation, and the conception of single essence (*ousia*), as being Origen's.[55] At Nicea, the participants framed a traditional creed with Origen's language in order to insist that God in God's identity is both Father and Son, both that which transcends all and that which creates all. That this language should have proven so successful at the time is quite comprehensible, when one remembers that Eusebius of Caesarea had been Origen's student, and had become a confidante to the Emperor. The great blow to Arius in the creed, of course, is the explicit denial of the creation of the Son by the Father. The term "of one essence" became the sticking point: Arius and some of his associates were exiled for refusing to subscribe to it. The old Pauline discipline of delivering a brother to punishment outside the Church (see 1 Corinthians 5, discussed in Chapter 2, pp. 54–55) had now acquired a literal meaning, derived from the force of the Empire. As the Son was not only the image of the Father, but also his reality, so the Emperor ruled with the reality of the Son's power, as well as in his image.

The close linkage between the Emperor and Christ, and therefore between heaven and the events of this earth, is what brought Christian history into being in the mind of Eusebius.[56] That same mind also and correctly sees, together with the Council of Nicea, that the essential unity of the Father and the Son is an absolute prerequisite for the Emperor to be offering a divine order in his rule of the Empire. What was at stake at Nicea was not episcopal quibbles about the right form of words, but one fundamental question, articulated in the realm of heaven and in the realm of the earth: can we at long last believe in unity?

The creed of Nicea answers that question without equivocation. The unity of God is expressed by the single essence, the unity of the Church within the now unified Empire, is articulated by the very fact of saying the creed. And the recitation of that creed has been an intrinsic act within the eucharist for Catholic and Orthodox Christianity, which may be said to come into existence[57] with the communal recitation of the Nicene Creed. The Council of Nicea did not put an end to the dispute, any more than the Council of Arles settled the question of Donatism. But the very persistence of the problems of what came to be known as heresies shows how deeply embedded they were in the very conception of the Constantinian settlement. Just as Donatists doubted that Catholics truly represented the Church in its fullness, so Arians doubted that the Son substantially represented the Father in his fullness. Both movements could in fact invoke traditional forms of authority (the blood of the martyrs, the wording of the Scriptures) in order to insist upon their claims. Both perpetuated strong attachments by Christians to perennial convictions: the Donatists, to the conviction of human unworthiness before God, the Arians, to the conviction of the inherently distinct majesty of the Father. But against them both – even while acknowledging those convictions – Catholic Orthodoxy maintained that the Christ who created the earth was one with God, and that the Emperor who ruled the world and ordered a single Church within it was Christ's image.

So primal was this assertion that it was manifested by creed, not argument. Scripture is not cited, but simply absorbed in the wording.[58] No dialects are developed, but the finest product of dialectical reason in the Church, Origen's teaching of the Trinity, is simply deployed.[59] No appeal to nature is involved, but reciting the creed is as certainly a sanctifying of human existence as anything Irenaeus said.[60] History finds no reference, but without the convictions of the creed in the consequence and sequence of events both human and divine, there is no history. [61]

Eusebius tells the story that Constantine himself suggested the term *homoousios* to the Council of Nicea; Grant and most historians naturally voice skepticism.[62] Grant's overall evaluation of the creed is representative:

All agree that though Constantine was a Christian, he was not a theologian. What the Nicene Creed did was maintain the picture of trinitarian theology as nonrational, not irrational but beyond reason, and based firmly on selected complexities of scripture and tradition. It rejected the position of Arius with its evident use of logic, in favor of a more traditional or flexible logic that had been employed since the time of the apostle Paul onward through Ignatius, Tertullian, and the later Origen.

In its description of the content of the creed, this is an accurate statement, provided we keep in mind that what is rejected in Arius' position is not logic as such, but only deductive logic, and what Grant calls "traditional or flexible logic" is so because it is interpretative, dialectical, inclusive of the natural world, and historical (as we have seen in *The Intellectual Foundations*).

But in any case the Nicene Creed has not been recited at eucharist as a confession of faith for better than sixteen hundred years simply because it is a pleasing amalgam of theological truisms. The very act of recitation constitutes a communal awareness, through the entire Church as Catholic and Orthodox, that Christ is essentially of God and that we, in our obedience to Christ's image (the Emperor, for the bishops gathered at Nicea), conform our lives to Christ. Christians of later times, of course, went on to differ over the objects of their civic obedience. But the basic conviction that such obedience is related to faith, that the kingdoms of this world stand in a dialectical relation to the kingdom of God (and are ultimately held to account by God), remains a hallmark of the Catholic, Orthodox faith. Whether the image of God in human conduct is a person or a principle, what demands our obedience is that it is God's image, and not a purely human arrangement. Just as God's spirit transforms us by faith, so his image commands our loyalty. Human society, the world of historical events and people's aspirations and ambitions and desires, belongs within the kingdom of God, and is ever on the road to encounter with him. What Augustine would later write in *The City of God* was, in effect, a commentary on the Creed: not on what it said, but on what it meant.

The Nicene Creed, and several creeds like it, simply cannot be understood as if it were a doctrinal innovation. It has been mistaken for that, and the mistake is perfectly comprehensible:

> With this Council the Church resolutely entered on the path which would eventually lead, in modern times, to such solemn "definitions" as the dogmas of the Immaculate Conception [of Mary], Papal infallibility, and the Assumption of the Blessed Virgin Mary.[63]

But the similarity is superficial. All of those modern doctrines (from 1854, 1870, and 1950 respectively) are more papal than conciliar, and actually do set out belief in what was for many and perhaps most believers innovative doctrines. Their speaking voice is the particular pope of the time, more than a council comparable to Nicea. Nicea uses a language rich in the four-fold logic of Christianity as it had been developed to that time, but it does not command mastery of that logic. Believers recite it regularly, without any necessary awareness of the biblical, dialectical, natural–theological, or historical resonances involved. Recognizing them enhances one's understanding, not one's faith.

The Nicene Creed is not an argument, does not forward the art of argument, and most believers do not think of it in a philosophical context. Church historians, whether from a Catholic perspective (so Daniélou and Marrou) or from a Protestant perspective (so Grant) tend to see it as the outcome of political forces, and in that they are certainly not in error. But the recitation of the creed, an effectively anonymous document, like the reading of the Talmud of the Land of Israel from the same century, is designed to make believers aware of how they stand in heaven and before heaven together. But the means to the end – unlike Talmud – is not by argument, although the Creed permits and encourages plenty of that. Rather, the Creed maps the contours of belief which the Church embraces as it is transformed by means of faith and obedience.

The Creed may indeed be "beyond reason" in its formulation, but not because its content is supernatural. It is so because it is of this world: the Church consciously stands before God as Father, Son, Spirit. That stand is taken fully in this world, by people of this world. When they do so, they speak with a conciliar voice in which the spirit of God and the apostolic succession and the vicarious episcopate and then the vicarious Imperium have all made their contributions. But none of them needs to be footnoted, and the whole is put forward as being as straightforward as a simple Christian could wish. After all, Constantine was not baptized when he acceded to the term *homoousios*, whoever had suggested it first. [64]

To say that Christ was of a single essence with God the Father was a dramatic statement, but scarcely a deep paradox. Those who accepted baptism, those who joined in the eucharist, would understand that God himself was transforming them personally in the baptismal waters with the spirit of Christ so that they could call on God as Father just as Christ did, and that God was present with them in the eucharistic offering of bread and wine which Christ himself had instituted. Their society was becoming God's society, and it seemed necessary to them, as it had seemed to the apostolic council in Jerusalem "good to the Holy Spirit and to us" (Acts 15:28), to set out how this was possible, how one might become part of it all. The Creed states how, in the understanding of Catholic Orthodoxy, we belong to the body of Christ, as it stands before God and makes the world new.

# NOTES

## PREFACE

1 A more technical treatment of the Eucharist is available in Chilton, *A Feast of Meanings. Eucharistic Theologies from Jesus through Johannine Circles*, Supplements to *Novum Testamentum* 72 (Leiden: Brill, 1994).

## 1 RECOVERING EDEN: THE THEORETICAL POLITICS OF RABBINIC JUDAISM

1 The power exercised by gentiles, e.g. the Roman government, never entered the picture since it was not a legitimate politics at all.

2 I do not distinguish crime from sin, since I do not think the system does. At the same time our own world does make such a distinction, and it would be confusing not to preserve it. That accounts for the usage throughout.

3 In line with the Mishnah's usage, I refer to God and God's heavenly court with the euphemism of "Heaven," and the capital "H" expresses the simple fact that "Heaven" always refers to God and God's court on high. The Mishnah is not clear on whether its authorship thinks God personally intervenes throughout, but there is a well-established belief in divine agents, e.g. angels or messengers, so in speaking of Heaven or Heaven's intervention, we take account of the possibility that God's agents are meant.

4 Chapter 3 spells out where God's direct intervention through Heavenly action of the activity of holy men and women is accommodated in Rabbinic Judaism, that is, charismatic authority.

5 The distinction between secular felony and religious sin obviously bears no meaning in the system, useful as it is to us. I generally speak of "felon or sinner," so as not to take a position on a matter unimportant in my inquiry.

6 Gentiles considered as individuals, not part of political entities, do not come under consideration. The sins or crimes that deny a person the world to come all pertain to beliefs or actions of Israelites (as M. 10:1D1, 2, and E make clear). The ethnic venue of "Epicurean" is not so self-evident as the others; I take it as meaning an Israelite who

maintains Epicurean beliefs or attitudes. The context surely requires that view.

## 2 APOSTLES AND BISHOPS: A POLARITY OF POWER IN EARLIEST CHRISTIANITY

1 For a full discussion of the kingdom in the preaching of Jesus, see Chilton, *Pure Kingdom. Jesus' Vision of God*, Studying the Historical Jesus 1 (Grand Rapids and London: Eerdmans and SPCK, 1996).
2 See Chilton and Neusner, *Judaism in the New Testament. Practices and Beliefs* (London and New York: Routledge, 1995).
3 Origen has occupied us particularly in Neusner and Chilton, *The Intellectual Foundations of Christian and Jewish Discourse: The Philosophy of Religious Argument* (London: Routledge, 1997), 70–86. He will not much concern us here: of unsurpassed importance in the study of Christian theology and philosophy, he is of marginal influence from the point of view of authority.
4 See Origen, *On Prayer* 23.
5 In his commentary on Matthew 18:23.
6 See K.H. Rengstorf, "*apostolos*," *Theological Dictionary of the New Testament* 1, ed. G. Kittel, tr. G.W. Bromiley (Grand Rapids: Eerdmans, 1978), 407–47.
7 See Leif E. Vaage, *Galilean Upstarts. Jesus' First Followers According to Q* (Valley Forge: Trinity Press International, 1994), 107–20.
8 D. Catchpole, *The Quest for Q* (Edinburgh: Clark, 1993).
9 Ibid., 188.
10 Named as amounting to 70 nations in the Hebrew text of Genesis 10, and to 72 in the Septuagint; see K.H. Rengstorf, "*hepta*," *Theological Dictionary of the New Testament* 2, ed. G. Kittel, tr. G.W. Bromiley (Grand Rapids: Eerdmans, 1978), 627–35.
11 See Chilton, *The Temple of Jesus. His Sacrificial Program Within a Cultural History of Sacrifice* (University Park: The Pennsylvania State University Press, 1992), 100–11.
12 G.B. Caird, *New Testament Theology,* ed. L.D. Hurst (Oxford: Clarendon, 1994), 224.
13 For a discussion of the extension and its theological underpinnings, see Neusner and Chilton, *Christianity and Judaism: The Formative Categories. II. The Body of Faith: Israel and the Church* (Valley Forge: Trinity Press International, 1996), 129–33.
14 So C.K. Barrett, *The Acts of the Apostles* I: The International Critical Commentary (Edinburgh: Clark, 1994), 108.
15 Barrett, 129–57, presents a fine analysis on how deeply influential the text of Joel is on the speech of Peter as a whole.
16 See Chilton, *Jesus' Prayer and Jesus' Eucharist. His Personal Practice of Spirituality* (Valley Forge: Trinity Press International, 1997). On the cultic meaning of both phrases, see Chilton, *Jesus' Baptism and Jesus' Healing. His Personal Practice of Spirituality* 2 (Harrisburg: Trinity Press International, 1998).

17 Lars Hartman, *"Into the Name of the Lord Jesus." Baptism in the Early Church*, Studies of the New Testament and its World (Edinburgh: Clark, 1997), 67–8.

18 Paul's insistence here that the "rock" was Christ might be intended to qualify the claims of the Petrine circle.

19 The assumption here and in Acts 2 is that spirit makes people more articulate than they normally are. That is also the way Paul believes tongues are properly to be conceived, as opposed to those who see the gift of tongues as resulting in incoherence (see 1 Corinthians 14).

20 See Hartman, 133–6.

21 For a discussion, see Chilton and Neusner, *Judaism in the New Testament. Practices and Beliefs* (London: Routledge, 1995), 99–104, 108–11.

22 The link between Jesus' preaching of the kingdom and his possession of the spirit is explored in *Jesus' Baptism and Jesus' Healing*.

23 Hartman, 140, citing Acts 8:37; 22:16.

24 See *The Intellectual Foundations of Christian and Jewish Discourse*, 26–46.

25 We have already covered the importance of Barnabas in *Judaism in the New Testament*, 99–100, 102, 104–8, 128.

26 How that occurred in ideological or theological terms is the topic of *Judaism in the New Testament*.

27 Paul's argument there is treated at some length in *The Intellectual Foundations*, 26–46.

28 See *Judaism in the New Testament*, 98–104.

29 See *The Intellectual Foundations*, 26–46.

30 See Chilton, "Purity and Impurity," *Dictionary of the Later New Testament and its Developments*, eds R.P. Martin and P.H. Davids, (Downers Grove: InterVarsity, 1997) 988–96.

31 In denying that his principal purpose was to baptize, Paul inadvertently shows us how vital it was to apostolic identity; see 1 Corinthians 1:14–17.

32 The difficulty might also be instanced in 1 Corinthians 16:12, if that refers to the same Apollos.

33 See Hermann W. Beyer, *"episkeptomai…,"* *Theological Dictionary of the New Testament* 1, ed. G. Kittel, tr. G.W. Bromiley (Grand Rapids: Eerdmans, 1978), 599–622.

34 See *Judaism in the New Testament*, 98–128.

35 A recent and very interesting study seeks to shelter 2 Timothy from that judgment, but the claim for some element of authenticity in the letter does not affect the present consideration; see Jerome Murphy-O'Connor, *Paul. A Critical Life* (Oxford: Clarendon, 1996), 356–9. For a general discussion, see Chilton, *Beginning New Testament Study* (London: SPCK, 1986 and Grand Rapids: Eerdmans, 1987), 71–3. The work is also published as *STUDI PERJANJIAN BARU BAGI PEMULA*, tr. Ny. C. Corputty-Item (Jakarta: Gunung Mulia, 1994).

36 See, for example, Abraham J. Malherbe, *Social Aspects of Early Christianity* (Philadelphia: Fortress, 1983), 60–91.

37 See pp. 98–128. This theme is also explored in our trilogy, *Christianity and Judaism: The Formative Categories*. The titles are *Revelation. The Torah and the Bible* (Valley Forge: Trinity Press International, 1995);

*The Body of Faith: Israel and the Church* (Valley Forge: Trinity Press International, 1996); *God in the World* (Harrisburg: Trinity Press International, 1997).

38  See *A Galilean Rabbi and His Bible. Jesus' Use of the Interpreted Scripture of His Time* (Wilmington: Glazier, 1984); also published with the subtitle, *Jesus' Own Interpretation of Isaiah* (London: SPCK, 1984), 90–8.

39  See *The Intellectual Foundations*, 26–31.

40  On "The Emergence of Gnosticism," see *The Intellectual Foundations*, 114–28.

41  It looks very much as if the principle stated before these qualifications, in 1 Corinthians 8:6 and Romans 14:14, has been elevated in 1 Timothy to an absolute standard which will not admit of such qualifications.

42  See pp. 104–8. The sources involved are Hegesippus, a second-century writer as cited by Eusebius, and Acts.

43  See Eusebius, *Ecclesiastical History* 2.1, 23; 7.19. In the first passage, he refers to Clement's *Hypotyposeis*.

44  See *Ecclesiastical History* 2.1, 23; 7.19.

45  His views are accessibly presented in *Jerusalem in the Time of Jesus. An Investigation into Economic and Social Conditions during the New Testament Period*, tr. F.H. and C.H. Cave (London: SCM, 1969), 260–2.

46  For this criticism, see Beyer (note 33, above), 618–19. Beyer develops some of the basic philological evidence in favor of the solution, but then opts for the hypothesis of "something new and distinctive." The problem with that hypothesis is the commonality of the term *episkopos* within Hellenistic culture. A successful solution must explain why it was taken up, not why it was invented. The application of *mebaqqar* to James seems to us to meet the case.

47  We here fill out the discussion in *Judaism in the New Testament*, 104–8.

48  See Vincent J. Rosivach, *The System of Public Sacrifice in Fourth-Century Athens*, American Classical Studies 34 (Atlanta: Scholars, 1994).

49  See Craig A. Evans and Peter W. Flint (eds), *Eschatology, Messianism, and the Dead Sea Scrolls* (Grand Rapids: Eerdmans, 1997), 151. For an accessible and interesting presentation of the texts in English, see Michael Wise, Martin Abegg, Edward Cook (eds), *The Dead Sea Scrolls. A New Translation* (San Francisco: Harper, 1996).

50  See John J. Collins, *The Scepter and the Star. The Messiahs of the Dead Sea Scrolls and other Ancient Literature*, The Anchor Bible Reference Library (New York: Doubleday, 1995). He develops his reading of the difference between this interpretation and that contained in the *Damascus Document* on pp. 64–5, following the lead of Joseph A. Fitzmyer.

51  Collins, 61.

## 3 WHAT ENDED WITH PROPHECY, AND WHAT HAPPENED THEN IN RABBINIC JUDAISM

1 Strictly speaking, we cannot use the word "canon" in the context of Rabbinic Judaism, since for that Judaism the corpus of authoritative truth, classified as "Torah," never is closed but may receive teachings, with the approval of the consensus of the sages, through all time. Since "canon" ordinarily refers in particular to a closed corpus of authoritative writings, therefore, the category does not pertain. But in a looser sense, "accepted writings as opposed to spurious ones," the word is used here. I discuss the matter further in my *Theology of the Oral Torah: Prolegomenon* (Kingston: McGill-Queens University Press, 1998).

2 See my *Rationality and Structure: The Bavli's Anomalous Juxtapositions* (Atlanta: Scholars Press for South Florida Studies in the History of Judaism, 1997).

## 4 CHARISMATA OF GUIDANCE IN PRIMITIVE AND EARLY CHRISTIANITY

1 See Henry George Liddell and Robert Scott, *A Greek–English Lexicon* (Oxford: Clarendon, 1901), 1715–16.

2 So, for example the King James Version and the New English Bible. The latter makes the equation even stronger by means of its paraphrase: "gifts of the Spirit."

3 See Ralph Schroeder, *Max Weber and the Sociology of Culture. Theory, Culture & Society* (London: Sage, 1992).

4 For further discussion, see Neusner and Chilton, *Christianity and Judaism: The Formative Categories. II. The Body of Faith. Israel and the Church* (Valley Forge: Trinity Press International, 1996), 143–62.

5 For a further discussion, see Neusner and Chilton, *Christianity and Judaism: The Formative Categories. I. Revelation. The Torah and the Bible* (Valley Forge: Trinity Press International, 1995), 112–17; *Judaism in the New Testament*, 60–97; *The Intellectual Foundations*, 26–46.

6 Eusebius cites Hegesippus as his source for the death of Symeon, as he does for the death of James.

7 Their interrogation might be linked to Vespasian's search for the family of David (*Ecclesiastical History* 3.12), although Eusebius himself claims Domitian was more comparable to Nero than to Vespasian (*Ecclesiastical History* 3.17).

8 See *The Intellectual Foundations*, 121–8.

9 For a plausible theory, see Raymond E. Brown, *The Community of the Beloved Disciple* (New York: Paulist, 1979), 99–103.

10 See Kirsopp Lake, *The Apostolic Fathers*, The Loeb Classical Library (New York: Putnam, 1919).

11 For 1 Clement, this is a probable allusion to the table of the bread of the presence as a type of the eucharistic table. Cf. Chilton, "Forgiving at and Swearing by the Temple," *Forum* 7 (1991), 45–50.

12 See *The Intellectual Foundations*, 26–31 by way of comparison.

13 *See Christianity and Judaism: The Formative Categories.* II. *The Body of Faith: Israel and the Church* (Valley Forge: Trinity Press International, 1996), 135–43.

14 See Robert F. O'Toole, "Hands, Laying on of," *The Anchor Bible Dictionary* 3 (New York: Doubleday, 1992), 47–9; Chilton, *The Temple of Jesus. His Sacrificial Program Within a Cultural History of Sacrifice* (University Park: The Pennsylvania State University Press, 1992), 27–42, 100–2, 109–11.

15 For a discussion of this technique within Mark and further discussion (with bibliography) see Joanna Dewey, "The Literary Structure of the Controversy Stories in Mark 2 – 3:6," *Journal of Biblical Literature* 92.3 (1981), 394–401.

16 See *The Temple of Jesus*, 123–5.

17 See the discussion in *Jesus' Baptism and Jesus' Healing.*

18 See Chilton and Neusner, *Jewish-Christian Debates. Communion with God, the Kingdom of God, and the Mystery of the Messiah* (Minneapolis: Fortress, 1998) for an extensive discussion.

19 Within the communities during the first century which heard Luke and Acts read, the irony that the movement in Antioch included an associate of the person responsible for John's execution (Luke 3:18–20, 9:7–9), and involved in Jesus' execution (Luke 23:6–12), was no doubt appreciated.

20 See M.H. Shepherd, "Elder in the NT," *The Interpreter's Dictionary of the Bible* 2 (New York: Abingdon, 1962), 73–5.

21 See David C. Verner, *The Household of God. The Social World of the Pastoral Epistles*, Society of Biblical Literature Dissertation Series 71 (Chico: Scholars, 1983).

22 The place of female elders in the Church, at a time when elders were barely distinguishable from bishops, has too often been overlooked; see Chilton, "Opening the Book: Biblical Warrants for the Ordination of Women," *The Modern Churchman* 20 (1977), 32–5; "The Gospel of Jesus and the Ministry of Women," *The Modern Churchman* 22 (1978–9), 18–21.

23 Such developments tell against the argument that 2 Timothy is authentic, while 1 Timothy is not; compare Jerome Murphy-O'Connor, *Paul. A Critical Life* (Oxford: Clarendon, 1996), 356–9.

24 To be sure, correct interpretation continues to be stressed; 2 Timothy 3:16–17 maintains expressly that "All Scripture is inspired of God." But the point of the entire statement is that it is inspired as *profitable for teaching* and like activities, and that authoritative teaching is here to be after the manner of Paul and others as apostles (see 2 Timothy 2:1–2). See Chilton, *Beginning New Testament Study* (London: SPCK, 1986 and Grand Rapids: Eerdmans, 1987), 11–12.

25 Verner, *The Household of God*, 180.

26 The term "priest" in English actually derives from "elder," *presbuteros*, so that priest, presbyter and elder are equivalent terms in respect of their common origin.

27 See *Judaism in the New Testament*, 175–88.

28 That is a prelude to developments in both Judaism and Christianity during the second century and later; see *The Intellectual Foundations*.

29 It is notable that Agabus here is associated with an unspecified number of other prophets. In our understanding, the period between the execution of Jesus and the burning of the Temple saw an increase in the claims of prophecy, as both Josephus and the Gospels would suggest. The source commonly called "Q" associates such prophecy with Jesus (see Matthew 23:34–6; Luke 11:49–51), and Luke–Acts attempts to turn that association in a global theology, in which Jesus is at the heart of all true prophecy. On the development of "Q," see Chilton, *Pure Kingdom. Jesus' Vision of God*, Studying the Historical Jesus 1 (Grand Rapids and London: Eerdmans and SPCK, 1996).

30 See M. Eugene Boring, "Early Christian Prophecy," *The Anchor Bible Dictionary* 5, eds D.N. Freedman, G.A. Herion, D.F. Graf and J.D. Pleins (New York: Doubleday, 1992), 496–502.

31 The fact that it seems difficult for bishops and deacons to exercise such control would seem to place the *Didache* within the first century, but the matter of dating is much disputed. See Robert A. Kraft, "Didache," *The Anchor Bible Dictionary* 2, eds D.N. Freedman *et al.* (New York: Doubleday, 1992), 197–8. In his classic study, Charles Taylor concluded that the treatment of prophets "is a sign of the Jewish character and early dating of the *Teaching*;" see *The Teaching of the Twelve Apostles* (Cambridge: Deighton Bell, 1886), 81.

32 Not until the rise of Islam was there a comparable challenge (and in somewhat similar terms). But by that time the identification of Christianity with Graeco-Roman culture made it largely immune (at least in the West) to what was in theological terms a serious competitor.

33 See Neusner and Chilton, *Christianity and Judaism: The Formative Categories*. II. *The Body of Faith: Israel and the Church* (Valley Forge: Trinity Press International, 1996), 165–8.

34 The date is proposed in F.L. Cross, *The Early Christian Fathers* (London: Duckworth, 1960), 102.

35 See Jean Daniélou and Henri Marrou, *The Christian Centuries. 1: The First Six Hundred Years* (New York: McGraw-Hill, 1964), 100–3.

36 In regard to that policy and its religious impact, see Chilton and Neusner, *Trading Places. The Intersecting Histories of Christianity and Judaism* (Cleveland: Pilgrim, 1996).

37 *To the Philadelphians* 6:1 attests the particular problem of the uncircumcised claiming to "interpret" Judaism.

38 See Daniélou and Marrou, 42–4, citing *To the Magnesians* 8:1, 9:1. In this regard, see *To the Ephesians* 9:1, 11:1–2, 19:1–3; *To the Magnesians* 10:1–3; *To the Trallians* 6:1–2, 9:1 – 10:1; *To the Philadelphians* 2:1–2, 6:1–3; *To the Smyrnaeans* 2:1 – 7:2. See Kirsopp Lake, *The Apostolic Fathers*, The Loeb Classical Library (New York: Putnam, 1919).

39 With his letter *To Polycarp* especially in mind, the similarity of Ignatius' work with the Pastoral Epistles is striking, and his familiarity with both the Synoptic tradition and the Pauline corpus is evident.

40 This theme is variously represented in Ignatius' letters, and the assignment of persons of the Trinity to clerical orders is subject to variation.
It should not be imagined that he has a fixed hierarchy of obedience in
mind, although what he says led to the development of such a conception. See *To the Ephesians* 4:1 – 6:2; *To the Magnesians* 2:1 – 4:1, 6:1 –
7:2, 13:1–2; *To the Trallians* 2:1 – 3:1, 7:1–2, 12:2, 13:2; *To the
Philadelphians* 3:2 – 4:1, 7:1–2; *To the Smyrnaeans* 8:1 – 9:1.

## 5 THE COMMANDING VOICE OF SCRIPTURE IN RABBINIC JUDAISM

1 G.E.R. Lloyd, *Polarity and Analogy. Two Types of Argumentation in Early
Greek Thought* (Cambridge: Cambridge University Press, 1966), 384.

## 6 THE CONCILIAR VOICE OF SCRIPTURE IN CHRISTIANITY

1 See Chilton, *God in Strength. Jesus' Announcement of the Kingdom*, Studien
zum Neuen Testament und seiner Umwelt 1 (Freistadt: Plöchl, 1979),
reprinted in "The Biblical Seminar" (Sheffield: JSOT, 1987), 136–43,
147–51.
2 See Robert Maddox, *The Purpose of Luke–Acts*, Studies of the New
Testament and its World (Edinburgh: Clark, 1982), 183; John T.
Squires, *The Plan of God in Luke–Acts*, Society for New Testament
Studies Monograph Series 76 (Cambridge: Cambridge University
Press, 1993) 187–9.
3 See pp. 104–5.
4 See Kirsopp Lake, "The Apostolic Council of Jerusalem," *The
Beginnings of Christianity* 5, eds F.J. Foakes Jackson and Kirsopp Lake
(Grand Rapids: Baker, 1979), 195–212.
5 The rendering of the Revised Standard Version here ("in assembly")
seems rather weak; see J. Rawson Lumby, *The Acts of the Apostles*,
Cambridge Greek Testament (Cambridge: Cambridge University
Press, 1904), 282.
6 Of course, these are just the people, and just the recognition of categories of people, one should expect to find in a synagogue (see
Martinus C. de Boer, "God-Fearers in Luke Acts," *Luke's Literary
Achievement. Collected Essays*, Journal for the Study of the New
Testament Supplement 116, ed. C.M Tuckett (Sheffield: Sheffield
Academic Press, 1995), 50–71. In the presentation of Luke–Acts, Paul
is careful to observe the traditional distinction, and is persecuted by
"the Jews" for his christology. It is much more likely that his profound
challenge of the very definition of Israel brought about discord. But
because Luke–Acts does not share Paul's definition, it is silent in that
respect.
7 See *Judaism in the New Testament*, 98–104; *The Intellectual Foundations*,
26–31.

8 That is the general position reached in David Ravens, *Luke and the Restoration of Israel*, Journal for the Study of the New Testament Supplement 119 (Sheffield: Sheffield Academic Press, 1995), 247–57.

9 See Eisenman, *James the Brother of Jesus. The Key to Unlocking the Secrets of Early Christianity and the Dead Sea Scrolls* (New York: Viking, 1996), 601.

10 See Anthony J. Saldarini's treatment of Eisenman's position in the *New York Times Book Review* (27 April 1997), 41.

11 Eisenman, 159, 600.

12 See Hengel, "Jakobus der Herrenbruder – der erste 'Papst'?" *Glaube und Eschatologie. Festschrift für Werner Georg Kümmel zum 80. Geburtstag*, eds. E. Grässer and O. Merk, (Tübingen: Mohr, 1985), 71–104, 81.

13 See J.B. Lightfoot, *The Apostolic Fathers* 1 (London: Macmillan, 1890), 414–20.

14 Or the view of the "Tübingen school" of the nineteenth century, as Hengel (p. 92) points out is the source of such contentions.

15 Cited by Hengel, 89.

16 Hengel, 90, citing the Pseudo-Clementine letter of Peter, 2.3ff.

17 Lake (note 4, above), 208.

18 Lake, 208–9, with a citation of the Greek text. For an English rendering and fine introductions and explanations, see John J. Collins, "Sibylline Oracles. A New Translation and Introduction," *The Old Testament Pseudepigrapha* I (Garden City: Doubleday, 1983). Collins dates this work within the first century, but after the eruption of Vesuvius in 79 CE (pp. 381–2). With due caution, he assigns Book 4 a Syrian provenience.

19 See John T. Squires, *The Plan of God in Luke–Acts*, Society for New Testament Studies Monograph Series 76 (Cambridge: Cambridge University Press, 1993) 121–54.

20 See Collins, 317.

21 He also cites 4:162–70.

22 Collins, 355.

23 Collins, 331.

24 See Otto Mörkholm, "Antiochus IV," *The Cambridge History of Judaism* 2, eds W.D. Davies and L. Finkelstein, (Cambridge: Cambridge University Press, 1989), 278–91, and, in the same volume, Harald Hegermann, "The Diaspora in the Hellenistic Age," 115–66.

25 Onias III, deposed as high priest by his brother Jason, lived in Antioch for three years until his assassination by Menelaus in 172 BCE. His son, Onias IV, is reported by Josephus to have fled to Ptolemy in 162 BCE, when Alcimus assumed the high priesthood (so *Antiquities* 12.387). Josephus also cites a purported letter from Onias IV to Ptolemy and Cleopatra (*Antiquities* 13.65–8), in which he asks for permission to purify and rebuild an old temple in Leontopolis for the cultic usage of Jews there. As part of his case, he cites his service to them in Syria and Phoenicia (*Antiquities* 13.65). During that time, he probably resided in Damascus, a crucial city within the history of the Essenes. See Uriel Rappaport, "Onias," *The Anchor Bible Dictionary* 5, ed. D.N. Freedman *et al.* (New York: Doubleday, 1992), 23–4.

26 See Günter Stemberger, *Jewish Contemporaries of Jesus. Pharisees, Sadducees, Essenes* (Minneapolis: Fortress, 1995), 125; Leland R. Deeds, *Cultic Metaphors: Sacrificial Ideology and Origins in Selected Scrolls from the Dead Sea* (Annandale: Bard College, 1996), 94–101.

27 See Morton Smith, "The Occult in Josephus," *Josephus, Judaism, and Christianity*, eds L.H. Feldman and G. Hata (Detroit: Wayne State University Press, 1987), 236–56, 248–50.

28 See Roger Tomes, "Why did Paul Get his Hair Cut? (Acts 18:18, 21:23–4)," *Luke's Literary Achievement. Collected Essays*, Journal for the Study of the New Testament Supplement 116, ed. C.M. Tuckett (Sheffield: Sheffield Academic Press, 1995), 188–97. Tomes rightly points out that there is considerable deviation from the prescriptions of Numbers 6 here, but Mishnah (see below) amply attests such flexibility within the practice of the vow.

29 See Josephus, *Jewish War* 2.590–4; Mishnah Menahoth 8:3–5 and the whole of Makhshirin. The point of departure for the concern is Leviticus 11:34.

30 For further discussion, see Chilton, *The Temple of Jesus. His Sacrificial Program Within a Cultural History of Sacrifice* (University Park: The Pennsylvania State University Press, 1992); "A Generative Exegesis of Mark 7:1–23," *The Journal of Higher Criticism* 3.1 (1996), 18–37; *Pure Kingdom. Jesus' Vision of God*, Studying the Historical Jesus 1 (Eerdmans: Grand Rapids, 1996).

31 See Mishnah Nedarim; Zeev W. Falk, "Notes and Observations on Talmudic Vows," *Harvard Theological Review* 59 (1966), 309–12.

32 Compare Exodus 20:12; 21:17; Leviticus 20:9; Deuteronomy 5:16.

33 As happens in Matthew 15:3–9.

34 See Chilton and Craig A. Evans, "Jesus and Israel's Scriptures," *Studying the Historical Jesus. Evaluations of the State of Current Research*, New Testament Tools and Studies 19 (Leiden: Brill, 1994), 281–335, 294–5.

35 So an as yet unpublished paper by Marcus Bockmuehl, given at the meeting of the Studiorum Novi Testamenti Societas in Birmingham in 1997. Of all the arguments adduced, the most attractive is that Jesus' statement concerning wine and the kingdom involves his accepting Nazirite vows. See P. Lebeau, *Le vin nouveau du Royaume. Etude exégétique et patristique sur la Parole eschatologique de Jésus à la Cène* (Paris: Desclée, 1966); M. Wojciechowski, "Le naziréat et la Passion (Mc 14:25a; 15:23)," *Biblica* 65 (1984), 94–6. But the form of Jesus' statement has not been rightly understood, owing to its Semitic syntax. He is not promising never to drink wine, but only to drink wine in association with his celebration of the kingdom. See Chilton, *A Feast of Meanings. Eucharistic Theologies from Jesus through Johannine Circles*, Supplements to *Novum Testamentum* 72 (Leiden: Brill, 1994), 169–71.

36 It is for this reason that the circle of James also sought to restrict the definition of who might participate in the full celebration of the eucharist. Mark 14:12–15 turns that meal into a Seder, in which only the circumcised could participate; see Chilton, *A Feast of Meanings*.

*Eucharistic Theologies from Jesus through Johannine Circles:* Supplements to *Novum Testamentum* 72 (Leiden: Brill, 1994), 93–108.

37 See the more global construction of Robert Eisenman, *James the Brother of Jesus. The Key to Unlocking the Secrets of Early Christianity and the Dead Sea Scrolls* (New York: Viking, 1996).

38 Indeed, there was even a place called Bethlehem of Nazareth, according to the Talmud; see Chilton, *God in Strength. Jesus' Announcement of the Kingdom,* Studien zum Neuen Testament und seiner Umwelt 1 (Freistadt: Plochl, 1979), 311–13.

39 See Chilton, "Exorcism and History: Mark 1:21–8," *Gospel Perspectives* 6 (1986), 253–71.

40 See D. Catchpole, "Paul, James, and the Apostolic Decree," *New Testament Studies* 23 (1977), 428–44. Catchpole even suggests that Paul's antagonists in Galatians 2 were delivering the ruling of the Council. Criticism of Catchpole has tended to run along the lines that he "discounts the historical value of Acts;" so Timothy George, *Galatians,* The New American Commentary 30 (n. p.: Broadman and Holman, 1994), 169, n.138. What is more to the point is that the people described as "from James" in Galatians 2:12 prompt separation from believing gentiles, not their maintenance of purity. They more likely correspond to those who claim the support of Jerusalem, but who are then denied support by the Council (see Acts 15:24).

41 Stephen Benko has suggested that Peregrinus was excommunicated during the second century for eating "meat that was consecrated to pagan gods," *Pagan Rome and the Early Christians* (Bloomington: Indiana University Press, 1986), 32.

42 See pp. 158–61.

43 That is, *recapitulatio* in the sense of Irenaeus; see *The Intellectual Foundations,* 111–28.

44 *Apokatastasis,* in the sense of Origen; see *The Intellectual Foundations,* 70–86, 156–8.

45 See Robert M. Grant, *Augustus to Constantine. The Rise and Triumph of Christianity in the Roman World* (San Francisco: Harper Row, 1990), 235–6.

46 Grant, *Augustus to Constantine,* 237.

47 Quoted in Grant, *Augustus to Constantine,* 238.

48 See Daniélou and Marrou (the latter in this case), 243–8.

49 See Chilton and Neusner, *Trading Places. A Reader and Sourcebook on the Intersecting Histories of Christianity and Rabbinic Judaism* (Cleveland: Pilgrim Press, 1996), 187–94.

50 See *The Intellectual Foundations,* 180–6.

51 See Daniélou and Marrou (the latter), 250, citing Athanasius, *De Synodis,* 16.

52 See *The Intellectual Foundations,* 75–6.

53 Daniélou and Marrou (the latter), 252.

54 See Robert M. Grant, *Gods and the One God,* Library of Early Christianity (Philadelphia: Westminster, 1986), 160–3. The text of the Creed is also as cited by Grant. The Creed as currently used was discussed, interpreted, and amended by councils at Constantinople

(381 CE), Ephesus (431 CE), and Chalcedon (451 CE). See T.A. Burkill, *The Evolution of Christian Thought* (Ithaca: Cornell University Press, 1971), 87–95.

55 *The Intellectual Foundations*, 84–6.
56 *The Intellectual Foundations*, 154–61.
57 As distinct from primitive Christianity during the period of the New Testament, and early Christianity between the New Testament and the fourth century. For a simple discussion, see Neusner (ed.), *God*, The Pilgrim Library of World Religions (Cleveland: Pilgrim Press, 1997), xvii–xx.
58 See *The Intellectual Foundations*, 26–46.
59 See *The Intellectual Foundations*, 70–86.
60 See *The Intellectual Foundations*, 111–28.
61 See *The Intellectual Foundations*, 154–67.
62 Grant, *Gods and the One God*, 162–3.
63 So Daniélou and Marrou (the latter), 252–3.
64 He was finally baptized shortly before his death in 337; see Grant, *Augustus to Constantine*, 247.

# INDEX